D0200642

Professor D.M. Nanjundappa

Planning for Social and Economic Development

Essays in Honour of Professor D.M. Nanjundappa

Edited by

R. BHARADWAJ

and

M.V. NADKARNI

SAGE Publications
New Delhi/Newbury Park/London

First published in 1992 by

Sage Publications India Pvt Ltd
M-32, Greater Kailash Market, Part I
New Delhi 110 048

Sage Publications Inc
2455 Teller Road
Newbury Park, California 91320

Sage Publications Ltd
6 Bonhill Street
London EC2A 4PU

Published by Tejeshwar Singh for Sage Publications India Pvt Ltd, photo-typeset by Pagewell Photosetters, Pondicherry, and printed by Chaman Enterprises.

Library of Congress Cataloging-in-Publication Data

Planning for social and economic development: essays in honour of Pro-fessor D.M. Nanjundappa / edited by R. Bharadwaj and M.V. Nadkarni.
     p.   cm.
  Includes bibliographical references and index.
    1. India—Social conditions. 2. India—Economic conditions. I. Nanjundappa, D.M., 1930-   II. Bharadwaj, Ranganath. III. Nad-karni, Mangesh Venktesh, 1939-
  HN687.P65   1992   306 .0954—dc20   92–20729

ISBN 0–8039–9444–3 (US-hbk)
       81–7036–302–0 (India-pbk)

Contents

Foreword

It gives me great pleasure to write the foreword to this volume of essays in honour of Professor D.M. Nanjundappa. As his colleague for many years in the Government of Karnataka, I watched with admiration his unique ability to operate within the rigidities of a bureaucratic framework and yet maintain intellectual integrity. Not content with remaining a theoretical academic, he brought his vast knowledge to bear on the planning process at the state level, improving its technical quality and influencing its policy orientation. His area of interest was not confined to Karnataka and his writings have touched a variety of national economic issues. Long before the phrase 'development with a human face' became fashionable, Professor Nanjundappa had repeatedly emphasised that growth, essential as it was, was not paramount and that the human being had to be at the centre of development. Investment in human development was as important as investment in infrastructure and physical resource development. But, if this is to be effective, given the limited availability of financial resources, the investments should be channelled towards the target groups and subsidies should be extended only to those sections of the community which have no capacity to pay for the services. This human concern has marked all the writings of Professor Nanjundappa.

We are privileged to have Professor Nanjundappa with us at the Institute for Social and Economic Change as UGC Emeritus Professor. We are sure that we can look forward to many years of his productive work.

T.R. Satish Chandran
Director, ISEC

Acknowledgements

The Editors wish to thank all the authors who kindly responded to our request and contributed essays which were specially written for this volume; T.R. Satish Chandran, Director, Institute for Social and Economic Change, Bangalore, for the Foreword as well as his support and encouragement for this endeavour; Sage Publications India for kindly agreeing to bring it out in good time; and to the publisher's referee for helpful comments.

R. Bharadwaj
M.V. Nadkarni

1

Introduction

M.V. NADKARNI and R. BHARADWAJ

India can be credited with having made an important contribution to the concept of planning in applying it to a developing country with a mixed economy. It neither went all the way to accept the Soviet model, nor accepted the sovereignty of the market. Even while allowing scope for market forces and private enterprise, India insisted that it needed stimuli and directions from the political process reflecting the aspirations of its people. These aspirations have to take the shape of planning to guide the economy through a democratic political process. Planning, however, could not be confined to the national level alone. Professor Nanjundappa is one of the few who gave expression to the need for planning not only at the level of states but further down as well, and played an active role in the task. We hope, therefore, that the present volume of essays in his honour is fitting both to the continued relevance of planning in India and to the person himself.

It is a reflection of the deep affection and regard in which Nanjundappa is held that eminent scholars have joined to contribute essays in his honour on themes with which he has been associated as a teacher, researcher, planner or as Vice-Chancellor. Not being just an academician, it was natural for him to give his attention to all matters which help in the formulation of economic policy and planning. The present volume, however, hopes to address itself to only some of his main concerns. There is a separate biographical note on Nanjundappa's career and work, which we need not summarise here.

In his paper on 'Economic Growth and Social Justice', V.K.R.V. Rao raises certain issues regarding both the goals and strategies of planning in India. Though the goal of planning is ultimately to help our people to realise their full potential and achieve the dignity they deserve as human beings, there is a tendency to mistake the shadow for substance by setting the goals and yardstick of performance in terms of economic growth. This led to imitating Western models of growth and technology, resulting in the persistence of mass illiteracy, unemployment and poverty. He also feels that the concept of freedom in a democracy means that common people should be in control of factors that affect their own lives and livelihood, which also, in turn, means their active involvement in the planning process at the grass-roots. He laments that instead it has been interpreted more in terms of freedom of private enterprise and market forces. According to him, development is a total process involving all aspects of life, not only economic, but also social, political, cultural and ecological. This is possible only when the basic needs of all are satisfied, and not by maximising growth rates which only creates affluence for a few. Social justice is thus not only an end in itself; it is also the best means. He thus places the human being at the centre stage of planning.

This finds a direct and sympathetic echo in Adiseshiah's paper on 'Education—Why, How and Whither of its Planning'. Since education is the prime mover of economic and social development, he calls for investment in it on a large scale as a matter of priority, rather than on a residual basis. At the same time it is equally important to see that this investment gets higher returns or achieves its basic objectives in a cost-effective manner. He lists a few positive gains here, mainly a significant widening of access to education through special incentives for the socially and economically backward, and building-up of a large cadre of educated and skilled men and women. Yet, he regrets, all this expansion has not led to the eradication of mass illiteracy. Moreover, there is a wastage at all levels, reflected in growing unemployment of the educated, drop-outs, and mismatch between types of skills needed and those available. It looks as though we have ignored the need for building a large base at the primary and local community levels, but focused on quantitative expansion at the top levels. This imbalance, he believes, ought to be corrected by giving local communities greater say in educational planning and developing the institutions that respond to their needs and potential. He also advocates a thorough reform in our examination system, greater autonomy to educational institutions, more flexibility and dynamism in curricula and methods of teaching, and opportunities for retraining and updating knowledge for teachers.

Adiseshiah's theme of education being the prime mover of development is taken further by Bharadwaj and Balachandran in their paper, 'Integrating Higher Education and Development: A Policy Perspective'. They emphasise that a strategy is urgently needed to make higher education serve the long-run goals of both efficiency and equity. It contributes directly to increase in the levels of living of recipients. Therefore, no individual wishing to have it should be denied access to it, and special efforts have to be made to improve the access of the poor to higher education. Under the present system, subsidy on education is uniform for all, instead of being designed in favour of the poor. At the same time, allocation to education per student has declined in real terms. This is because of the lack of appreciation of the linkage between education and development and the contribution it makes to improvement in skills and productivity.

The importance of increase in productivity as a source of economic growth should be taken seriously in India, since it has the dubious distinction of being one of the few countries where growth in total factor productivity has been negative, and the entire growth in national income is accounted for by growth in total factor input, while other countries like South Korea have achieved high growth rates through increase in productivity (Page 1990: 113). In his essay, 'Beyond Output Growth: Human Resource Management for Improved Productivity', Abdul Aziz makes the point that we cannot afford to follow the policy of increasing production at any cost, and that productivity improvement through better management of resources, specially human resources, should be the concern of economists and policy-making in future. Promotion of a proper work culture and commitment among the working class has to receive high priority. This is not a simple question of giving monetary incentives, but of promoting worker participation in decision-making and giving scope to their creativity. He argues that henceforth higher priority has to be accorded to improving the quality of human beings and their work than to merely building up more and more capital stock.

There can be no scope for improving the quality of human beings who are not employed or grossly underemployed. In their paper on 'Planning for Employment: What Has Been Our Experience?', Rayappa and Nagaraju review our rather dismal record in this respect. They note that employment became an integral part of the planning process only from the Sixth Plan onwards. Even the net additions to the labour force were underestimated and employment-generating sectors did not receive the priority they deserved. The approach seemed to leave the problem to be solved by the general process of economic development, with some marginal relief through employment guarantee programmes on a casual basis in the rural sector. Such an approach created tremendous tension in society since a large labour force, young in age, had little productive opportunities for themselves, and resulted in serious unrest, though expressed in terms of caste, regional or linguistic issues. Since employment elasticity of the GNP has been declining, serious attention must be paid to the nature of growth strategy pursued, directly encouraging employment-promoting activities. The country has enough potential for it since inadequacy of rural schools, health services, proper transport and communication facilities in the rural areas is also an indication of the scope for employment. A greater expansion of employment in the service sector rather than in the manufacturing sector need not necessarily be unproductive per se, unless persons employed there are inclined more to disservice than service through negative work attitudes. The Eighth Plan is expected to reorient development policy, particularly to meet basic needs and provide employment, as the two go together. The thrust on employment in the rural sector and small towns is also expected to reduce the pressure on cities. Rayappa and Nagaraju emphasise the need for clear and more dependable sector-wise assessment of the magnitude of underemployment and unemployment, separately, in order that suitable strategies can be adopted. They add that it is also important to assess the employment-generating potential and relative cost of different economic activities under alternative technologies, so that suitable priorities can be given.

Job opportunities as well as general development efforts could be under severe strain in the context of a rapid population growth involving huge additions in absolute numbers every year. Ramesh and Shanta Kanbargi, in their paper on 'Rapid Population Growth and Economic Development in India: An Overview and Assessment', argue that while persistence of poverty and unemployment owes quite a bit to rapid population growth, family planning efforts too have not been imaginative enough to understand factors behind population growth and evolve policies accordingly. Indirect methods of promoting female literacy, enhancing the status of women and improving health facilities for them and children in the rural areas and small towns, particularly child survival rates, could probably go a long way, more than the direct methods of popularising family planning. It is the lack of imaginativeness and seriousness in these policies which are responsible for our failure both on the poverty and population fronts, contend the authors.

It would, however, be escapism to lay all the blame on population growth, and ignore poverty and deprivation arising from inequity in land distribution and exploitative relations. Land reforms assume a great significance in this context. In his paper, 'Land Reforms: The Next Phase', V.M. Rao reviews the status and implementation of land reforms and pleads that they still need to be a part of a comprehensive planning-cum-programme in the interests of both poverty alleviation and optimum use of land resources. He believes that while the land reforms programme has thus far paid more attention to equity, the task of raising productivity as a part of the programme has been relatively ignored. This was particularly so regarding consolidation of holdings and improving the viability of small holdings by promoting appropriate cost-effective technology and crop mix for them, and supporting such holdings outside the market framework through the development of common lands. The ancillary activities needed for small and marginal farmers also need more attention, now that their number is rising. Improving the literacy and skills of landless labour and marginal farmers deserves higher priority. The task of promoting an equitable distribution of operational holdings with reasonable lower as well as upper limits, and preventing the emergence of dominant landowners is still unfinished and has to be taken up in the next phase of land reforms, argues the author. He also gives clear guidelines about how and where land records have to be improved, and pleads for a greater clarity in concepts and definitions as, for example, in the case of 'personal cultivation', so that loopholes can be avoided in implementing land reforms. He also indicates what incentives and disincentives would be needed to make a more equitable, productive and sustainable use of land resources possible. His suggestions are designed to promote both equity and development.

Improving the availability of food to the poor is among the important ways of helping them. India did, on the whole, not only achieve self-sufficiency in food by the mid-1970s, but even the economic access to food has improved as judged from the decline in the proportion of per capita income required to purchase a quintal of wheat or rice (Tyagi 1990: 52). Not only have the relative market prices of cereal foodgrains declined, but the public distribution of foodgrains and a few other essential items of consumption at subsidised prices has formed a part of our economic system. Yet, as Radhakrishna and Ravi show in their paper on 'Food, Nutrition and Prices: Some Macro Issues', per capita consumption of foodgrains has levelled-off even before much improvement could be made in the nutritional status of the poor. This requires an examination into various dimensions of the food problem from a demand perspective, which this paper provides. While a change in tastes has come in the way of increasing per capita cereal consumption among the poor, they are unable to increase the consumption of non-cereal foods because the prices of such foods are very high. As the authors point out, subsidising non-cereal items, even for the poor alone, could make a significant demand on government revenues. On the other hand, the prospects of a substantial rise in the relative income of the poor are also dim. Production of non-cereal foods, however, would respond to high prices and demand, particularly if research and extension are stepped up towards technological change in this direction, which, apart from increasing production, should also reduce cost per unit of output. Planning for agricultural development may have to give more attention to this factor henceforth, taking care to see that per capita availability of cereals does not decline as it constitutes basic food.

One of the worrying features of agricultural development in India is that quite a few states have not shown the necessary dynamism in this regard, and even among those which have, development has tended to taper off both in respect of production and productivity. Karnataka is one of the states of the latter type which had made some mark by extending the benefits of technological change even to semi-arid rain-fed areas, but is now facing a slow-down. Bisaliah's paper, 'Three Epochs of Technology-Extension Nexus in Karnataka Agriculture: Some Policy Issues', reviews the experience of the state. The three epochs are: (E1), marked by old technology and the old extension approach (1955–56 to 1967–68); (E2), marked by new technology still combined with the old extension approach (1968–69 to 1978–79); and (E3), marked by new technology with a new extension approach (1979–80 to 1987–88). He explains how the old extension approach based on a multipurpose extension worker has now changed to the Training and Visit System emphasising 'knowledge transfer'. While the earlier emphasis was on 'contact farmers'—mainly the 'progressive farmers'—the emphasis now is on 'contact group'. The new system is more sophisticated and aims at a continuous upgradation of knowledge of both the extension worker and the farmers. In spite of this, however, increase in productivity was lower in E3 than in E2, except in the case of oil-seeds for which it was higher. The author suggests that this could well be due to lack of continuous technological upgradation and 'fine tuning of technology' to suit different climatic situations and soils. He observes significantly that the rate of advancement in technology is limited by the advancement in basic science and knowledge. If basic knowledge is static, applied research cannot be expected to be very dynamic. He believes that agricultural research policy has to aim at a balanced mix of basic and applied research for best results. This apart, his analysis shows that even the 'new' extension system itself has some shortfalls. It is yet to focus more on laggards in development than on 'progressive' elements. The emphasis also appears to be more on using cash inputs than on promoting a balanced mix of cash and non-cash inputs which may have a synergetic impact on productivity.

Both agricultural and non-agricultural development have come to depend a lot on energy, particularly commercial energy. Recurrent oil shocks, the latest arising out of war in the Middle East affecting supplies from Iraq and Kuwait, have proved our vulnerability. In his paper on 'Planning and Energy: Some Macro Issues', Satish Chandran appraises the present system of planning in India for energy in the context of a close link between energy and development in our country and highlights issues where further attention is needed. Though inter-sectoral (inequality) in energy consumption had declined over the years, reflected in agriculture steadily improving its share from 10 per cent in 1970–71 to 24 per cent in 1987–88 (see Table 4 in his paper), there still remains the problem of interpersonal inequality in energy consumption, particularly in high quality energy sources. Thus, both to promote economic development and reduce inequality, there is no alternative to significantly stepping up energy supply. The author finds, however, that over the last four decades, planning for energy has succeeded neither in ensuring adequate availability nor in reducing inequality. Demand for energy has to be estimated well in advance and projects to meet it have also to be started well in advance. This is not done, and the gap between demand and supply is never bridged. Different sources of energy must also be planned in an integrated manner, but there is no proper coordinating agency in the planning system. The author does not see bright prospects for reducing the demand for energy or reducing energy intensity of development in the near future, though saving energy wherever possible is a goal worth pursuing. However, he makes it clear that the demand for energy depends not only on growth but also its content. If the main thrust of economic development is on employment generation in agriculture and labour-intensive industries, improving skills and knowledge, meeting basic needs and enhancing the quality of life, then the requirement of energy would be relatively less.

Development and energy issues can hardly be separated from environmental issues. In his paper, 'Planning and Environmental Concern', Nadkarni probes into them, and pleads that negative externalities have to be anticipated and their prevention or minimisation has to be incorporated in the planning process right at the start, instead of trying to correct them after the damage is done. Problems of poverty and underdevelopment also involve environmental concern in the form of lack of sanitation, unhygienic drinking water, etc. If we ignore the adverse environmental impact of ill-conceived development projects, environmental problems arising out of poverty and underdevelopment get compounded rather than resolved, because, environmental damage hits the poor more than others. Planning, however, does not end with an environmental impact assessment of projects. The long-term planning of policies and their implementation are equally necessary. One of the tasks of planning is to see what alternative strategies are feasible and what each alternative implies in terms of environmental costs. If the rationale of planning is that economic development cannot be left completely to free market forces and be subjected to certain broader values, the use of environment too cannot be left to the free market and should be subjected to the same values. We have no right to take liberties with the environment in the name of poverty alleviation, since its unsustainable exploitation has only aggravated poverty.

It would be interesting to see at this stage whether the role of planning in India has increased or decreased over the years. On the one hand, the government is taking on more responsibilities for social welfare; on the other hand, with increasing 'liberalisation' of the economy, the private sector is expected to take up more responsibilities of economic growth. If the size of plan outlay in the public sector is accepted as a broad—though not perfect—indicator of the role of planning and the state, we find that its proportion to GNP at current prices has steadily increased over the years. During the Third Plan period (1961–62 to 1965–66) it was 9.4 per cent, which increased to 13.6 per cent during the Sixth Plan period (1980–81 to 1984–85), and further to 14.8 per cent during the first four years of the Seventh Plan (1985–86 to 1988–89). However, capital–output ratios have also increased over the years, offsetting the impact of the increase in the proportion. This is so even with respect to the increase in the proportion of GNP invested. Since an increase in capital–output ratio would have occurred in both the public and private sectors, the trend in the proportion of public sector plan outlay would indicate that the role of planning has increased, and not decreased, in spite of liberalisation. However, the trend towards increasing costs even in real terms, plus inflation, could both lead to a tremendous pressure on finances, since the government needs many times more resources than before to perform a given task.

Atul Sarma discusses the problem of financing the plans in his paper, 'Financing the Plan: Resource Crunch or Lack of Political Will?' He is perplexed by the fact that there is a severe resource crunch and resort to higher levels of deficit financing even in periods when national income has shown a higher growth rate. He reviews the role played by different sources of plan finance. While the shares of current revenue and net inflow from abroad have declined, more so the latter, the shares of domestic capital receipts and deficit financing have increased. What is most poignant, deficits have emerged on current account at fairly significant levels. The author says, 'This means that even the expenditure of a house-keeping nature has now to be met by borrowed funds or by money creation'. The author suggests that government revenues are not income elastic mainly because the government lacks the will to hurt so many interest groups and thus chooses only soft options.

With the private sector assigned a greater role in economic growth, the importance of large-scale enterprises or the corporate sector is also expected to increase further. This calls for a closer look at the state capital markets in India. R.H. Patil provides an analysis of their role and functioning in his paper, 'Capital Markets in India'. Since the public sector companies too have entered the bond market, capital markets cannot be considered the exclusive preserve of the private sector, not to mention the influence exercised by public sector Mutual Funds and Unit Trust of India. The author shows that secondary markets for stocks in India have not developed to the same extent as in other emerging markets such as Brazil, South Korea and Taiwan, let alone stock exchanges in developed countries. Moreover, development of the capital market within the country is highly unequal, with the Bombay Stock Exchange exercising overwhelming influence even on companies which are located near other stock echanges. A heartening feature of capital markets now is the rise of the small investors, but their interests need to be protected. This also means that markets have to be brought closer to the investors, who are now slowly spreading beyond the traditional centres like Bombay. The author pleads for greater attention to the development of over-the-counter type of markets, instead of simply opening more and more stock exchanges, which would also make the latter more efficient. The question, however, is how far capital markets can be managed to take into account plan priorities in industrial development and whether Mutual Funds and Unit Trust of India can play a role in this regard.

Foreign capital, including aid, has been a crucial source of finance for economic development both in the public and private sectors. India can get more capital only if its economic performance is satisfactory. Sumitra Chishti, in her paper on 'India in the World Economy—Challenges and Prospects in the Nineties', shows that this performance has been mediocre. To add to this, India faces a serious debt problem now, making it very vulnerable. It looks as though there has been hardly any planning on this front. The author finds that India's international trade environment is beset with long-term problems and uncertainty. Prospects of achieving a major breakthrough on the export front are bleak. Changes in Eastern Europe and the break-up of the Soviet Union have further added to uncertainties. The author feels that on the whole the environment for increased capital flow is not as congenial now to India as in the years immediately after Independence. To top it all, Chishti also points to the major erosion in the solidarity of developing countries in seeking collective solutions to their international economic problems. Are we then likely to opt for a more 'inward looking' solution than in the past, emphasising self-reliance and import substitution? This involves a price in the form of continuation of high cost production structures, bottlenecks, scarcities, inefficiencies and inflation. Or, do we opt for incurring more and more debts, accepting any conditionality imposed, so that we keep our flow of imports—essential and non-essential alike—undisturbed, whatever be the cost in terms of our independence? Can we strike an honourable balance? Though the author offers no ready-made solutions, the picture she has painted should make our planners and political leaders sit up and take a hard look at the alternatives we face.

The last two papers in the volume are exclusively on the Karnataka experience, but should nevertheless be of general interest. Though it is easy to say that the planning process should be decentralised even up to the village level, we seem to have a long way to go to achieve this ideal. In his paper on 'District Planning Experiment in Karnataka', S.G. Bhat gives a review of the state's experience and difficulties faced. In practice, even grass-roots planning seems to depend on the same bureaucracy which has also to prepare state-level plans which are hardly evolved from people as such. The information base of district-level planning is far from adequate. Even the new *zilla parishads* do not have the necessary powers to raise resources to supplement the assistance provided to them. The size of the 'district sector' in the state plan is only about 25 to 28 per cent, which does not appear significant. What is most worrying is that there are forces at work which are against building up grass-roots institutions.

Apart from the question of reflecting peoples' aspirations and involving peoples' representatives in the planning process, it also needs inputs from subject experts outside the government bureaucracy. That is how Planning Boards were set up in several states, but they were hardly active. The idea was pursued in a new form to draw high-level expertise, and the Economic and Planning Council (EPC), popularly known as the Think Tank, was set up in Karnataka. G. Thimmaiah offers 'An Insider's Evaluation' of this experiment in his paper. He feels that on the whole its contribution, particularly to the policy of political decentralisation in the state, was noteworthy. The Council even started reviewing the progress of implementation of projects and programmes in the state. It looked as though the Council was also used to break the monopoly of IAS officers in development administration, as the EPC became the major forum for discussion of policies. It also generated a lot of new data and information which helped the planning process. The author is of the view that the experiment was so useful that district level Think Tanks could be started to achieve similar benefits. With the fall of the government and imposition of the President's Rule in 1989, the Council stopped functioning and was later formally abolished by the Congress (I) government. It is not clear if this decision was based on an objective assessment of the usefulness of such an institution outside the rigid framework of government bureaucracy. What is more clear, however, is that it is not easy for the planning process even at the state level and below to free itself from the domination of the bureaucracy.

The aim of the present volume was not to cover all aspects and fields of planning. We hope, however, that it succeeds in conveying that planning is not and should not be a purely bureaucratic process, and should have enough openness to learn from people and independent outside expertise. Nor can it be confined to purely stepping up growth rates and investments. Though everything may be done in the name of human welfare, the human being is not yet at the centre stage of the development process.

REFERENCES

Page, John M., Jr. (1990). 'Pursuit of Industrial Growth: Policy Initiatives and Economic Consequences', in Maurice Scott and Deepak Lal (eds.), *Public Policy and Economic Development: Essays in Honour of Ian Little*. Clarendon Press: Oxford.

Tyagi, D.S. (1990). *Managing India's Food Economy: Problems and Alternatives*. Sage: New Delhi.

2

D.M. Nanjundappa: His Life and Work

M.V. NADKARNI and ABDUL AZIZ

Dogganhal Mahadevappa Nanjundappa (born 25 October 1930) will be long remembered, particularly in Karnataka, as an eminent economist, as an able administrator and as a pioneer who developed the Planning Department in Karnataka as one of the best organised among the states. He rose to the top in Indian economics, having been elected President at the Annual Conference of the Indian Economic Association in 1981, and again as President at the 32nd Annual Conference of the Indian Society of Labour Economics in 1991. He also excelled as a planner, being associated with the planning process in Karnataka from 1972 when he left the comfortable position of Professor and Head of the Department of Economics at Karnatak University, Dharwad, in favour of an economic practitioner's role and rose to the position of Secretary and Commissioner for Planning and Institutional Finance, Government of Karnataka.

As if this was not enough, he brought glory and distinction to the position of Vice-Chancellor, first at Karnatak University, Dharwad, from 1981 to 1984 and then at Bangalore University from 1987 to 1990. In both cases, he put the Universities back on the rails, brought discipline in both academic and administrative work, and breathed new life in the environment which had become stale. That he completed his full term as Vice-Chancellor with unsullied reputation was an achievement in itself, but he also set a model in academic administration for others to follow by providing an energetic and committed academic leadership. Though he worked at the state level and at state universities, he always stood above partisan politics, caste groups and vested interests. Apart from his academic excellence, he was also respected by all as a man of utmost integrity.

Nanjundappa was born in a lower middle class family in a remote village (Dogganhal) in an economically backward district (Chitradurga). His father, Mahadevappa, had a petty job in the government and some land under cultivation. His primary schooling was in the village itself, but he had to move out for middle and higher school education. This meant a considerable financial strain, which he had to overcome by doing part-time jobs off school hours. By the time he completed his Secondary School Leaving Certificate examination in 1946, his father had moved further up in the government hierarchy and was able to set up home in Davangere town. Nanjundappa also secured a merit scholarship with which to pursue his college education at Davangere. Though his economic position was not smooth enough, he pursued higher education with distinction, always achieving a good first class and a top rank. He completed B.A. (Hons.) in 1951 and M.A. in Economics in 1952 with first rank, both from Mysore University. For his distinguished performance at the M.A. level, he was awarded the Sir Hugh Daly Gold Medal, which also won him the Government of India Research Scholarship to pursue research. His thesis, 'Economic Policy and Full Employment in India', was awarded the Ph.D. Degree at Mysore University in 1957. He also taught at the same University for a brief period (1952 to 1954).

Basically a product of the Indian education system, he represented one of the best examples of its output, but he also complemented his training by exposure to some of the best academic institutions abroad. He was selected Smith-Mundt Fulbright Scholar for post-doctoral study at Harvard during 1963–64, and Hallsworth Visiting Research Fellow at Manchester (1968–69). During this period, he also had the opportunity to work at the London School of Economics and at Oxford. He was a recipient of the British Technical Cooperation Award twice (in 1973 and 1980) for study at Sussex. He was a Consultant to ESCAP (UN) on block-level planning (1980) and prepared draft guidelines on the theme. He has participated in several international seminars. During his visits abroad, he had a chance to interact with such celebrities as J.K. Galbraith, Arthur Smithies, A.R. Prest, Ursula Hicks, B.S. Yamey and Michael Lipton.

After his doctorate at Mysore, he worked with the Government of India, first in the Ministry of Commerce and Industry (1956–59) and then in the Ministry of Community Development (1960). Even while in central government service, he was engaged in research and completed many studies involving regional surveys and planning reports on small-scale industries and area development reports for several districts.

But his heart was in teaching, and he soon got the opportunity he needed. He became Head of the Department of Economics of Karnatak University in 1960 where he continued as Professor and Head till 1972, providing academic leadership to colleagues and bringing up students. Being his students ourselves, it was our privilege to be taught by such a popular teacher, who took his lectures seriously, introduced the latest and best texts, and cared for the progress of each student. He organised several all-India conferences and seminars and made the Department one of the most active.

His research work at Karnatak University did not take long to draw the attention of the Government of Karnataka. G.V.K. Rao, the then Development Commissioner and Devaraj Urs, then Chief Minister of Karnataka, were particularly impressed by his work and sought his help in improving the planning process and practice in Karnataka. It was thus that he joined the Government of Karnataka as Economic Advisor in 1972, became the Special Secretary for Planning in 1976, and Secretary in 1978. After a break from 1981 to 1984 when he was Vice-Chancellor at Karnatak University, he resumed the position of Secretary and Commissioner, with charge of both planning and institutional finance this time. He continued in this position till 1987, when he was requested to take the position of Vice-Chancellor at Bangalore University. He was also appointed Advisor to the Governor for the brief spell of President's Rule in Karnataka in October 1990. He retired from the post of Vice-Chancellor after completing his term in 1990, and was reported to have expressed his unwillingness to continue for another term though offered. Instead, he preferred the offer of UGC Emeritus Professorship and is presently affiliated to the Institute for Social and Economic Change.

Nanjundappa is one of the small number of academic economists who had the opportunity to participate in policy-making at the state level. His academic background helped him in going beyond official statistics and in conceptualising the relation between economic theory and economic problems, which was necessary for policy-making and for operationalising the policy. Academic economists who have such a gift are rarely available at the state level. It was Karnataka's good luck that not only did Nanjundappa devote himself to the task of economic development as a practitioner economist at the state level, but made a tremendous success of it as well. He developed and strengthened the Planning Department in Karnataka and professionalised economic policy-making and the planning process at the state level. He took enormous pains to improve the data and information available to the Planning Department and initiated numerous special studies in this regard, both within the Department and outside. He prepared a significant number of studies, besides guiding and finalising many more, which ranged from documents of policy analysis to sectoral studies and plans and evaluation reports. It is because of his foresight and endeavour that the Planning Department was in a position to provide support even in preparing district- and block-level plans and create conditions of success even for the decentralised planning process, apart from state-level planning.

It is inevitable for a man of this stature to hold innumerable honorary positions. To mention only a few, such as Member, Indian Council of Social Science Research, Member, Panel of Economists of the Planning Commission, and Editor of learned journals, may not do full justice to him or the institutions, but should suffice for the purpose here.

In terms of academic output, Professor Nanjundappa has been prolific, not counting the numerous reports and plans prepared or finalised by him as an economist with the government. His writings have a wide range, covering such diverse areas as development planning, public finance—including government finance, local finance and university finance—irrigation economics, transport economics, industrial economics and public policy. Working for a state government, he could not afford the luxury of narrow specialisation. It will be preposterous on our part to claim to have a close and thorough knowledge of his work in all the areas in which he has worked. Nevertheless, we shall make an attempt to capture and present his salient contributions in select areas, particularly since many of the issues raised by him have a continued relevance today.

His academic writings have a more or less common world-view. He believes in state intervention and planning, not so much because the private sector has its limitations in promoting economic growth and development requiring state investment and support, but more because it is only through state intervention and planning positively in favour of the poor and the less privileged that social and economic development can really be launched in developing countries. He believes that even if the private sector and the market are allowed a good scope, they need to be constantly monitored and moderated to reduce inequity and exploitation and keep them well under control. At the same time, Nanjundappa is concerned about efficiency of planning and state intervention, including state investment, so that distortions created by ill-advised interventions do not reduce resources available for development and aggravate inequity. For him the primary aim of planning is not maximising rates of economic growth and finding resources for it, but improving the quality of life of people, giving them a sense of fulfilment through full employment, and raising their productivity. It is in deference to this world-view that the title of this volume was selected.

The theme which first enthused him was the problem of unemployment in the country and public policy needed to tackle it—the theme which formed the subject of his doctoral thesis and in which his interest continued thereafter. Readers will recall that Arthur Lewis had in the early 1950s talked about the phenomenon of disguised unemployment—defined as labour whose marginal productivity was close to zero (Lewis 1954). The question of whether or not disguised unemployment obtained in the under-developed economies had been subjected to empirical verification (Schultz 1964). When its existence was actually accepted both theoretically and empirically, there arose the question of measuring the extent of disguised unemployment. Nanjundappa was one of the earliest to have attempted to measure disguised unemployment at the field level by developing an appropriate methodology and using it for a field study in north Karnataka (Nanjundappa 1968). His concern for the disguisedly unemployed rural labour force subsequently gave expression to the evolution of a scheme of employment guarantee under the Employment Affirmation Scheme evolved by him as Economic Advisor and Planning Secretary, Government of Karnataka. Though this scheme had a precursor in the Employment Guarantee Scheme that was implemented in

Maharashtra, Karnataka was the first state *after* Maharashtra to have adopted the scheme, thanks to Nanjundappa's persistent pleas to, and persuasion of, the Government of Karnataka.

With the change in planning strategy at the national level from growth to employment orientation since the launching of the Fifth Five-Year Plan, the state plans too had to fall in line. However, the exercise of evolving an employment-oriented plan required reliable and appropriate data on the employment potential of the numerous plan schemes. Kahn had talked about employment multiplier—that a given increment in investment would cause, by establishing backward and forward linkages, an increase in employment by some multiplier. Though it appeared very elegant and attractive, this theoretical construct needed to be operationalised such that in the field context the employment effect of investment was fully captured. As part of this task, Nanjundappa looked upon investment as an activity that created an asset; an asset that was to be operated and maintained if it were to yield a stream of income. Therefore, he argued that investment would generate employment at three stages, viz., creation, operation and maintenance of the asset. This part of the employment was described as on-site direct employment. According to him there was also another component of employment, viz., indirect off-site employment which is generated on account of the activities of supplying inputs needed by the asset and also the consumer goods required to satisfy demand created by new incomes generated, as also on account of the induced social and economic infrastructure. It is this conceptualisation of the process of employment generation which he communicated in a note that helped the Institute for Social and Economic Change (ISEC) in estimating the employment potential of the plan schemes in response to a request from the Government of Karnataka (Aziz and Rayappa 1978).

Public finance has for long been a field of special interest to Nanjundappa, both as a teacher and researcher. He was one of the earliest to raise the issue of centralisation of resources under Indian fiscal federalism and argued for a change in the devolution mechanism (Nanjundappa 1966, 1974). In a perceptive essay, he also attacked the practice of financing major development projects out of budget funds, which needlessly slowed the pace of development itself. Besides limiting funds for development due to budgetary constraints, even the limited funds were not rationally allocated since many projects used to be (probably still are) sanctioned without proper project formulation and economic appraisal. He therefore advocated that those projects whose end products were of the nature of a trading activity should be taken out of the present system of central assistance and budgetary finance in order to evolve sound investment programmes and ensure an optimum use of resources. He advocated the setting up of a National Development Bank or sectoral banks such as the National Power Development Bank and National Forest Development Bank for financing the development projects (Nanjundappa 1976a: 57–67). He also deplored indiscriminate subsidisation and wanted subsidies to be restricted to situations where (*i*) external economic benefits do not get reflected in the incomes of purchasers and cannot be traced to beneficiaries who can be charged for by the state in other ways, and (*ii*) the phenomenon of indivisibility prevails and as such, costs are difficult to cover (ibid.: 57–58).

He critically scrutinised the theme of developing local government institutions, both in urban and rural areas, and their financial base (Nanjundappa and Nadkarni 1967; Nanjundappa 1976a: 137–51), much before the din about *panchayati raj* in Karnataka had started in the 1980s. While emphasising the need for building these institutions and for starting the development process from below, he also cautioned that 'it will detract from the dignity and autonomy of a self-government body if it is to depend entirely on finances provided from above' (Nanjundappa 1976a: 140). He also observed significantly that proper financial planning for local bodies could promote the efficiency of even state budgeting. He believed that 'a relatively high rate of locally financed investment can be achieved together with autonomy, thereby preserving the link between individual sacrifice and benefit, and providing incentive for the release of new energies necessary to transform an economically stagnant village into a dynamic one' (ibid.: 151).

There is so much talk today about primacy to rural development in the country. Michael Lipton had raised the question of urban bias in the planning process in the less developed countries. It was Nanjundappa, who, in his Presidential Address to the Indian Economic Association in 1981 (Nanjundappa 1982), tried to quantify the extent of this bias in Indian planning. This exercise was also elaborated in a separate book (Nanjundappa 1981).

But Nanjundappa is not a populist who would advocate mindless subsidisation of agriculture in the name of correcting the urban bias. He asserted that 'there ought to be a proper economic correspondence between investment made on irrigation projects and the payment which the beneficiaries make towards the use of water' (Nanjundappa 1976a: 69). He did not change this stand later, in spite of the farmers' agitations in Karnataka and elsewhere, protesting against levies or charges on irrigated crops or for water use. At his Sri S. Nijalingappa Endowment Lecture at Bangalore University later, he was forthright in attacking the inequitable impact of investment in irrigation—particularly major and medium irrigation—and on income redistribution, and called for a policy of 'charging for irrigation on a full cost basis' so that it pays for itself and the government can have funds enough to meet the needs of the rural poor and other investment requirements, thus also softening the iniquitous impact of major irrigation in the process. He also took care to advocate that there should not be cost over-run, that time schedules be maintained and underutilisation of irrigation potential avoided so that farmers are not compelled to pay for the inefficiency of the government (Nanjundappa 1987).

It is not surprising that he turned his critical look at Indian industry as well, which in fact he did much earlier. He took a keen interest in the Monopolies Inquiry Commission's Report in 1965, wrote on 'Restrictive Trade Practices and Public Policy' for the Indian Economic Association's Annual Conference in 1966, and pursued the problem of resale price maintenance at the London School of Economics in 1969–70, around which time he was also studying road-user taxation at Manchester and Oxford. He published his results in India at his favourite University at Dharwad (Nanjundappa 1971). Resale price maintenance refers to the practice of manufacturers who fix uniform retail prices for their respective brands below which their goods should not be sold in the market. A trader who does not fall in line attracts sanctions not only from the manufacturer whose price is cut but also from all manufacturers who are party to the collective agreement. The practice is often labelled a conspiracy against the consuming public. Nanjundappa advanced an alternative theory of resale price maintenance for a developing economy. Instead of being a manufacturers' or dealers' movement as in developed countries, he showed that in India it was the result of government policy itself.

Being a teacher, another favourite theme of Nanjundappa is investment in human capital. In contrast to the role of monetary or financial resources, the role of real resources has been emphasised in the process of development of the less developed countries. Since human resource was conceived as one such real resource, Nurkse, Lewis, Todaro and others outlined the need for human resource mobilisation for development. Based on the realisation that the supply of skilled and professional categories of human resource is not elastic enough, it was felt that the available human resources have to be developed to make them more productive through education and training. This calls for investment of financial resources in education and training. Besides, in the context of resource allocation, a question that bothers the planner, allocation of resources to education must be justified. In the literature on the subject three criteria of resource allocation to education have been suggested: (*i*) the extent of contribution of education expenditure to the growth of national income, (*ii*) the magnitude of economic benefits/returns from education in relation to costs, and (*iii*) computation of educational requirements independent of market values. After duly examining the relative appropriateness of these criteria, Nanjundappa advocated that from the point of view of optimum allocation of resources in the underdeveloped economies where competing investment expenditure is common, the rate of return criterion would offer a powerful decision tool (Nanjundappa 1965). Of course, he admitted that educational expenditure did have a consumption and maintenance component too, as suggested by his student (Nadkarni 1965); yet he took the entire educational expenditure as investment on human capital formation. The position taken by Nanjundappa has two important policy implications: (*i*) to the extent that human capital formation through education and training is found to have greater contribution to growth (as stressed by Schultz [1960]), educational expenditure should get greater priority in the scheme of resource allocation for economic planning; and (*ii*) since the returns to elementary school education are found to be higher, priority should be given to school education rather than higher education.

His interest in the financial aspects of human resource development subsequently led him to study the most vexed question of financial allocation to higher education and more particularly, to university education (Nanjundappa 1976a: 91–102, 1976b). In his own words, 'the present system of financing higher education through grants does not score well either on equity or on benefit principle. The balance of the argument is in favour of bringing about a closer alignment between the costs of education and price students pay in the form of fees.' But he also hastens to add, 'this is not to suggest that universities can and should behave exactly like business firms . . . this should not and cannot happen' (Nanjundappa 1976a: 95–96). He believes that some subsidisation is inevitable here, but it should be open and selective so that a rational allocation is possible. His scheme calls for treating expenses on higher education as a loan to students to be repaid in convenient instalments when they begin earning. Such a measure has the potential of reducing wastage without having to sacrifice access to higher education for those who seek it.

Professor Nanjundappa found similar anomalies in the field of investment on roads and road financing, marked by wastage, inefficiency and inequity. He conducted research on this problem at the Universities of Manchester and Oxford from 1968 to 1970. Being durable investments, he pointed out that roads were eligible for borrowing on capital account, making it possible to float bonds. He advocated the establishment of a tax system which took into account road usage and wear and tear, and argued for pricing of roads for their optimal use and development. He also developed a scientific method of computing road costs for the purpose of pricing (Nanjundappa 1973).

In her Foreword to this book (ibid.: viii) Lady Ursula Hicks remarks significantly: 'To my mind the special merit of Dr. Nanjundappa's book is that although he is well read in the international literature, both his analysis of the problems and his proposals for solving them are related closely to Indian conditions. They are, however, *relevant* to practicable policies in most low income, developing countries . . .' (emphasis added). These remarks are significant, because they apply to Prof. Nanjundappa's other work as well. What is more, much of what he said even earlier has not lost its relevance today. For him academic excellence was not an obective in itself. Even while he strove for it, his overriding consideration was the relevance for policy in Indian conditions.

REFERENCES

Aziz, Abdul and P.H. Rayappa (1978). 'Employment Potential of Plan Schemes'. Institute for Social and Economic Change: Bangalore (unpublished).

Lewis, Arthur (1954). 'Economic Development with Unlimited Supply of Labour', *Manchester School Journal*, vol. 29, no. 4: 1–18.

Nadkarni, M.V. (1965). 'Some Definitional Aspects of Investment in Human Capital', *Indian Economic Journal*, Conference Number, Part III, December.

Nanjundappa, D.M. (1965). 'An Appraisal of the Criteria for Investment in Education', *Indian Economic Journal*, Conference Number, Part III, December.

———. (1966). 'Resource Transfer from the Union to the States—Case for Lesser Centralisation and More Flexible Scheme of Devolution', *Indian Economic Journal*, vol. 14, no. 3, October–December.

———. (1968). *Surplus Manpower and Economic Development in Mysore*. Government of Mysore: Bangalore.

———. (1971). *Resale Price Maintenance in a Developing Economy*. Karnatak University: Dharwad.

———. (1973). *Road User Taxation and Road Finance in Indian Economy*. Jawaharlal Nehru Memorial Institute of Development Studies: Bombay (distributed by Popular Prakashan, Bombay).

———. (1974). *Inter-Governmental Financial Relations in India*. Sterling: New Delhi.

———. (1976a). *Development with Social Justice*. Oxford and I.B.H.: New Delhi.

———. (1976b). *Working of University Finances*. Sterling Publishers: New Delhi.

———. (1981). *Area Planning and Rural Development*. Associated Publishing Company: New Delhi.

———. (1982). 'Rural Urban Conundrum in Indian Planning', *Indian Economic Journal*, vol. 29, no. 4: 1–18, April–June.

———. (1987). *Irrigation Investment and Income Redistribution*. Bangalore University: Bangalore.

Nanjundappa, D.M. and M.V. Nadkarni (1967). *Local Taxation in Urban Areas*. Karnatak University: Dharwad.

Schultz, T.W. (1960). 'Capital Formation by Education', *Journal of Political Economy*, vol. LXVIII, no. 6, December.

———. (1964). *Transforming Traditional Agriculture*. Yale University Press: New Haven.

3

Economic Growth and Social Justice

V.K.R.V. RAO

THREE MAJOR PROBLEMS

Planning for economic development cannot be content merely with targets for economic growth and increase in production. It has also to ensure equitable distribution and alleviation of poverty. This needs a philosophy and a development perspective, which were indeed behind the thinking of both Gandhi and Nehru, and the Indian Constitution. No one seems to remember Gandhi's criterion for economic choice, viz., that while taking economic decisions, the planner or the administrator, as the case may be, must think in terms of giving priority to helping the poor out of their poverty. This absence of philosophy of development behind planning and economic growth is regrettable. Quantitative targets without regard for the distributional implications are creating an environment within the country that has become allergic to growth because it does not involve either mass participation or fulfilment of mass needs.

At the dawn of Independence, India had many priorities and problems to tackle. I shall refer to only three major problems that confronted the country and which continue to confront it today.

1. National Integration.
2. The role to be assigned to the people in the government.
3. Economic and social development.

In fact, these problems are interlinked in terms of their solution; and, while they needed to be tackled individually, they also needed to be dealt with in a coordinated and integrated manner. Unfortunately, the first two did not receive the attention they deserved. National integration was taken for granted, while the active role that people should play in government was not given much attention. In fact, attention was concentrated on economic development. The newly-freed Indian people were expecting freedom to bring about a nationally-oriented utilisation of their natural and human resources, a substantial increase in the national product, a significant rise in their levels of living, and release from poverty and unemployment. Economic growth became the major goal of development; and it was expected to solve all their other problems. In this, they were also influenced by the general obsession with economic growth that they found all around them, whether in the capitalist or the communist states, or in the victorious or defeated states that emerged from the Second World War. In fact, the rate of economic growth became the yardstick for measuring national achievements; and in the process the objectives behind economic growth were either taken for granted or assumed a secondary role.

There is no denying the fact that in macro terms the last four decades have seen a considerable increase in national product in India; there has also been a perceptible increase in per capita product. But the decline in the poverty of the masses has not been significant, nor has there been any noticeable movement towards reducing inequalities in income and wealth in the country. The propertied and similar classes which constitute the 'above poverty line category' of the Indian masses, and those who joined them, grew in power, influence and economic well-being and resources; but the vast majority of the population remained largely outside the boundaries of this progress and found no visible improvement in either their economic or social conditions. It is true that production increased, and with it a pale imitation of Western affluence, sometimes conspicuously vulgar, appeared in the country. Large houses, modern hotels, fleets of cars and tarred roads for travel, and shops for the sale of luxury goods came up; but these were outside the purview of the poor masses, who became either passive and awe-struck with admiration, or were imbued with an inner resentment that spent itself in futile longings and a non-participant or deadening role in national economic development. Sometimes this led to unrest and violence, but was speedily put down by the government, which was run directly by or in close cooperation with the minority that constituted the elite and other vested interests in property, wealth, and the new production process. Economic development was leading to the creation of a dual society in the country and causing disillusionment among the masses who had been expecting Independence to free them from their nagging problems of poverty, unemployment, and low social and economic status.

APING THE WEST AND HOPING FOR THE BEST

All this happened not necessarily from mala fide action on the part of the ruling classes in the country. Economic growth was then conceived of as a diffusionary process that would automatically spill over areas and classes, and would give the masses of the population as well as all the areas in the country a significant share of its dividends. In actual fact, this did not happen. Oases of affluence and economic well-being surrounded by Saharas of poverty and economic backwardness appeared in India. The theorists of economic growth have also changed their perception and given up their belief in its automatic diffusionary effects over all the regions and people of the country. They are now talking in terms of having to provide for in-built elements in the growth process that would lead to a more equitable distribution of the dividends from development, of a better distribution of incomes and assets as a positive factor for stimulating and accelerating economic growth, of placing the objective of maximising employment in the technology used for increasing production, and of making direct attacks on poverty by differential treatment of target groups of the poor in rural areas. More light also seems to be dawning in development literature on human resources, social obstacles and people's participation. There is now more talk of the difference between real development and mere economic growth, not only with respect to the developing countries but even with regard to the developed nations with their much larger per capita national products.

The path that development took in our country was based on a mistaken application of the Western model of development, involving capital intensity, use of modern technology and urbanisation, without taking into account our abundant labour supply, the extensive prevalence of illiteracy and the lack of skills among our labour force, the predominantly rural character of our population, and the prevalence of a commercial rather than an industrial bias in our entrepreneurship. It took the West many decades to develop their industry and urban civilisation, with a harsh transition from their original rural status, made possible by the absence of a parliamentary democracy, lack of class consciousness among their working class and/or organisation on their part, and the absence of an informed and progressive public opinion. Their problem of initial capital accumulation had also been solved by their conquest or colonisation of other countries. Combining this with their advance in science and technology, and with the dynamism and austerity of their early capitalist classes, they were able to achieve a rate of economic growth and a level of national income which took them beyond the demographic transition stage, and enabled them to go ahead with their capital-intensive production and allied use of labour-saving technology. The problem of accumulation is crucial to economic development, and especially so at its earlier stages. Once development has taken place and achieved momentum, the rate of accumulation in terms of the percentage of the national product saved declines; savings become largely involuntary on the part of corporate groups and higher income households, consumption need not diminish on the part of the masses, and resource mobilisation and its productive utilisation become easier. This, in brief, was the history of development in the Western countries.

When the newly-independent countries, including India, thought of going in for economic development, they saw as their model the contemporary developed countries with their capital-intensive production, their urban concentration and styles of living, their unequal incomes and wealth sought to be softened by the welfare expenditure of their governments, and their high levels of technology. They forgot not only the history that had preceded and explained this development, but also their current status in production, capital supply and technological skills that constituted the base of their continuing economic growth. They thus opted for a model of growth that was based on capital-intensive industry, neglect of agriculture and the masses who worked in agriculture and rural areas, and failed to develop the human resource potential in their abundant labour supply. Neglecting human resource development, they embarked on a programme of capital-intensive economic development that necessitated the large-scale dependence on foreign aid in both capital and technology and brought in the demonstration effects of Western affluence and its corrupting impact on their own domestic elites. The results of this purely economistic approach to development, based on a model unsuited to their social, economic and resource conditions, led to the creation of a highly inegalitarian society, with pockets of affluence mainly confined to urban areas, rural stagnation, growing unemployment, and continuing poverty among their masses. The result was disillusionment and a search for alternative ways of development.

ECLECTIC MIXTURE

An alternative model of economic development requires that priority attention be paid to such factors as illiteracy, lack of industrial or technical skills, vast inequality in the possession of not only land but also of other productive assets, and dominance of agriculture and the rural sector in the economy with distressingly low output per worker. The inevitable result was more one of confusion than of ideological confrontation, and lack of a clear understanding among their people of the ideological implications of development on their own welfare and their own role as active participants in the development process. In India, the developmental model adopted contained an eclectic mixture of two ideologies. On the one hand, we shared with Western capitalist countries their political system of parliamentary democracy, adult franchise, periodic elections and fundamental rights or basic individual freedom. We also shared with them, on the economic front, private property and a large role for private enterprise and the profit motive, not only in agriculture but also in industry, trade, services and other sectors of economic activity. From the socialist model we borrowed centralised planning, a dominant public sector in industry, transport, energy and credit, public regulation of private economic activity, administered prices, a battery of controls and a bulging bureaucracy. But we did not have the advantage of a social and economic revolution preceding development. Nor did we back our development with the necessary institutional changes in social relations and property rights, or an understanding and positive participation by the people or committed cadres of party workers. We also failed to pay special—let alone priority—attention to human resource development. India succeeded in setting up the formal framework of a socialist pattern within the context of a mixed economy and a parliamentary democracy, but failed to bring about a socialist transformation of Indian society and the development of its human resources. At the same time, it is an unquestionable fact that there has been substantial economic development in India. While its per capita product still puts it in the group of least developed countries, it is now one of the major industrialised countries in the world on a macro or national basis, with an extensive and deepening industrial structure, use of modern technology and a large supply of scientific, technical and professional personnel. There has been economic growth but it has not been accompanied by the expected measure of social justice.

I do not believe that India's decision to go in for a mixed economy to secure economic growth with social justice was wrong; but where we did go wrong was in the choice we made between two alternative means of operating the mixed economy. In what may be called Type A, the state agencies and the public sector provide external economies to a fast-growing private sector and offer no effective opposition to the increasing concentration of economic power in private hands. The basic decisions regarding production, distribution, savings and investment in this case are taken either by the private sector or, in response to its pressure, by the state agencies. In Type B, the state uses the public sector as 'commanding heights' of the economy to determine the main direction of the country's economic development. In this pattern, the private sector, while being allowed to grow, is prevented from generating concentration of economic power; and its development is subordinated to the overall demands of development in the country. In this way, the state converts the commanding heights into lucrative heights as well, ensuring thereby an acceleration in the tempo of capital formation and resource mobilisation. The Indian experiment with a mixed economy tended to conform to Type A rather than Type B. Hence its failure to bring about the desired socialist transformation.

This failure was also facilitated, and, in fact, was the result of the political pattern or power structure associated with Type A in a mixed economy functioning within the framework of a parliamentary democracy. The power structure associated with Type A turned out to be a political alliance of the intermediate classes with the upper classes, resorting to socialist ideology only to delude the masses and win their electoral support, while in fact using all levers of power, patronage, and influence to facilitate a type of capitalist development which was in favour of vested interests and narrow sections of Indian society. An alternative power structure would have been an alliance of the intermediate classes with the have-nots, using socialist ideology to release mass energy and initiative on a vast scale, and the levers of power to promote the process of socialist transformation of the economy in the interests of the widest sections of Indian society, especially those at the bottom. This latter political pattern would have gone well with Type B and enabled the mixed economy to have ushered in a socialist trans-formation. What occurred, however, was the choice of the former political pattern, with the power structure being constituted by the intermediate classes in combination with the upper classes and vested interests; and what obviously suited them was Type A of the mixed economy, which certainly could not be expected to usher in a socialist transition.

What was wrong, therefore, was not so much the framework of the strategy as the neglect of its political economy. There was no clear identification of the political and socio-cultural conditions for effective implementation of the economic strategy. The failure thus lay in taking a narrowly economic rather than a politico-economic and macro-sociological view of the process of socialist transformation and not formulating the political and social strategy required. The missing element in the Indian strategy has been, therefore, the absence of mobilisation of the political, social, ethical and cultural forces needed for socialist transformation.

The Indian experience has shown that under a purely economic or purely political pattern of parliamentary democracy, economic growth with social justice is bound to be thwarted by vested interests and the power structure on the non-economic plane. What is needed in order to secure social justice along with economic growth, or vice versa, therefore, is a comprehensive and integrated approach to development that would take into account not only economic factors relevant to growth or political factors pertinent to a parliamentary democracy, but also the socio-cultural factors relevant to both justice and growth, the direct and indirect influence exerted by vested interests, the composition and bias of the power structure, and all the variables on the non-economic parameter

that could either facilitate or obstruct the path to a socialist transformation.

Thus, the failure on the part of the authorities concerned to take
into account the effect of unequal distribution of productive assets
and the social, political and cultural condition of the rural masses
brought about the non-achievement of social justice, even when
there was some spectacular success in economic growth in the
agricultural arena. The freedom conferred on private enterprise
did not help the poor but led to a strengthening of the vested
interests in the rural economy and the creation of a powerful kulak
class that inevitably had its impact on the rural power structure to
the detriment of the rural poor and social justice to which they
were entitled.

In actual fact, the political and economic freedom embodied in
political democracy became a fertile ground for the dominance of
the socio-political system by vested interests and the elite and
privileged classes, who used the framework of the political system
to strengthen their control over the power structure, and their
share in the dividends from economic growth at the expense of the
masses, who were given a titular right to vote them out of political
power. The failure to take into account the socio-political, cultural
and economic conditions of the masses—that basically determine
both growth of production and betterment of distribution—and give
these factors priority attention led even well-intentioned economic
planning and the freedom enshrined in political democracy to fall
below targeted growth rates, to stand in the queue for foreign aid
with all its implications for national sovereignty, and to opt for
deficit financing and inflation while at the same time failing to
solve the problems of mass poverty and unemployment.

The presence or absence of political freedom did not seem to
make much difference as far as the achievement of social justice
was concerned, as long as no notice was taken of the relevance of
the social, political, cultural and economic conditions of the people
on either economic development or political articulation, and no
attempt made to giving priority to the measures needed to bring
them in line with the needs of both economic growth and social
justice.

There can be no two opinions on the need for economic development to be linked with both equity and freedom. In fact, economic development without equity would result in social and

political tensions of a magnitude that could endanger the very achievements of economic growth, while economic development with unrestricted freedom for the private individual and private enterprise is bound to lead to social injustice that could well stall the process of economic growth. Planning for development has to be on an integrated basis that would ensure economic growth with social justice without jeopardising individual freedom. This is easier said than done; and its implementation depends not only on national factors and their appropriate functioning but also on international factors and their impact on the power structure, social tensions, and national economic and political policies.

A FEW SUGGESTIONS

I shall now put forward a few suggestions aimed at making possible economic and social development in India, along with the achievement of equity or social justice and the maintenance of freedom or individual civil liberties and opportunities for growth.

The first, and, in some ways, the most important suggestion is to bring about the people's active participation in the development process and in planning it as well. The people at large, both classes and masses, have to be made aware and accept the implications of development with equity. This includes the necessary changes in their social and cultural attitudes, their work ethic and industrial discipline, their urge for increased consumption and its qualification by increased accumulation, self-reliance in economic effort, restraints on individual holdings of income and wealth, and on the unrestricted play of individual freedom and private enterprise. Above all, the adoption of dialogue, debate, compromise and a conciliatory approach to the resolution of internal differences and disputes is salient to create the necessary social, political and economic background for a successful attempt at achieving development with equity and freedom. People's conscious acceptance of the goal of development with equity and freedom, and their active participation in the development process cannot be obtained without a comprehensive, nation-wide programme of information, communication and education, both formal and informal, backed by all possible media—including the modern media such as radio and TV and the traditional media such as folklore, folk songs, plays and puppetry—and an open debate and discussion on the issues and actions involved. In the final analysis, it is the people's power and their active participation that is the best guarantee of ensuring development of the kind we desire. For too long now we have neglected the people and left the stage free for the elite and the privileged classes. This mistake has to be rectified if we want the desired development; and this requires a comprehensive and integrated approach, combining the economic with the social, political and cultural factors involved.

The second suggestion is to dissociate the concept of freedom from that of the economic freedom associated with private enterprise, market forces and the profit-maximising motive, and place it on a firm footing of social equality, reduction of economic disparities within the limits of tolerance and functional efficiency, equality of opportunity, concern for the maintenance of cultural diversities and non-disruptive social deviance, encouragement of creativity and innovation directed to the developmental goals, and protection of basic civil liberties for all its citizens.

Third, in determining economic targets for development, we should primarily take into account the limits set by our human and natural resources and the need for fostering self-reliance and abandoning dependence. What is required as the goal of economic development is that it will give all the people in the country a reasonable national minimum living standard and a happy and culturally satisfying life, rather than the multitude of material possessions associated with Western capitalist affluence and its social and psychological tensions. Apart from philosophical reasons and the traditional belief that links plain living with high thinking and a happy life, achieving a per capita product of the type that Western capitalist countries now have is beyond our natural and human resources. It can only be achieved, if at all, by abandoning self-reliance and submitting the nation to a state of dependence, and providing a high level of living only for a minority consisting of the privileged classes while imposing much lower levels of living and consequent frustration and discontent on the vast majority of the non-privileged population. There could be room for a moderate measure of inequality in incomes, but this should largely be of a functional, and not of a rentier character. The important thing is not to get lost in a competitive contest for affluence with the capitalist nations and their high per capita incomes. Sophisticated technology could be used, not for capital-intensive capitalist development, but to reduce the drudgery of labour—agricultural, industrial, transport and other kinds, including household labour mainly undertaken by women. It could also be used to provide collective facilities either for consumption or for labour-intensive production.

In general, the technology used in our region should be adapted to the availability of domestic resources, be ecologically benign and sustainable, aim at the development of human resources rather than the large-scale use of expensive machinery and technology. If developing nations set limits to their economic growth in this manner, think in terms of a largely egalitarian society, and concentrate more on human resource development, people's participation would be easier, and the development process would not cause the hardships, tensions and conflicts generated by the efforts of unequal economic growth.

Of course we cannot escape some of the demonstration effect of the affluent lifestyles of the most developed countries in this world of travel, tourism and global communications, but we can counteract this by (a) appropriate education in the superior ethos of a less affluent lifestyle, and (b) by backing this action by preventing demonstrative opulence and conspicuous consumption within our national frontiers. I do not believe that the development I am arguing for can be consistent with the five-star hotel culture of the affluent styles of living that we are providing in selected pockets of the countries of the developing world on the plea of promoting tourism and earning foreign exchange. In fact, it is high time that these countries took a second, and a whole look at the tourist industry, and worked out the social and total development cost-benefit ratio of the investment incurred on its promotion to attract affluent tourists to spend their foreign currency in our countries.

A primary aim of our developmental effort should be the development of our human resources. We must not forget that development is for the promotion of domestic human welfare and not for the sacrifice of the domestic citizen at the altar of the competitive raising of economic growth rates. Nutrition, health, literacy, skills, education, culture, social awareness, humaneness, spiritual and ethical values, compassion, fraternity, secularism, respect for human dignity, service of fellow-men, self-reliance and the work ethic—all these are required for human resource development;

and necessary inputs for the purpose should be built into the developmental process. Instead of merely compiling indices of national product, I would also suggest the compilation of indices of human resource development as a measure of the success achieved by the developmental effort. If at all we want to enter into international competition in development, the criteria used should be the quantum and rate of human resource development rather than that of material production and affluent lifestyles.

Development, whether of material or human resources, cannot be achieved without saving and investment. Accumulation and work motivation are the basic sinews of economic growth and the socio-political system should be oriented to provide both. Financing of development should be through domestic resource mobilisation and not by resort to inflation. If foreign borrowing is resorted to, it should only be for productive investment, returns from which should make the borrowing self-liquidating within a defined period. Foreign grants should be avoided as far as possible, as charity is not a two-way process in terms of its psychological effect on the donor and the recipient. The *bakshis* mentality is as bad in international economic relations as it is accepted to be in domestic economic relations. Development is a national challenge and the response should come from within and not through charity from without. As long as there is no world state, no world government, and no world finance minister or world public finance, developing nations should rely much more decisively on domestic effort and domestic resource mobilisation than on foreign philanthrophy. It is better to cut the coat according to the cloth, even if it means a shorter coat, than to go in for a larger coat at the expense of national self-respect and self-reliance and the risk of falling into 'dependence'.

There is also no escape from planning, if development is to succeed in achieving its goals; but planning should leave adequate scope for genuine decentralisation that could release the dormant energies of the people and secure their active participation in local and regional development, the results of which they can see and the main dividends from which they would be able to acquire. While there has to be centralised planning with regard to the national infrastructure in food; energy; transport; science; technology and credit, and in areas like large production units; capital-intensive economic activity; and defence, decentralised and participative planning should be the rule for local and regional development and for the establishment of small production units, maximising of employment, securing the fulfilment of basic human needs and aiding in the establishment of integrated rural and urban communities that would be viable in terms of political participation, social equalisation and economic growth. Steps should also be taken to see that the bureaucracy, which is both the prop and the bugbear of planned development, is effectively oriented in the social, political and economic goals of development, with ample room for feedback and interaction between it and those who are the expected beneficiaries of its functioning. Above all, the planning machinery should provide for monitoring and progress reporting at periodic intervals of the developmental efforts at the central, regional and local levels. These exercises should be open documents and subjected to public debate and discussion, so that the people at large are drawn into an understanding of the planning process, made aware of their own responsibilities and contributory potential in the matter, and induced to play a positive and participatory role in the developmental effort. There should be integrated rural development of village clusters for the creation of viable rural communities, and planned urban development to curb the growth of large urban agglomerations in favour of small and medium towns. A rural–urban continuum should be created, based on mutual exchange on equitable terms, reduced rural–urban disparities, and the evolution of a nationally operative style of living that would cut at the roots of the growing rural–urban dichotomy that is now such a conspicuous phenomenon of development in our country.

In conclusion, I would declare myself to be an optimist with regard to the developmental prospects of our country and the region as a whole. However, we have to move fast in the direction that I have outlined; and we have to draw on the basic and humanising roots in our diverse spiritual and religious heritage. Development requires positive participation by the people and needs a spirit of self-reliance, respect for human dignity, and confidence in our ability to march together towards the goal of economic betterment, social growth and freedom for individual growth and happiness. It is a total process and involves all aspects of life, not only economic, but also social, political, religious, cultural and ecological. I hope that the people from both classes and masses will rise to the occasion.

4

Education—Why, How and Whither of its Planning

MALCOLM S. ADISESHIAH

NEED FOR RENEWAL: THE WHY?

Education is a sector of the economy and, in my view, is wrongly classed under social services. It is of course a social service, it is a consumption item, it is a good which is enjoyed for its own sake. But it is also the engine of economic development, it is a subject which involves costs and benefits, and it is, after defence, the sector that calls for the largest share of the annual budget of the country (which is usually also measured in terms of the percentage of the gross domestic product that is appropriated). It is therefore appropriate that it should be weighed in the balance from time to time in order to see how, when and where it needs change and renewal; it needs to cast off the worn-out and outdated and be replaced by the needed techniques of today; it requires an analysis of how the huge investment that it involves can be made optimal in the sense of getting a higher/better return, and how its proliferating expansion which faces the resource crunch can be arrested.

This is also the right time for such an overall reappraisal because it is now four decades since certain educational and linked employment obligations were made part of our Constitution by our founding fathers, and it is necessary to see how far we have been able to meet them. It is nearly three decades since the last review of the system by the Kothari Commission took place, which resulted in the 1958 parliamentary resolution on the National Educational

Policy that was to be followed (GOI 1958). Again, we should see how far we have been able to carry out these directives. And, most recently, parliament has after a year's public discussion set forth the National Policy on Education—1986, along with a Programme of Action which makes precise the timing and the steps involved in executing that Policy (GOI 1986a, 1986b). And so, in this call for a renewal of our educational system at all levels, it is appropriate that we take a fresh look at the various facets of educational development in India—the educational plans, the techniques used for their formulation, their substance, content, and end result in terms of a happy and contented people with rising standards of living over the past four decades since we took in hand, as a people, our national and educational development.

There is, of course, the problem of the very short period of time that has elapsed for the attainment of what has been termed as the end result. Further, raising the abysmally low living levels of the people does not depend on education alone, but is the result of the manner of functioning of all sectors—primary, secondary and tertiary—of the social structure created, and of the political will of the people and their government.

Hence, in creating a balance sheet of the development of education over the past four decades, we can identify the elements of its strengths and of its weaknesses over this period, and the direction in which it is helping to move the living levels of the people. Most of this paper will be devoted to the plus and minus aspects of the short-term balance sheet, and will make no more than a brief, passing reference to the longer-term issues of the direction in which it is helping to move society.

THE HOW

Educational development over the past four decades has four *positive* achievements to its credit.

First, it has thrown open the doors of education at the point of admissions at every level—primary, secondary and higher levels—to all the people of India—rich, middle income and poor, rural and urban, forward and backward, with special incentives to the backward, which, in part, is compensation for the discrimination faced

by them in the past. There has thus occurred an impressive quantitative expansion in all facets of education.

Second, there has, as a consequence, been a veritable explosion
in education, measured by the number of institutions and enrolled
students. In elementary schools the expansion was from 1 lakh
with 21.3 lakh students in 1951 to 6.3 lakh schools with 727 lakh
students in 1985. At the second level the expansion was from 0.07
lakh schools and 2.2 lakh students in 1951 to 0.57 lakh schools with
9.4 lakh students in 1985. And, in universities, from 18 universities
and 61,000 students in 1951 to 150 universities with 3.5 million
students in 1985. This is roughly a three-fold increase in educational
institutions and a six-fold increase in student enrolment (NIEPA
1985; GOI 1986c).

The third factor, resulting from the above two, is educational
manpower. India has the second largest (next only to China) pool
of educated and skilled men and women in the world, estimated at
over 120 million. In the more specialised field of sciences (including
the social sciences) and engineering, India has the third largest
cadre of scientists in the world at 32 million after the United States
(90 million) and the erstwhile Soviet Union (82 million) (UNESCO
1987).

Fourth, there has been the development of institutions of excel-
lance at every level—the school, the science faculties of universities,
the engineering, medical and agricultural specialities, and the
research institutions both in the natural and life sciences and other
social sciences, notably economics. These peaks of excellence are
few and far between, but in a sense that is the nature of peaks, to
open up vistas of what might be, what will be.

The educational development of the country also records a
number of *setbacks*.

The first is the familiar one—familiar to all sectors of our Five-
Year Plans—of a gap, in some cases a growing gap, between
targets and attainment. The most serious gap is with regard to the
pledge of education for all, set forth in the Constitutional obligation
of universal elementary education, whose attainment target was
1962, but which today, after nearly three and a half decades, is still
elusive. This difference between targets and actuals characterises
the higher secondary system as well, which in 1960 established as a
target 50 per cent of its entrants flowing into its vocational stream.
Three decades after launching these institutions (+2), a mere 2.2

per cent of the entrants appear to have opted for the vocational stream (NIEPA 1985).

A second setback is the wide and widening gap between education and the employment market, highlighted by the fact that our 840 employment exchanges report that over 30 million men and women registered with them in 1988 are looking for employment. About half of these job-seekers are the educated unemployed—that is, those who have passed high school (matriculation/SSC) and above that level with higher qualifications. Some of these 15 million educated job-seekers are already employed but are looking for better jobs, some are students who want to earn money to pay their way through school and college. But indications are that over half comprising this group are really unemployed. Furthermore, this figure of some 7 to 10 million boys and girls who have been educated and trained at various levels, including the highest university level, and have not been able to find employment for over two years must in fact be increased several times because the catchment area of the employment exchanges is the urban areas. The educated rural unemployed do not have access to the exchanges because there *are* none in the rural areas. What is disturbing is not only the high absolute number of the educated unemployed, but their rapid multiplication over the time period from 0.5 million in 1960 to 7 to 10 million in 1988, which means that the education–employment link is currently set in the wrong direction. Within this widening gulf between education and employment, the number of those being educated for non-existent jobs or for jobs which are limited and specific from the +2 to the university graduate and post-graduate levels is growing each day. Thus, education is no longer a preparation for life, insofar as it has a decreasing relevance for the labour market which is its home, and even more seriously so, in relation to the various levels of skills demanded.

A third overall setback of the education system as it has developed is the enormous, continuous and growing wastage built into every part and level of the system.

The most familiar wastage that everyone is acquainted with is the fact that 52 out of every 100 students enrolled in Standard I drop out before Standard V and 82 before Standard X. This wastage continues through the higher secondary (Standard XII) and the graduate and post-graduate courses of the university and its affiliated colleges. In Standard XII, only nine of the 100 who enrolled in Standard I remain. At the college/university level, a survey conducted in Tamil Nadu in 1989 found that there were colleges in which no student had cleared the B.A. course, and in a majority of colleges the figure was 30 per cent. The wastage in the professional institutions—engineering, agriculture and medicine—has not been computed but in terms of cost is very high.

Another contributor to the wastage is the outmoded examination system at every level. In high school, higher secondary and university (undergraduate and post-graduate), what is tested is memory and not powers of reasoning, and the system of evaluation is an arbitrary arithmetical one. As far back as on the eve of Independence, the Radhakrishnan Commission noted that if there was only one reform possible in higher education, that should be the abolition of the examination system and its replacement with a scientific system of evaluation and self-evaluation for the student and teacher (GOI 1948). The existing examination system is not only unscientific and anti-learning, but has become the source of all forms of malpractice such as cheating, corruption and nepotism, which are gathering force every day.

Behind this examination malaise is the wastage involved in the outmoded and outdated curricula and syllabi in our educational institutions. Particularly at the university and college levels, the content of the sciences is not keeping pace with the fast expansion of knowledge and the rate of its change characterising our world. The result is a further widening of the gap between the educated and the employment market demand, giving rise to the phenomenon of the 'unemployables'.

This adds up to another form of educational waste, starting with the educated unemployable, going on to the full-time educated unemployed, the educated underemployed and the educated misemployed. Except for the full-time educated unemployed, there is no precise figure for the other forms of wastage in this area, but that it is high and at a level that a poor country like India cannot afford is obvious.

A final form of wastage are those who are left out of the school system: children of school-going age (6 to 14 years) who are not in school. Their number is rather large at two levels of computation: First, there are about 20 million children of this age group not in school on the first day of the school year. Second, by including in the category of the left out those who drop out of school (referred to earlier), the number of children without education swells to over 50 million; children who will join the adult illiteracy cohorts of the 21st century. In this form of wastage should also be included the 280 million adult illiterates of today; over the past four decades, the percentage of illiteracy has decreased from about 80 per cent in 1951 to 60 per cent in 1988, but because of the weak holding powers of the school system and the increase in population, the absolute numbers have increased from 200 million in 1951 to 280 million in 1988 (NIEPA 1985).

The tragic feature of all this wastage in the education system is not merely the squandering of our scarce resources in terms of money, equipment, library and buildings. The tragic element is that education wastage is the wastage of the human person—of the men, women and children of this country. There is no more calamitous a waste than this.

Finally, a weakness of the education system as it has developed is that it has not helped to counter the poverty of the people and correct the inequalities in the social structure: in fact, it has in some ways contributed to enlarging the number of the poor and to increasing the inequalities in the distributional system. Insofar as education has led to educated unemployment, mis-employment and unemployability over the past four decades, it has had the effect of increasing the poverty-ridden cohorts. Further, one of the strengths of the system was that it has thrown open its portals to those who had been kept out of it for centuries—the children and adults from the Scheduled Castes, Scheduled Tribes, backward communities and girls and women. But this is true only at the level of admissions. When we turn from entrance to outcome, we find that 80 per cent of those who complete school and university belong to the top 20 per cent society, a feature that has continued year after year at every level of education. As all forms of education are free and are heavily subsidised by the state, and its tax income to the extent of 80 per cent is from indirect taxes which are paid by the poor majority of society, the education system has proved to be a conduit for transferring resources from the poor majority to the well-to-do minority. In that sense the education system has been an instrument in making an unequal society more unequal (Adiseshiah 1986).

THE WHITHER: THE WAY OUT

Is there a way out of this rather serious impasse? Yes, there is, the broad outlines of which have been set forth by the National Policy on Education (1986) and the Programme of Action approved by parliament. All that is needed is for our Five-Year and Annual Plans to carry out fully and faithfully their provisions.

1. First, our educational plans should now concentrate not on quantitative expansion, but on consolidating the institutional gains that have been made and that must now provide incentives as well as compensatory learning programmes for those who are or have been excluded from the system.

This involves action at two levels. At the first level our plans should follow the Approach of the National Policy on Education, 1986, with regard to the imperative of educational equality, involving ensuring that women and girls, children and adults from the Scheduled Castes and Tribes and other backward classes are brought into the system—both its formal part and its vast, uncharted informal (adult literacy) part. As this effort at pulling in the deprived and discriminated into the educational system goes alongside the serious, if not successful, effort to alleviate the poverty of the families in this group, and makes available to them some assets so that their incomes might increase on a self-sustaining basis, educational planning can succeed in bringing into the educational stream those who have been thus far excluded from it.

The second level is that educational equality in the formal sector involves not only equality in admission into educational institutions as set forth above, but also some move towards equality in educational outcome. This means that the next three or four plans should provide for a remedial learning system for the newly-admitted, first-generation learners, some what along the lines of the tutorial system which flourishes at the private unofficial level in all states which enables backward students to catch up with their peers and even successfully pass the difficult IAS, IPS and IFS competitive tests (TNBCE 1973; University of Kerala 1985). Only provision for such compensatory learning systems in our plans can ensure that those who successfully complete school and college also include the first-generation learners from the various groups who have so far been denied education. The implications of equality for the informal sector (adult literacy) will be dealt with later.

2. Educational planning should be part of the way of life of the local community. This involves action at two levels. At one level, the elementary and secondary school plan and programmes should be developed at the local *panchayat* union level so that the schools respond to the needs, potentials and resources of the local community, making educational plans area-specific. This involves reversing the present trend implied in the National Policy on Education which increasingly centralises educational programmes in far away Delhi—such as the programme for a national curriculum (which is a contradiction in terms), for a national testing service, for a national (lecturers) selection service, for a national council of teachers, etc. Education is an intensely personal process, rooted in personal needs, and the further our educational plans move the schools and colleges and their contents and appurtenances from the students and their teachers, the more will the educational plans move in an anti-education, anti-learning direction.

This objective also ensures action at the second level of localisation. As educational plans arise out of the *panchayat samiti* level, the elementary and secondary schools will no longer function in isolation, but in and with the local community: higher secondary schools, colleges and universities will not only gear their learning programmes towards how to learn, which is their primary purpose, but will also respond to the skills needed by the local farming, artisan and commercial community. For this purpose, their learning programmes will be based on surveys of the *panchayats* with regard to the resources available, the skills needed and the employment called for, both those in current demand and those in potential development. This is the only way to begin to close the educational–employment gap from the educational end.

Finally, there are several problems associated with the entire education system, but pointedly focused on the higher education system, so that they are dealt with here in relation to universities and colleges in particular.

The first group of problems is for the system to shed its preoccupying and useless burden of running a heavy workload involving an unscientific and antiquated examination system. I have recently been engaged in assisting the formulation of the educational plan for Tamil Nadu, where a body known as the Directorate of Examination has swollen four-fold in staff and budget in the last decade, and which holds the examinations for the secondary and higher secondary systems. This kind of organisation exists in all states. At the university level, there is in every university a Comptroller of Examinations with a continuously swelling department year after year. Here clear guidelines for the reform of the examination system are laid down in the National Policy on Education, which every educational plan should embody, and which involves: (*i*) the abolition of the present external, memory-testing, end-of-the-year or end-of-the-course examination system; (*ii*) replacing this with the semester system and its accompanying continuous internal assessment, involving appropriate changes in the learning material and teaching methodology; (*iii*) substituting the present essay-type questions with objective short answers set by those who teach the courses (instead of the present highly confidential and anonymous question papers set by those who have not taught the course); (*iv*) moving to a credit system in place of a fixed core and optionals curriculum, replacing marks with grades in assessing learning attainments. What the National Policy on Education does not say is who is to administer this reformed system of evaluation. My answer is not the NCERT, the State Director of Examination, the UGC, or the university: it should be designed and operated by each learning unit, the high school, the higher secondary, the college and the university departments.

A second group of problems is for some decentralisation in educational institutions: at the school level, every school being given some freedom to experiment with the syllabus in relation to its local environment; in the case of the university, (*i*) to replace the system of affiliated colleges which is a non-academic control of colleges peculiar to this subcontinent with a system of autonomous colleges (which is what any college ought to be) so that they can develop according to their creative potential, and (*ii*) to give the departments of the university autonomy, which will free them from strangulation by the Board of Studies and the Office of the Registrar.

A third group of problems relates to the vocation of the teacher. There is a technical problem in this matter. In my student–teacher days, a teacher was regarded as one who was born and not made, as one who had a higher education degree, and for the university, a post-graduate degree (to which today a first research degree, M. Phil., is attached). At the rate at which knowledge is expanding, the greater level of maturity of students today, and the new development in the art of communication, it is clear that all teachers need to be trained—for pre-primary, school, college and university.

Today's teacher is not born; he or she has to be made. Thus, the academy of teacher training set up in each university meets a felt need of the teacher and the educational system.

There is also the group of problems relating to the teacher—his or her level of emoluments, conditions of work and prospects for the future. This has to be guided by the union of teachers to which everyone concerned—the school, college, university and governments—has to be responsive. And then there are the moral problems of the teachers. How is their work to be assessed? Just as the teacher assists in the evaluation and self-evaluation of his or her students, students too can assist in the evaluation and self-evaluation of their teachers. The moral standards displayed and maintained by the teacher will, in the end, be a reflection of the morals of students of society at large. Not much mileage will be gained by appealing to the 'sacred vocation' of teachers and the need for them to set an example to the students and society. This they should, but that can be assisted by a moral overhaul of the society in which they function.

A final group of problems is to make what is learnt and taught relevant to the local communities' needs and potential. This can be achieved very simply by testing classroom, library and laboratory learning with conditions existing in our poverty-stricken villages and urban slums. This is particularly necessary from the secondary and higher secondary levels onwards. Thus, the students and teachers of physics can test their learning in helping the farmers and artisans to repair their instruments; the students and teachers of chemistry can help test the chemistry of the soil and discuss with the farmer its relation to the crops, seeds and fertilisers he uses; the students and teachers of biology can attend to the problems faced by the dairy and poultry farmers; the commerce students and teachers can help the village cooperative keep its account books; the students and teachers of political science can assist the *panchayats* to run their affairs and relate their activities to the expressed needs of the people of the village or block. Above all, all the students, led by the students and teachers of language, should engage themselves two hours each week in making available functional literacy to the adult illiterate in the villages. Such a programme will have several effects: first, it will require each curriculum-setting authority—the committee at the school level and the Board of Studies at the higher education level—to prescribe in its curriculum and textbooks the application of the learning centred around the local rural/urban conditions. Second, this part of the work of students and teachers applying learning to local conditions is not an extra-curricular activity, but a part of the students' curriculum. It should be assessed like their mathematics or social studies or language, and form part of the evaluation of their performance before declaring them outstanding, good, average or poor. Third, it will enrich the learning programme, providing a feedback to the curriculum committees and boards correcting their current theoretical prescriptions, in line with what the test to the local conditions indicates. Above all, it will be a means of bringing education and the community closer, enabling students and teachers to face and sensitise themselves to the crucial problems of unemployment, poverty and inequality in our country.

REFERENCES

Adiseshiah, Malcolm S. (1986). 'Culture of Poverty', *Bulletin*, vol. 5. IASSI, New Delhi.

Government of India (1948). *Report on Universities*. Ministry of Education: New Delhi.

——— (1958). *Education and National Development*. Report of the Ministry of Education: New Delhi.

——— (1986a). *National Policy on Education*. Ministry of Human Resources Development: New Delhi, May.

——— (1986b). *Programme of Action*. Ministry of Human Resources Development: New Delhi, August.

——— (1986c). *Challenge of Education—A Policy Perspective*. Ministry of Education: New Delhi.

University of Kerala (1985). *Report of the Commission Constituted to Inquire into the Working of the University of Kerala*. Trivandrum.

NIEPA (1985). *Basic Educational Data*. National Institute of Educational Planning and Administration: New Delhi, February.

TNBCE (1973). *Towards a Functional Learning Society*. The Tamil Nadu Board of Continuing Education: Madras.

UNESCO (1987). *Statistical Year Book, 1986*. UNESCO: Paris.

5

Integrating Higher Education and Development—A Policy Perspective

R. BHARADWAJ and K.K. BALACHANDRAN

THE THEME

Although research concerning the *process* of development has identified access to and delivery of education as a limitation to the *speed* of development, efforts at integrating it with the process of socio-economic transformation have as yet not resulted in satisfatory solutions. Consequently, the activity is treated as an 'add-on' to the process of development, and the sector continues to operate in an 'open-ended' fashion receiving periodic financial 'allocations' from the administration. As a result, we have not yet been successful in devising a suitable public financing mechanism for higher education which would enable us to reconcile the demands of equity, quantity and quality.

This paper articulates, in terms of a simple formulation, a perspective for incorporating higher education integratively in the context of the development process.

EDUCATION AND DEVELOPMENT: TRANS-DISCIPLINARY CONSENSUS

The role of higher education in the course of social and economic change through the intensification of skills and homogenisation of society has been widely noted in the literature. Years ago Marshall referred to it as a 'national movement'; and in our own times, the Education (Kothari) Commission identified classrooms as places where the destiny of India is shaped (GOI 1966). A number of studies during the late 1950s and early 1960s by Theodore Schultz, Edward Denison, Gary Becker, John Vaizey, Harry Johnson, Robert Solow and others, had demonstrated the role of education in accelerating the process of development. Till the late 1950s, physical capital was considered the key button which, if pressed hard enough, would set the development process in motion. However, the studies conducted on the nature and causes of economic growth over a long historical period in the developed countries revealed that while physical capital undoubtedly played an important role in economic growth, it was by no means as dominant as many economists had earlier visualised. If the growth of national product over a (long) period is such that physical capital alone does not account for the whole increase, the remainder or 'residual' must be due to a variety of other factors. Although varying estimates had been made by economists about the components of the 'residual' factor in economic growth, it was broadly accepted that a substantial portion of it, or of the gains in productivity, could be attributed to improvements in knowledge, skills and capacities of the people or, in short, in the *quality* of 'human stock'. The economists produced historical case studies of countries which enjoyed superior economic growth as a result of having paid greater attention to raising the educational level of their people than did other countries. The developments in Japan and Germany after the Second World War are generally regarded as the classic examples of education being deliberately utilised as a countributing factor to rapid economic and social change.

Thus, the attempts to explain the 'residual' ended up in discovering (or rediscovering) that upgrading human resources through education (and health) could have long-run positive effects on the efficiency of human beings as productive agents. Investment in education, therefore, is an investment in the productivity of the population. Like economists, sociologists too maintained that education, particularly higher education, brings about a change in the individual, promoting greater productivity, modern attitudes, values and beliefs about work, and quality of life. The political scientists observed that education encourages individuals to take an active interest in public affairs, and perform their duties and exercise their rights as members of a community. It prepares young people for citizenship. It is one of the important means for the creation of an open society and political democracy. In the absence of education, the very functioning of democratic institutions becomes a mockery; in fact, they become tools for exploitation of the gullible by the demagogues.

The 'externalities' of education are so pervasive that the list could be extended further: for example, education enhances a person's capacity to absorb, diffuse and utilise new knowledge and deepens his/her professional competence and entrepreneurship; it is the basic key that unlocks the door to technological break-throughs; it sharpens international competitive edge and enables the country to attain certain comparative trade advantages; it has an influence on family welfare, and so on. Education, in short, has many indirect effects of a permanent and far-reaching nature on society.

Particularly in the case of less developed countries, it was argued, there has been a tendency to invest too little in human resources, relative to what is invested in physical resources, as they enter upon the process of development; or, in other words, the human dimension of development tends to be neglected. These countries should therefore regard most of their outlay on education as an 'investment', and not as 'consumer outlays', since economic and social progress must be even more important for them than for the advanced countries. It was also pointed out that it is in the countries with a high degree of education that there is a readiness to accept change and development that are appropriate to a modern economy. The potentially productive talents of a larger number of people in the less developed countries have remained untapped and inert behind the massive barrier of their illiteracy and poverty. Lack of education made people poor, and poverty prevented them from pursuing their education. As Marshall has put it, 'There is no extravagance more prejudicial to the growth of national wealth than that wasteful negligence which allows genius that happens to be born of lowly parentage to expend itself in lowly work' (1925: 211; see also 126, 204, 213, 216, 217). A literate and educated populace should therefore be regarded as productive and desirable, for, to tolerate illiteracy and undereducation would mean allowing the wastage of human talent potentially available for society's progress. An uneducated populace is more like a giant chained to the ground who, for all his writhing, cannot rise to his feet.

By the mid-1960s, there was general agreement among economists, sociologists, educationists, planners and policy-makers in many developing countries that education is a key change agent, or a catalyst of change, in moving countries along the development continuum. Basically, it is an activity which contributes to the enrichment/enhancement of human resources.

The emergence of human resource development as a major concern has further deepened the perception. Higher education, in particular, was no longer perceived as a 'luxury' or a privilege (and pleasure) confined to a favoured few. Provision of it has been accepted as a collective responsibility of the society; it cannot then be expected to function satisfactorily in the absence of some kind of public action. *Since it is treated as a societal issue, it has to be planned in the context of a societal background, not in the context of the individual or market place.* Therefore, access to higher education, and equality of higher educational oportunities, assume great significance. As the notion that higher education is the key to productive life and national prosperity has come to be accepted, discrimination among individuals has to break down, for who can be denied the chance to become productive and useful to society? Furthermore, schools and colleges have a direct influence on the levels of aspirations and expectations among individuals, especially among the socially and economically disadvantaged groups in developing countries. Thus, a new horizon has now been opened in the concept of higher education as an investment enhancing human resources for development.

THE CURRENT SCENARIO IN INDIA

Quantitative Expansion

Even before Independence, Indian leaders and the people had realised that in the transformation of the economy in particular, and society in general, higher education would have to play a determining role. With freedom, fresh vistas were opened to develop human potential and expertise which could be used in a progressive realisation of economic goals and social objectives. The Government of India, in coordination with the state governments, was anxious to initiate immediate steps not only for a radical reform of the entire higher educational system built during the British period, but also for large-scale expansion that would bring higher educational facilities within the reach of the majority of youth who had long been denied this opportunity. The twin objectives of making available sufficient middle- and upper-level trained manpower to the country in its programme of economic development, while at the same time meeting the rising expectations of the vast section of the young people, did introduce some important new dimensions to the policy of growth and financing of higher education in the country. In other words, the government was keen to pursue the three goals of quantity, quality and equality simultaneously.

Since 1950, the government has vastly increased the proportion of resources devoted to the sector of higher education and the most impressive expansion has taken place in enrolment in universities and colleges. With over 150 universities and deemed-to-be universities and 6,000 colleges (accounting for a total enrolment of 4 million students), and an annual expenditure of about Rs. 1,000 crores, higher education in India has become a truly large system. The average annual growth rate of enrolment during the period 1950–51 to 1981–82 has been about 10 per cent, despite constraints on resources. The percentage of students in higher education to total population in the age group 17 to 23 years increased from 0.8 in 1950–51 to 5 in 1981–82. There are now 2.5 lakh teachers serving in the system.

Over the years, the government, both at centre and the state level, has assumed the major responsibility for financing the higher education system. At the time of Independence, fees and other contributions met nearly 60 per cent of the recurrent expenditure of higher educational institutions; the rest was met by government grants. Today, the central and state governments meet about 80 per cent of the recurrent expenditure; their percentage share has doubled over the years. The private sources of finance have ceased to make any appreciable contribution to higher educational development. The 'mixed' government subsidy–fee system has gradually turned out to be a near total subsidy system.

Quality

Qualitative improvements in education constitute the essence of the enrichment of human resources. Unfortunately, quality has been the major casualty in the process of expansion of higher education. Academic standards are relaxed, ignoring the fact that only if the people supplied by the system achieved certain minimum standards of competence could they play their part in economic development. The qualitative aspect has not received the attention it deserves, and the entire process of expansion is proving to be self-defeating.

An important question that arises in this context is: Why there has been no acceleration in economic growth despite the continued growth of the higher education sector? Though India can claim to have the third largest pool of scientists and technologists in the world, next only to the United States and the erstwhile USSR, it has been rated very low in terms of productivity. Are we approaching a situation of diminishing returns from higher education? This is unfortunate, especially when international competitive forces, particularly in skill-oriented activities, are operating in full measure. Deteriorating quality is further aggravated by inadequate financial resources.

Justice in Access to Education: A Mirage?

Equalising opportunity for higher education is considered one of the examples of the 'spill-over' effect made possible by large public expenditure on higher education. The concept crops up in almost all discussions on financing higher education today. Theoretically, as Marshall has pointed out, one starts here from the assumption that every individual is a candidate for every position in society, so that public policy must aim at eliminating the effects of differing social and economic environments on the critical turning points in peoples' lives. The practical implications of this are vast. The ability to profit by higher education is spread among all classes of people. There are great reserves of untapped ability in society; if offered the chance, they can rise to the top. A great deal of talent of the higher level will be lost to society under an inegalitarian system of education. If needed, latent or slow development of talent must also be fostered and brought to fruition so that all are stretched to their maximum potential.

No individual, whatever be his economic and social status, sex and rural–urban differentiation, desiring higher education should be denied the opportunity, is the avowed goal of the educational policy-makers (in all countries, especially the developing ones). Greater efforts, therefore, must be made to enlist the socio-economically backward sections of the population in higher education and thus attain equity in economic opportunities over time.

If we go back into history, we find that the development of higher education tended to be justified in terms of the provision of what was called a liberal education for the 'elite' rather training for careers. Higher education proved more attractive later when it was known that if pursued, it would directly or indirectly be of some advantage in finding employment or building careers. This, as well as the egalitarian spirit that was pervading the world over, shifted the emphasis in favour of democratisation of higher education.

As far as India is concerned, after nearly four decades of experience with the attempt to promote the goal of equality of higher educational opportunity, serious doubts are now being raised about its actual implementation. *The so-called higher educational boom, instead of equalising opportunities, has in fact legitimised, or even aggravated, inequality over the years.* Most of the seats in the existing higher educational institutions have been appropriated by those belonging to the middle and upper income strata of society, leaving the vast masses out of the ambit of benefit. Over two-thirds of India's university/college entrants belong to the top 30 per cent of society. Those who really come from 'poor' families do not constitute more than 5 per cent of the total student population. The utopian hope of access to higher education, or, in other words, democratisation through higher education, has thus failed to occur although higher education remained the focus of the myth of equality. This has got further exacerbated as the benefit of subsidy has gone mostly to students belonging to the well-off sections of society. Under the existing system, everyone is entitled to the *same* amount of the generous public subsidy regardless of his/her capacity to pay. For the majority of the students it has meant money that their parents or they could well have afforded, while for others, the minority (the weaker sections), the subsidy is inadequate, and they are not in a position to take advantage of university/college education. The main reason for keeping fees low in university, colleges and other professional/technical institutions was to help the poor families and promote equality, but what has taken place is the monopolising of seats available in colleges and universities by the well-to-do classes of society. The present arrangement under which over two-thirds of the expenditure on higher education is met by public funds is, in short, neither equitable nor efficient. Under the existing situation, to defend grants for higher education on the grounds of social and economic justice is therefore a monstrous perversion of the truth.

Provision of more higher educational opportunities (and facilities) does not automatically mean greater participation on the part of the less advanced economic and social classes. Several studies reveal that the majority of children belonging to the economically/socially weaker sections do not even cross primary school level. The drop-out rate at this stage is as high as 70 per cent. As a consequence, the pool from which higher education draws its students is biased in favour of higher income classes owing to the situation at the school stage. The dice are already loaded in favour of the 'haves' from the beginning itself! *Educational inequality has in fact been compounded at each successive level, and hence the greatest at the higher education level.* Under the circumstances, even if efforts are made to set up more higher educational institutions all over the country and seats reserved for economically/socially backward groups, we cannot ensure that boys and girls from those groups *will* enrol themselves. Obviously, there are other factors that inhibit them from entering higher educational institutions, and these need to be clearly identified. If equality of opportunity (and access) at the higher educational stage has to be really effected, efforts will then have to be directed at first enlarging the intake of children of economically/socially weaker sections into schools and in bringing down the tremendous wastage on account of drop-outs. More positive steps will have to be taken to alleviate the economic and other disadvantages of children who find it difficult to reach the higher education stage. These measures are missing in India, or are inadequate. The heaviest cost of expansion of the higher education system in India is that a good number of really gifted children, who possess the potential of attaining higher standards, are deprived of the higher education that they deserve, due mainly to economic and other reasons. A major part of the pool of ability continues to remain outside the system.

NEED FOR A NEW PERSPECTIVE

The foregoing discussion brings out the inequity in higher education, underlining how the objective of increasing access to higher education to the less privileged could not be materialised. The 'add-on' view of education resulted in a type of public financing and administration in which operational rigours went against, *albeit* unwittingly, any justice in access. It is, therefore, required to place the problem in a different perspective, and view education as a societal issue. As education draws from earlier generations and leaves behind intellectual capital for succeeding ones, considerations of inter-generational equity become a corner-stone for any attempt aimed at integrating education and development. The students are financed through the savings of the community made in the earlier period and the former mainly derive the benefits through higher income after completing their education. Since investments in higher education have a time dimension, it is obligatory for the individual beneficiaries to see that the system is sustained over time. There is also an imperative need to upgrade quality so that the system can contribute creatively to the collective well-being of the community. And, qualitative improvements can be brought about only if adequate resources are made available. As the *Challenge of Education* puts it, 'the resource implications of qualitative changes in education would be far greater than that of mere quantitative expansion because in such an initiative additional per unit requirements for quality upgradation will be needed for new as well as all the existing institutions' (GOI 1985: 62). If the system fails to achieve this objective, it would mean forfeiting its right to public support.

Higher education in India is regarded as a social and private investment, shared by the government (major proportion), and students and their families. Consequently, the entire issue of the public financing of higher education has been bogged down, in recent years, in the controversy over the divergence between 'social gain' and 'private gain'. Since the latter is more, an increase in fees is recommended by some, but keeping in view the income distribution of the people, one feels that it has the dangerous potential of pricing out the poor from obtaining skills for better living. Therefore, a fee hike may not be favoured under these circumstances. The state, at the same time, finds it difficult to extend more funds due to a severe resource crunch; whatever little is allocated comes too late (and with many preconditions), and is so thinly spread that the general system suffers. The per student expenditure has suffered considerable dilution over the years due to rising prices, leading to a sharp slump in academic standards. And, to top it all, a good number of those who manage to obtain access to and get good grades from the heavily subsidised professional institutions, leave the country embodied with the skills acquired. In the process, the nation suffers a new type of 'resource drain'.

Since the late 1970s a crisis has been looming large in the higher education sector. An integrated plan of action, whereby the triangle of equity, quality and equality could be squared as far as possible, has yet to be evolved; so far this has been set aside as a 'second-order' problem. *A clear recognition of the fact that education is the chief component of development and social progress has yet to emerge among the planners and policy-makers.* There is perhaps no sector of national activity where the government—both at the centre and state levels—has dragged its feet as that of education. Education, especially for the weaker sections of the population, continues to be treated as a 'welfare activity', although it is those at the base of the socio-economic pyramid who meet a sizeable share of the taxes that go to subsidise the education of the privileged who occupy the apex, enjoying the best and highest paying jobs. Cuts in investment in education are most often resorted to in order to counteract short-run financial stringency. Whenever the government budgets go awry, educational schemes are invariably the first casualty of the cuts. While there is a general recognition of the advantage of modern techniques in other sectors of the economy, and large funds are provided for their adoption, a similar attitude towards education has unfortunately been absent. Though the expenditure on education, as a percentage of the GNP, has increased from 1.31 per cent in 1950–51 to about 4 per cent in recent years, it compares unfavourably with the corresponding position in many developed, and even some other developing countries. The percentage share of the education sector in total plan allocations has consistently declined over the successive Five-Year Plans.

To disentangle this, we could perhaps look at the issue from a different perspective, viewing higher education as a societal issue. Basically, higher education is an activity which endows the recipient with a capacity to perform better and earn more, or, in other words, it *enhances* the individual's potential and thus contributes to the enrichment of human resources.

As students of development literature are aware, human resource development entails two types of costs: (*i*) the *essential cost*, which includes food, clothing, shelter, housing, and a minimum level of education; and (*ii*) *enhancement cost* which directly contributes to increases in productivity and levels of living. Higher education constitutes the major component of the enhancement cost. This cost can be broken down into three categories: current cost, fixed cost, and cost on continuous quality upgrdation. One has to obtain the economy-wide implications of these costs and also obtain the economy-wide returns from these investments.

To articulate the above empirically, a standard open Leontief system appears to be tailor-made. It will enable us to obtain, by embedding the educational structure, the direct and indirect economy-wide estimates of costs and benefits in terms of 'resources used' and 'resources augmented'. The public financing of higher education, determining taxes and grants, would have to be anchored to such an approach if the system has to be charted gradually towards the desired goal of providing justice in access to higher education, keeping the inter-generational equity as the welfare criterion.[1]

Accordingly, in actual practice, the most critical component turns out to be the planning and administrative orientation. We conclude with a few general observations on this question.

PLANNING OF EDUCATION

Planning education for a developing country is a challenging task. It involves a conceptualisation that should take into account inter-temporal, mutually reinforcing parametric variations iteratively. In practical terms, this means financing educational targets under a gradually changing rate and pattern of economic environment due to developmental efforts which also, in turn, interacts continuously with education. Educational administration therefore requires the creation of a network which, while bringing out the interaction between each type of expenditure with the additionalities to operational skills, also provides a set of norms for allocation of

[1] A forthcoming study, 'An Econometric Analysis of the Growth and Financing of Higher Education in India (with special reference to the role of the Government)' undertaken jointly by the authors of this paper provides empirical results obtained with the new approach.

available funds, given the developmental goals. If ushering in the new technologies is the goal, then development of human potential to meet the challenge becomes the aim of educational administration. That is, the broad financial efforts need to be further divided into their finer components—teaching, research, administrative and supporting staff; libraries; equipment and appliances; laboratories; etc.—in different types of institutions. The benefit in financial terms as measured by skill enhancement, contribution to development or any factor, in each line of specialisation may be correspondingly worked out. We will then be able to obtain a benefit-cost matrix which will give us the interactions involved and also the rate of benefit in each line of educational investment. Considering the fact that educational expenditure is now regarded as investment in human capital for national development, every effort must be made to see that we get the most out of the available resources by optimum use. These issues assume special significance in the present context of the rethinking among policy-makers on the existing design of programmes for higher education in the country so that it can be transformed into 'one vibrant with a commitment to development and change'. The challenge of the future is surely a challenge of change. The years lost have now to be made good.

REFERENCES

Government of India (1966). *Education and Development: Report of the Education Commission* (Kothari Commission). Ministry of Education: New Delhi.
——— (1985). *Challenge of Education—A Policy Perspective*. Ministry of Human Resources Development (Department of Education): New Delhi, August.
Marshall, Alfred A. (1925). *Principles of Economics*. Macmillan: London.

6

Beyond Output Growth: Human Resource Management for Improved Productivity[1]

ABDUL AZIZ

THE CONTEMPORARY ECONOMIC CONCERNS

The basic concern of economists after the Second World War was the question of promoting economic growth at rates high enough to ensure a sustained rise in the standard of living of the people. The achievement of this goal, to the extent possible, however, did not generate the all-round applause that the economic philosophy of the time deserved. For, along with the rise in the average standard of living, the developed and the developing societies faced the challenges of acute unemployment, inflation, and balance of payments disequilibria. Attempts made to resolve these economic ills by promoting higher rates of capital formation as a means of creating productive capacities and production surpluses did not lead them anywhere; for, these problems became further accentuated rather than subsided. It has come to be increasingly realised today that this failure is due to a serious mistake committed in the past by the policy-makers. It is said that, in their anxiety to achieve higher levels of output, the policy-makers did everything to increase production; increased production *at any cost* appeared to have been their concern at the time. Production levels were, no

[1] I wish to thank Professors V.M. Rao and M.V. Nadkarni for their useful comments on an earlier version of this paper.

doubt, pushed up by creating capacities through higher levels of capital formation—physical as well as human. And higher levels of capacity creation did expand production potential and even facilitated higher levels of production. But along with the rising production levels, costs also increased more or less commensurately, not merely because of the excessive heating of the economy following inflationary financing of government expenditure, but also because of the less efficient use of factors. As a result, the general price level tended to rise year after year even in the face of a continuous rise in production. This outcome is the result of the policy-makers' emphasis on production rather than on productivity—a mistake that has landed present-day economies into the paradoxical situation of rising production levels accompanied by rising prices.

If we accept the proposition that negligence of the productivity imperatives in the growth process is partly at the base of our contemporary problems, it then follows that the future concern of policy-making has to be, among other concerns, promotion of higher levels of productivity. Contemporary economic theory—the Keynesian and the post-Keynesian (and the policy originating from it)—hardly focused itself on productivity. Its concern has all along been on the goal of keeping the economy on the pedestal of full employment equilibrium and, once this goal is attained, to take the economy along the steady growth path. Productivity concern did not figure in the scheme of things at all. There is a reason for this which originates from the assumption which the Keynesian theory proceeds with, viz., supply, i.e., productivity, is demand-controlled and, therefore, it is determined by demand. So long as demand levels are maintained at higher levels, productivity too is said to be maintained at a higher level. Hence, in the Keynesian system productivity was taken for granted; it was considered ever-present if demand was created. It is this kind of misconception about productivity which made subsequent writers, particularly the followers of Keynes, maintain a cold attitude towards productivity. Most of the growth models which emerged during the post-Keynesian era sought to raise output growth rate by increasingly building the growth promoting factors, viz., capital and labour. Technology was looked upon as a factor that released the productive forces inherent in labour and capital. But by subsuming technology in the factor of capital or the skills of the labour force, the growth theories did not explicitly give to productivity the place it deserved in the growth constructs. The result is that there is today a tendency in theory and policy to seek expansion in output/production by an expanded use of inputs or resources; the idea of accelerating growth by intensively using the available resources, though fully recognised, has, however, not found full expression either in the theoretical constructs or in policy parameters.

THE PRODUCTIVITY CONCERNS

The point we have been labouring is that the productivity concern has not adequately reflected itself in contemporary theory and policy to the extent deserved, and that it should become the future concern of economists in larger measure. If the productivity concern were to reflect itself in theory and policy, the question arises as to how and where it should be brought into the scheme of things. In other words, the question more specifically to be addressed is: along what route should productivity be brought back to the mainstream of economics? A cursory look at the history of economic thought suggests that productivity had been the concern of the classical economists, especially of the neo-classical economists who strived to maximise output by the efficient allocation and full utilisation of resources. On the one hand, resources in this framework are expected to be put to use such that they are most efficient, and on the other hand, none of the resources are expected to remain idle and underutilised. It is these twin concerns of the neo-classical school that were expected to lead the economy to the attainment of maximum output of the given resources. Implied in the neo-classical construct is also the requirement that the resource allocation pattern ought to be such that yield from each one of the factors of production—capital, human resources and physical resources—and the overall yield of these resources in combination should be maximum, given the state of knowledge. Productivity, therefore, was seen as an outcome of efficient utilisation of various factors of production. If this is how productivity is now to be understood—as it should be—then the route through which it could be brought back to mainstream economics is clear. That is, it can come in as a growth agent.

When we argue that productivity should be brought back to the mainstream of economics as a growth agent, we do not mean to treat it as a factor of production; it in fact is synonymous with growth itself and by reason of that cannot by itself act as a growth promoting agent. What we mean by this statement, however, is that the actual growth promoting agents, viz., physical and human capitals, should be so managed as to promote higher levels of productivity so that given the quantum of these resources higher growth can be obtained.

HUMAN RESOURCE MANAGEMENT FOR IMPROVED PRODUCTIVITY

From what has been presented above it is clear that productivity improvement through better management of resources should be the concern of economists as well as the philosophy that should underline economic theory and policy in the years to come. Development of human and physical capital as agents of growth has received more than adequate attention during the last three to four decades. The time now seems to be ripe for a shift in emphasis from capital building to capital management. The imperative of physical capital resource management is, no doubt, important considering the enormous quantum of the capital that has now been formed by all societies—developed and developing alike. However, for reasons to be stated shortly, managing human resources, in our view, appears to be more urgent and important. But none of the growth models had ever explicitly considered human resource management in its structure. The reason for this is that until recently, both in the developed and developing economies, physical and human capital formation was looked upon as a crucial factor in initiating and sustaining growth. Management of human capital was taken for granted by implicitly assuming that either human resource management was a non-issue, or, where it was considered to be important, the entrepreneur–manager was assumed to have in his armoury all the tools of managing human resources. But with the tremendous awakening that has come about among the workers, followed by their unionisation, a new worker culture has emerged—a culture to be reckoned with by the managers of the economy whose concern is to optimally combine the factors of production. It is true that unionism had emerged in the West a long time ago and that this problem is not a new one to managers in that region. But certain recent events have created a new situation in Third World countries which calls for a tremendous amount of input from the managers to effectively manage human resources. The factors contributing to the emergence of this 'situation' are: (*i*) the opening up of the communication channels which expose the working class to the consumerist culture of the West and the competitive unionism, which, in the process of enlisting support for their organisation, promises the impossible to the workers, who are then led to asking for more and more benefits; (*ii*) the introduction of a new production technology which calls not only for new skills and periodic updating of skills, but also a tremendous degree of commitment from the worker towards the maintenance and operation of the machine with which he works; and (*iii*) the misinformed worker now indulging in the practice of labour-hoarding which has adversely affected the productivity level of the organisation in which he is working.

These developments have serious consequences. Thus, asking for more and more through aggressive wage demands, i.e., seeking wage hikes in excess of productivity growth which, by building up inflationary pressures will, via increased wage costs, raise capital costs and thereby capital–output ratios. The rising capital–output ratios are further fuelled by certain management practices which are so much part of the organised corporate industry which enjoys an enormous degree of monopoly in the output market. Second, the neglect on the part of the worker with regard to maintenance of machines shortens the life of the machine, forcing the economy to allocate more resources for the replacement of capital rather than for *new* capital formation. And, finally, the hoarding of labour, besides increasing the supervisory costs, causes the economy to maintain more than a socially necessary workforce, leading to the emergence of an involutionary process—a situation of work-sharing and underutilised labour time. The rise in capital–output ratios, the diversion of financial resources for capital replacement rather than for capital formation, and the underutilised workforce will surely bring down the growth rate of the economy given the savings ratio. It is in this context—of a possibility of the workforce decelerating the growth rate of the economy—that we have to see the role of the managers of the economy; they could manage human resources in such a way that not only is the growth of the economy not affected adversely, but its full potential is also possibly realised.

SYSTEMS OF HUMAN RESOURCE MANAGEMENT

Human resource management for promoting growth will call for two strategies: (*i*) to nurture a positive attitude among the work-force towards work, machines, co-workers and supervisors; and (*ii*) to cultivate among the working class a perspective of what consequences their actions as a collective group will create for the economy as a whole. Both these requirements will have implications for developing a human resource management system which emphasises promoting work culture and commitment among the working class towards the goal of national development. As part of achieving this objective, different systems of human resource management have emerged in the countries of the world—each being specific to a given economic system. A brief review of these systems will be in order here.

In a pure capitalist economy, the manager, guided by the eco-nomic rationale of profit maximisation, generally employs two sets of tools of human resource management: (*i*) effective supervision, and (*ii*) a system of incentives covering employee remuneration and promotion, or a combination of (*i*) and (*ii*). In the devising and application of these instruments he is guided by the consider-ation of cost-effectiveness, such that as long as the extra cost of employing these intruments does not exceed the returns on their account he has the incentive to employ them. This approach to human resource management, which emerged in 19th century England and was labelled scientific management, has been employed even in the socialist economies, though to a limited extent. But this dimension of human resource management leaves open the question of workers' commitment to work, machines, co-workers and supervisors.

In the socialist economies, like the erstwhile USSR, for instance, largely non-monetary incentives were deployed to secure the commitment of the workforce to the goals of the enterprise and the economy. In these economies the political leaders strove to impress upon the working class that the extra labour put in by them in terms of extra time and intensity of effort would generate higher levels of national output which, although might not have immediately and directly benefited them, would strengthen the national economy, giving them a tremendous sense of satisfaction. It is this feeling of being able to contribute towards the strengthening of the national economy which was supposed to serve as an instrument of human resource management in the socialist countries. In later years, these countries tried supplementing this tool with a mild dose of monetary incentives. A combination of monetary and non-monetary incentives was considered to be a more potent instrument of human resource management in these countries.

In spite of the so-called failure of the socialist experiment, a revolutionary method of managing human resources employed in the former socialist countries like Yugoslavia and Czechoslovakia deserves mention here. Deriving its logic from the wider philosophy of a participatory economy, the political leadership promoted a system of labour-managed enterprises—a device that facilitated a mechanism of automatically managing human resources. The participatory economy is conceptually composed of firms controlled and managed by those working in them. Management vests with all and is on the principle of one vote for one person. There is income-sharing after meeting expenses relating to material and other operation costs incurred and some reserves. The sharing of income is to be equitable, i.e., it is equal for labour of equal intensity and quality, and governed by a democratically agreed upon income distribution schedule. The working community need not have full ownership of capital assets; capital and machinery can be borrowed on a rent payment basis.[2]

In mixed economies like ours, the tools of human resource management to be evolved have to be a hybrid of what the capitalist and socialist economies have evolved. To be more specific, a system of incentives to motivate the worker to give his or her best to the organisation has to be evolved. This should be supplemented by a participatory management scheme (as distinct from the participatory economy) as a means of getting the workforce committed to the goals of management. Under this scheme, the workers should be formally given an opportunity to participate in decision-making at various levels such as at shop, plant and even at the

---

[2] For an excellent account of this system see Vanèk (1971).

board level. While the incentive schemes would ensure highr levels of productivity through increased intensity of effort by the workers, there remains the problem of workers' commitment to the organisation, machinery and the co-workers. This problem is expected to be solved by evolving a scheme of participative management.

Participative management can be conceived as a device of sharing management authority with the workers as part of the strategy of creating a workforce that is committed to the goals of the industry and the economy. By agreeing to share authority, the management may appear to be losing some amount of power and authority. However, this is not thought to be so. For, there is a theory which holds that power is not subject to a 'zero-sum game' where, if workers gain power, management loses it. It is argued that under the participative management scheme, the total amount of control can increase with both parties benefiting, thus giving rise to the 'non-zero-sum game' position. How total control increases following sharing of power between labour and management has been explained by A.S. Tannenbaum (1968: 14–15). According to him, participative management on the one hand extends control of management to areas of decision-making which traditionally do not fall under its purview, and on the other hand it leads to increased amenability of workers for control by the management. Theoretically, therefore, sharing power of decision-making with workers facilitates return flow of power to management. If that were so, the management would not in effect lose power but instead may gain more power than what is shared with the workers. This leads to an increase in total power. This point of how participative management would lead to (*i*) management extending control over areas of decision-making which traditionally are not their own, and (*ii*) workers allowing themselves to be made amenable for management control has been illustrated by a study carried out in Karnataka by the present author. The illustration apart of the mechanism of control sharing, the study brings out a very important point that is relevant to the subject under consideration. It shows how, under the scheme of participative management, it became possible for the industrial managers to exercise control over worker-behaviour variables such as absenteeism, worker indiscipline, wastage of material and improper maintenance of machinery, which otherwise are not amenable to traditional management control. The ability of the management to exercise control over these variables led to better maintenance of machines, waste control, reduction in absenteeism and improved worker discipline, and this, in turn had a favourable effect on the productivity of the enterprises (Aziz 1980). It therefore appears that sharing of decision-making power at the shop and plant levels under the scheme of participative management holds out immense possibilities of improving productivity by facilitating a better management of human resources.

SUMMING UP

Productivity should be the chief concern of economic policy in the years to come. Improved productivity should be increasingly achieved through better management of resources, particularly human resources. Monetary incentive systems have a role in this but democracy in decision-making at the work place appears to hold out a good potential as an instrument of promoting productivity. Therefore, the policy-makers should treat democracy at the work place as an economic input for improved productivity. If this logic is accepted it should also be the concern of policy-makers to develop decentralised decision-making institutional structures as a means of promoting, as also sustaining, higher levels of productivity in future.

Before concluding, one point ought to be emphasised. The paper, no doubt, all along underlines the need to promote productivity in future rather than merely building the capital stock and, as part of achieving this goal, calls for priority to human resources management as imperative. While doing so, the focus of the paper remains only on organised labour. But the solution to stagnant productivity levels cannot be found in the management of organised labour alone. The problem of low productivity is a societal problem—a problem that is at the root of *all* segments of the workforce in society and not of just one segment like organised labour. After all, the characteristics of a workforce which go against productivity improvement are not unique to any one particular segment of the workforce. If organised labour exhibits such characteristics these are shared by other segments of the workforce as well. And, what is more interesting is that the possibility of such characteristics being acquired from the elite segments of the workforce such as managers, bureaucrats and technocrats cannot be ruled out. Instances of highly paid and respected government employees and professionals resorting to work stoppage, hoarding of labour, asking for more and more benefits—monetary and non-monetary—are not uncommon in contemporary society. Therefore, if human resource management as a means to improved productivity is to be the concern of economists and other social scientists for the decades to come, the focus should be on the management of the entire workforce of the society. Perhaps this imperative is more compelling in the case of the elite segment of the workforce. The question of who should manage the elite workforce and what systems of human resource management are appropriate to them falls outside the scope of the present paper.

REFERENCES

Aziz, Abdul (1980). *Workers Participation in Management*. Ashish Publishing House: New Delhi.
Tannenbaum, A.S. (1968). *Control in Organisation*.Tata-McGraw Hill: Bombay.
Vanek, Jeroslav (1971). *The Participatory Economy: An Evolutionary Hypothesis and a Strategy for Development*. Cornell University Press: Ithaca.

7

Planning for Employment: What has Been Our Experience?[1]

P. HANUMANTHA RAYAPPA and G. NAGARAJU

THE FIVE-YEAR PLANS AND EMPLOYMENT

Planning for employment has been one of the major concerns of the planners in our country since Independence. In fact, over different Five-Year Plan periods, there has been an increasing recognition of the importance of providing employment. In spite of this emphasis on employment, the magnitude of unemployment and underemployment has been increasing over the years, while the rate of growth of employment has been slackening. This is indicative of the fact that all is not well on the employment front in the economy. As a result, in the approach to the Eighth Five-Year Plan, employment generation has been accorded a central place. Here, two pertinent questions arise: (*i*) What have been the objectives, programmes and strategies for employment of our Five-Year Plans and what has been their impact? (*ii*) What is the intended approach in the Eighth Five-Year Plan for employment generation?

Since the inception of Five-Year Plans in 1951, poverty and unemployment have been considered the twin problems confronting the Indian economy. The First Five-Year Plan was launched with a modest total outlay of about Rs. 2,000 crores; however, some did not consider it to be a plan in the real sense of the term (B. Prasad 1983). The thrust of this plan was on agriculture, irrigation and the

[1] We wish to thank Professors Abdul Aziz, M.V. Nadkarni and V.M. Rao for their help in the preparation of this paper.

development of infrastructure. It was estimated that about 9.7 million jobs would be created by the end of Plan period. In the Second Five-Year Plan the emphasis shifted to heavy industry, although it was conceived to promote labour-intensive, small-scale industries on a supplementary basis. Rural works were also emphasised as a strategy to tackle the problem of unemployment and underemployment (which was estimated to be 15.3 million persons). The distinction between rural and urban unemployment was duly recognised in the Plan document.

The expansion of employment opportunities commensurate with the increase in the labour force over the Plan period was conceived as one of the principal aims of the Third Five-Year Plan. At the beginning of the Plan period, the backlog of unemployment was estimated at 9 million persons, which was later realised to be a gross underestimate. Even though the need for a supplementary programme of rural works was recognised during this time, not much money was spent on this programme during this period.

At the end of Third Five-Year Plan, there was a plan holiday from 1966 to 1969, when Annual Plans were drawn up and implemented. During this time rural diversification was adopted as one of the strategies for the generation of employment; rural works programmes were also emphasised as severe droughts and famines affected the economy.

The Fourth Five-Year Plan once again emphasised labour-intensive programmes including agriculture, rural electrification, rural industries and the development of infrastructure. These included area development schemes like developmental/relief work in drought-prone districts, employment guarantee programmes and other community development projects. Agricultural schemes such as extension of area under cultivation, multiple cropping, introduction of high yielding varieties (HYVs), and irrigation were given a fillip in order to help generate additional employment in the rural areas. New projects undertaken by the states and the centre were sought to be given an employment orientation.

The Fifth Five-Year Plan had a life span of four years and had to be prematurely terminated with the change in government at the centre in 1977. With redistributive justice as a principal objective, promotion of wage- and self-employment for the poorer sections of society were emphasised during this time. Several poverty alleviation programmes such as Small Farmers Development Agency

(SFDA), Marginal Farmers and Agricultural Labourers Development Agency (MFAL), and Drought-Prone Areas Programme (DPAP) were pursued.

In the Sixth Five-Year Plan, employment became an integral part of the Plan with varied employment-oriented programmes integrated within it.

The central objective of the development strategy of the Seventh Five-Year Plan was the generation of productive employment with expansion of employment opportunities consistent with the increase in productivity. However, it is evident that throughout the different plans, while employment generation was *one* of the important objectives of planning, it never appeared as the *central* objective.

On the basis of the historical background of planning for employment during the planning era, certain criticisms have been advanced. First, there were no dependable estimates of the extent of underemployment and unemployment in the country. The rate of growth of population was underestimated and hence the net additions to the labour force were not fully accounted for. There was no proper diagnosis of the problem of underemployment, particularly in the rural areas. Second, sectoral outlays were not consistent with the plan objectives, with a general inconsistency between pronouncements and plan allocations to different sectors. In particular, the employment-generating sectors did not receive the priority they deserved. Third, employment targets could not be achieved in full measure because of shortfalls in the performance of various sectors in the economy. 'In conclusion, wrong strategies and weak implementation have been solely responsible for the non-fulfilment of removal of poverty and unemployment in the country' (B. Prasad 1983).

TRENDS IN EMPLOYMENT

What have been the trends in the growth of employment in the country?[2] First of all the average rate of growth of employment in

[2] The quantum of employment generated during a particular plan period is estimated by the Planning Commission. Usually, the estimation is based on the total plan expenditure and the ratio of employment generated per unit of investment or per unit of increase in output in different sectors of the economy. Of course, this procedure is subjected to criticism because of the difficulties in computing the ratio of employment generated per unit of investment. However, in the

the economy has remained lower than the rate of growth of the labour force. While the rate of growth of employment was 2.1 per cent between 1951 and 1986, the rate of growth of the labour force during the same period was 2.5 per cent. And, as can be seen from Table 1, the growth rate in total employment has been declining from 2.8 per cent during 1972–73 to 1977–78, to 1.5 per cent during 1983 to 1987–88. More or less the same trend is visible in the other sectors as well, viz., rural, urban, organised and unorganised, even though the decline in the rate of growth of employment varies. The performance of the rural sector which holds a major share in total employment has been disappointing as it has exhibited the lowest growth in recent years.

Table 1: *Growth Rates of Employment—Rural, Urban, Organised and Unorganised Sectors*

Sectors	1972–73 to 1977–78	1977–78 to 1983	1983 to 1987–88	1972–73 to 1987–88
Growth rate of total employment	2.82	2.22	1.55	2.21
Growth rate of rural employment	2.52	1.74	0.95	1.75
Growth rate of urban employment	4.31	4.10	3.79	4.00
Growth rate of organised sector's employment	2.48	2.42	1.36	2.11
Growth rate of unorganised sector's employment	2.84	2.20	1.55	2.21

Source: Abstracted from Planning Commission (1990a).

The share of the organised sector in total employment has remained low (around 10 per cent) and its rate of growth has also seen a progressive decline. Another important shift has been the increased proportion of wage labour. In rural and urban areas together, there has been an increase in casual wage labour from 23 to 30 per cent, with a steady decline in self-employment from 61 to 56 per cent, and salaried regular employment from 16 to 13.5 per cent (Planning Commission 1990a).

The employment elasticity of the GDP during the period 1972–73

---

absence of a better alternative, the same method is being followed with a few modifications in the procedure (GOI 1970).

to 1977–78 was observed to be 0.6 which decreased to 0.4 during the period 1983–84 to 1987–88 (Planning Commission 1990a). The percentage growth of the GDP required for 1 per cent increase in employment has continuously increased from 1.04 in 1951 to 2.44 during the period 1978 to 1983, and to 3.57 during 1983 to 1987 (P. Prasad 1990). This fact can be taken to mean that increasing output in the economy is because of increase in its capital content.

UNEMPLOYMENT AND UNDEREMPLOYMENT

Difficulties in obtaining precise estimates of unemployment and underemployment in developing countries are well-known. The definitional as well as estimation problems involved in arriving at these estimates in the Indian context have already been highlighted (GOI 1970). The main sources of data on unemployment in India are the decennial censuses, National Sample Survey (NSS) reports, and registrants at the employment exchanges. The unemployment estimates based on census data are considered underestimates as the information sought there is on the usual-status criterion. The data available at the employment exchanges suffers from inaccuracies on at least two counts. All those who are unemployed do not necessarily register with the employment exchanges, and those who register their names need not be unemployed but could be looking for alternative job opportunities. National Sample Survey data is considered relatively more reliable and is more widely used because of the superior methodology used in its collection and its national coverage. Generally, the criterion of time has been followed in estimating the magnitude of unemployment and underemployment in the country. However, it has been argued that this only provides a lower limit of the extent of underemployment in the rural areas and hence, is usually an underestimate (Rath 1983). The Dantwala Committee (GOI 1970) also felt that the magnitude of underemployment could not be explained satisfactorily in terms of man-years. A better criterion would be that of income levels and the terms and conditions under which this labour would be available to the market (GOI 1970). Raj Krishna has provided four criteria to estimate unemployment and underemployment: time criterion, income criterion, willingness criterion and productivity criterion (Raj Krishna 1976). However, no estimates of unemployment and underemployment are available based on these criteria.

The estimates of unemployment and underemployment for a given time period vary from one plan document to the next. These discrepancies can be noticed both with respect to the backlog of unemployment and underemployment, as well as to the net additions to this backlog. Moreover, it was felt that the figures on backlog of unemployment were seriously underestimated. Table 2 provides unemployment rates (percentage of unemployed to total labour force) as provided by the Planning Commission.

Table 2: *Rates of Unemployment (Percentage of Unemployed to Labour Force) during 1983 and 1987–88*

Unemployment	Residence (Rural, Urban and Total)	1983	1987–88
Usual permanent status	R	1.91	3.07
	U	6.04	6.56
	T	2.77	3.77
Weekly status	R	3.88	4.19
	U	6.81	7.12
	T	4.51	4.80
Daily status	R	7.94	5.25
	U	9.52	9.26
	T	8.25	6.09

Source: Abstracted from Planning Commission (1990a).

The Table shows that the latest data available indicates that the unemployment rate according to the usual-status criterion increased from 2.77 per cent in 1983 to 3.77 per cent in 1987–88. On the other hand, though the unemployment rate based on the weekly-status criterion did not change much during this period, the unemployment rate based on the daily-status criterion came down from 8.25 per cent to 6.09 per cent. This implies that there has been a shift from underemployment to open unemployment. It should be cautioned here that although these rates do not appear to be alarming, the absolute numbers involved are very large in the Indian context. The underemployment rate for both sexes combined has increased only slightly from 3.94 per cent in 1977–78 to 3.97 per cent in 1983. Though the marginal underemployment rate has declined during this period, moderate and severe underemployment have increased from 7.70 per cent in 1977–78 to 8.16 in 1983. The incidence of underemployment is the highest among agricultural labourers (Satyapaul 1988). Added to these is the problem of unemployment among the educated which has acquired a serious dimension over the years. Their numbers has increased from about 2.1 million in 1971 to 14.7 million in 1986.

POVERTY ALLEVIATION PROGRAMMES AND EMPLOYMENT

Keeping in view the relationship between unemployment and poverty, the Indian government has undertaken a number of poverty alleviation programmes aimed at improving the employment opportunities among the poor, both in rural and urban areas. These programmes fall under two broad categories: (i) self-employment, and (ii) wage employment. In the first category, loans and subsidies are given to poor households to help them be self-employed, in agriculture, industry, service or business. A major programme under this category is the Integrated Rural Development Programme (IRDP). The self-employment programmes, however, have certain limitations in achieving their set objectives. Especially with regard to the poorest of the poor who lack entrepreneurial abilities, and in areas where market links are poor, the self-employment schemes do not help them to cross the poverty line. Hence, a parallel approach of providing wage employment was necessitated. The important schemes under this category are the National Rural Employment Programme (NREP), Rural Landless Labourers Employment Guarantee Programme (RLEGP), which, of late, have been converted into the Jawahar Rozgar Yojana (JRY). Under these programmes, activities of community interest are undertaken and the poor provided with employment through work on these.

During the Sixth Five-Year Plan, Rs. 1,766.8 crores were spent on the IRDP and 165.62 lakh beneficiaries were covered in the country. During the Seventh Plan, Rs. 1,782 crores were spent till March 1988, covering 110.55 lakh beneficiaries. During the Sixth Plan, Rs. 1,873 crores were spent and 1,775.18 lakh man-days of employment were generated under the NREP. During the same period about Rs. 380 crores were spent on RLEGP and 2,600 lakh man-days of employment were created. Under the Employment Guarantee Scheme (EGS) of Maharashtra, a unique wage employment scheme, it is estimated that a total amount of Rs. 2,900 crores were spent up to 1988–89, which generated 21,657 lakh man-days of employment in public works such as roads, irrigation works, other agriculture-related activities, and social forestry. The EGS has provided, on average, 105 days of employment per beneficiary, contributing to about 30 per cent of their family income (Acharya 1989). The total expenditure incurred on major employment schemes (RLEGP, NREP and JRY) and the extent of employment generation during the Seventh Plan period are provided in Table 3.

Table 3: *Performance of Wage Employment Programmes during the Seventh Five-Year Plan*

Year	NREP		RLEGP	
	Total Actual Expenditure (in lakh rupees)	Employment Generated (lakh man-days)	Total Actual Expenditure (in lakh rupees)	Employment Generated (lakh man-days)
1985–86	53195	3164	45317	2476
1986–87	71777	3954	63591	3061
1987–88	78831	3708	65353	3041
1988–89	53885	2276	36429	1681
Total	257688	13102	210690	10259
1989–90 (JRY) up to December 1989			119577	4566

Source: Government of India (1988–89 and 1989–90). *Annual Report*, Department of Rural Development: New Delhi.

These apparently well-conceived employment-oriented poverty alleviation programmes have also fallen short of their expected performance. The cost of providing employment per man-day has greatly increased over the years under wage employment programmes. For instance, under the NREP, cost per man-day which was Rs. 5.25 in 1980–81 increased to Rs. 14.74 in 1984–85, Rs. 16.81

in 1985–86 and Rs. 23.67 in 1989–90. The wage employment programmes had limited success as they created only a fraction of the total employment needed in the country. Wages paid to the workers did not always conform to the minimum wages prescribed.

There is also the view that their income effect and nutritional impact on the beneficiaries is limited due to low wages and low employment. The impact of these programmes should be evaluated not only in terms of the percentage of the poor who cross the poverty line, but also in terms of sustained employment generation. Several loopholes in the implementation of these programmes— wrong identification of beneficiaries, leakage of benefits, inflation of the number of man-days of employment generated, easy working conditions under the scheme—have also plagued the programmes.

APPROACH IN THE EIGHTH PLAN

The Planning Commission set up by the National Front Government at the centre has prepared an Approach Paper on the Eighth Five-Year Plan entitled, 'Towards Social Transformation', which was recently approved by the National Development Council. The paper begins with a few criticisms of the approaches in the earlier Five-Year plans and their shortcomings, and a reorientation of the development strategy in the Eighth Plan has been outlined. As it is only an Approach Paper, details about total plan outlay and sectoral allocations have not been provided. What has been attempted here is to cull out the important pronouncements on employment planning from this Approach Paper to see the direction in which it attempts to plan for employment generation.

At the outset, the Approach Paper points out that even after four decades of planning the task of ensuring full employment and even a moderate minimum standard of living to everyone remains unfulfilled. The attainment of these basic tasks must be the central concern of development strategies in the 1990s. According to this Paper, meaningful development consists in mobilising the skills, strengths and creative capabilities of the masses and with their cooperation. The Eighth Plan is expected to reorient development policy in such a way that it gives primacy to the immediate and urgent needs of the poor, namely, employment opportunities to all at minimum wages, access to adequate means of livelihood and skills, and other basic necessities such as food, education, health and housing. It adds that growth should be widely distributed across regions and sections of the population and is of a kind which can absorb the increases in the labour force and backlog of the unemployed in large parts of the country.

In operational terms, according to the Paper, the problem is one of tackling unemployment and underemployment. Migration from rural areas to cities in search of employment will be mitigated by greater opportunities for gainful employment proposed to be created in the rural areas. The guarantee of the right to work, reserving at least half of the total public outlay for the benefit of the rural areas, and emphasis on village and small-scale industries are envisaged. For achieving full employment the pattern of investment has to undergo substantial shifts from high capital/labour to low capital/labour activities. The Approach Paper points out that there are many sectors and sub-sectors in which the pattern of investment can be reordered so as to maximise the use of labour.

While there are certain welcome changes in the perception of planners regarding employment planning, many of the pronouncements did appear in the earlier plans as well. The new and promising pronouncements, such as the right to work, increase in the share of plan outlay for the rural areas, a decentralised approach to planning, and greater emphasis on welfare aspects such as health, education and environment are notable. However, the Approach Paper repeats some of the slogans that appeared in earlier plans: emphasis on small-scale and village industries, shift from high capital/labour-intensive activities to low capital/labour activities, higher rate of growth of employment at a level of 3 per cent per annum, etc. The paper is also silent on how the performance of various sectors would be improved by improving the implementation of the programmes.

As poverty and conditions of unemployment and underemployment are said to be closely related, any perspective on poverty alleviation/removal should keep in view the need for deliberate planning for the creation of employment. For this, there are a few prerequisites which should not go unmentioned. Even though none of them might be new, they are worth repeating.

PREREQUISITES

First, there is need for a clear understanding of the nature and magnitude of employment, unemployment and underemployment in the country, both at the aggregate level and more so at the disaggregated level. In this connection the recommendations of the Dantwala Committee may be worth recalling (GOI 1970). The Committee had noted that the estimates of employment potential on an aggregate basis could not be made at the level of the economy as a whole. Hence, information on segments of the labour force classified by region, rural–urban residence, status or class of worker, and educational attainments should be attempted and the likely demand for different types of labour should be appraised. Therefore, it is only necessary and appropriate that employment and unemployment situations are analysed separately among these categories of workers. The employment position of women, children, the elderly and weaker sections should be dealt with separately.

Second, it is necessary to know the sectoral composition of the labour force and the changes that have taken place in it over different plan periods. In the process of development, even though a shift from agricultural activities to non-agricultural pursuits was visualised, it has not materialised to the extent desired. However, some changes have occurred within each sector and sub-sector and it is important to identify these changes and capture the factors responsible for them.

Third, the employment potential of different sectors and sub-sectors differs and similar is the situation with respect to different plan schemes. While planning for employment generation, it is necessary to have a fair idea of the employment potential of these plan schemes. A study carried out at the Institute for Social and Economic Change clearly indicated that the employment potential (both direct and indirect) of different plan schemes not only varies but is different at each phase of each category (manual, skilled, etc.) of their construction, operation and maintenance (Aziz and Rayappa 1979). Estimation of such parameters is very crucial in the process of planning for employment generation.

Fourth, efficiency at work and productivity of workers depend not only on their educational levels but also on other factors like health, nutrition and housing. Provision of these to the poorer sections should receive adequate priority in the Eighth Plan. The technological content of plan schemes has to be carefully probed and designed. Modernisation of the same, age-old, time-consuming and less remunerative occupations usually pursued by deprived sections may also be considered in the light of human resource mobilisation and development.

Finally, the provision of employment at the existing wage rates will not help in alleviating the problem of poverty as a majority of the poor who lack productive assets and who are mainly dependent on wages for sustenance will continue to live below the poverty line. Therefore, a hike in wages is essential if they have to move out of the poverty trap. This is possible by improving the productivity and efficiency of the worker, which can be improved by adopting improved skills. Therefore, the formulation of an appropriate wage policy is considered an essential element for the maximisation of employment and the minimisation of poverty.

REFERENCES

Acharya, S. (1989). *Intervention into Labour Market: Case Study of Maharashtra Employment Guarantee Scheme*, ILO (ARTEP): New Delhi.

Aziz, Abdul and P.H. Rayappa (1979). 'Estimation of Employment Potential of Some Plan Schemes in Karnataka: A Survey'. Institute for Social and Economic Change: Bangalore (mimeo.).

Government of India (1970). *Report of the Committee of Experts on Unemployment Estimates* (Dantwala Committee Report). Planning Commission: New Delhi.

Planning Commission (1990a). 'Employment: Past Trends and Prospects for 1990s'. Working Paper, New Delhi (mimeo.).

────── (1990b). 'Towards Social Transformation: Approach to Eighth Five Year Plan, 1990–95'. Draft, New Delhi.

Prasad, Brahmananda (1983). 'Employment Strategies of the Indian Five Year Plans: Reasons for Their Failure', in A. Robinson et al. (eds.), *Employment Policy in a Developing Country*, vol. 2. Macmillan Press.

Prasad, Pradhan (1990). 'Prospects of Development and Employment Growth', National Seminar on Agricultural Labour, National Council for Rural Labour: New Delhi, 8–9 March.

Raj Krishna (1976). *Rural Employment—A Survey of Concepts and Estimates for India*. World Bank Staff Working Paper Number 234.

Rath, N. (1983). 'Measuring Rural Unemployment in India: A Methodological Note' in A. Robinson, et al. (eds.), *Employment Policy in a Developing Country*, vol. 1, Macmillan Press.

Satyapaul (1988). 'Unemployment and Underemployment in Rural India', *Economic and Political Weekly*, vol. 23, no. 29: 1475–83, 16 July.

8

Rapid Population Growth and Economic Development in India: An Overview and Assessment

RAMESH KANBARGI and SHANTA KANBARGI

T he population of India nearly doubled over a period of thirty-four years from an estimated 344 million people at the dawn of Independence to 685 million people in 1981. There has been a further increase in 1991 to 844 million (provisional estimate) and the population is expected to cross the one billion mark by the turn of the century.

The population was observed to have grown at more or less the same rate during the decades 1961 to 1971 and 1971 to 1981—at about 2.2 per cent per annum—but at a slightly lower rate of 2.1 per cent per annum during 1981 to 1991, demonstrating the very limited impact of the birth control programme being pursued since 1952. Such a high growth rate observed in India and other less developed countries is unprecedented in the history of human-kind. In contrast, in the more developed countries of today, annual natural growth rates were seldom above 1.5 per cent as they passed through their demographic transition from high to low fertility and mortality levels. At the prevailing growth rates observed in these countries it may take over 100 years to double their populations.

What are the consequences of such rapid population growth on the efforts of the governments in the poor countries to remove poverty and improve the levels of living of the masses? In this paper we have tried to examine the interrelationship between population growth and economic development, focusing on the selective research carried out in India and elsewhere.

ECONOMIC CONSEQUENCES OF RAPID POPULATION GROWTH

It was Malthus who really brought the issue of population to the focus of scholarly attention. He first brought out the conflict that exists between population and the levels of living as a major issue in the maintenance of human welfare (Malthus 1798). He argued that the main source of poverty is in the confrontation that exists between population growth and scarce resources and, that the population grows faster than food production. But the sustained economic growth in Western Europe and North America in the 18th and 19th centuries was accompanied by rapid population growth of a nature which the world had never known. Agricultural and industrial developments improved the levels of living of the people. Health and sanitation facilities were expanded, resulting in a significant fall in mortality levels. This led to a change in the views of economists on the relationship between population growth and economic development. A growing population was considered to be necesary to bring about economic growth because it stimulates demand, improves the labour force and leads to technological innovations.[1]

But the situation soon changed. The Second World War was followed by a dramatic decline in the levels of mortality in the developing countries due to borrowed health technology and other factors. However, fertility levels remained high and the population of these countries began to show accelerated growth rates. The experience of Western Europe and North America, therefore, was found to be irrelevant for developing countries and growing populations were increasingly considered a threat to development efforts. Economists renewed their interest in 'population' as an issue in the development process and were once again drawn to this puzzle. Macro-economic models were developed to study the impact of rapid population growth on economic development in these countries. The analytical models of Leibenstein (1954) and Nelson (1956) who treated population as an endogenous variable

[1] For instance, Kuznets (1966: 20) defined economic growth as a sustained increase in population attained without any lowering of per capita product. Other economists also argued the positive effect of population growth on economic development. See also Hirshman (1958), Boserup (1965), and Glover and Simon (1975).

which is influenced by income are the best examples. They argued more or less like Malthus, that increasing income leads to increasing populations, downward pressure on per capita incomes, and thus to a low-level equilibrium trap. The classic work of Coale and Hoover (1958) is one of the most widely acknowledged mathematical models of the economy of India to study the impact of a growing population. Their study concluded that in about thirty years per capita income in India could be lower by 40 per cent under high fertility assumptions as compared to low fertility assumptions.

The Coale and Hoover model virtually opened a floodgate for studies examining the relation between population growth and economic development that came out with conflicting findings.[2] More recently, Jung and Quddus (1984) examined these relations for twenty-five developing countries and nineteen developed countries using time series data and cautioned against assuming a simple relationship. Similarly, Leibenstein argues that 'there are very few hard data and very few good studies directly measuring economic consequences of population growth.' The question cannot be answered by the usual method of subtracting the population growth rate from the rate of economic growth since it is not known whether the contribution of additonal population is negative, zero or positve (Leibenstein 1985: 136). Nonetheless, some macro studies examined the consequences of rapid population growth on education and found that future expenditure would be adversely affected because of the increase in the absolute number of students (Jones 1975a); similarly, health costs would go up (Jones 1975b). Such studies provided strong hints to the planners in Third World countries about the likely costs involved in the process of development accruing because of population growth. Some studies tried to estimate the value of prevented birth under specific assumptions (Demeny 1961; Enke 1967; Zaiden 1968) which provided the necessary support for several developing countries to pursue the family planning programme and justified the expenditure incurred on these programmes on the grounds that it was comparatively more effective than the expenditure on other development programmes. As a result of these research findings and the continuing debate, today, most of the developing countries have accepted

---

[2] For more details on these models see Birdsall (1977).

birth control programmes indicating the general agreement on the arguments that a growing population hinders development and it should be checked to accelerate development.

THE CASE OF INDIA

The growing population of India has long been considered by many economists as an important factor behind poverty. Birth control was advocated by many as early as the 1920s, and indeed a birth control clinic was opened in the city of Poona in 1923 and another in Bangalore in 1930 by the then Princely State of Mysore. In the 1930s, several economists emphasised the likely adverse impact of a growing population on employment and agriculture (Thomas 1934–35; Karve 1936; Wadia and Merchant 1943). The Indian National Congress advocated an anti-natalist policy as early as 1938 and constituted a Committee on Population under the Chairmanship of Dr. Radha Kamal Mukerjee. The Committee suggested the opening of birth control clinics in India to control population growth (Shah 1949).

The first Census of free India in 1951 showed 41.4 million people over the previous Census of 1941 (Table 1) and, in addition, the country was faced with food shortages. The Planning Commission which came into existence in 1950 recognised early that population control is most essential to planned development in India. The document of the First Five-Year Plan which was presented to parliament in December 1952 and was approved contained a 'Population Control Programme' with a budgetary provision of Rs. 65 lakhs. India thus became the first country in the world to adopt family planning as an integral part of the development programme which has since remained the single most important policy intervention to achieve the national demographic goals set forth from time to time. Today it is the second largest programme in the world, next only to China, in terms of budget, personnel and people covered.

Underlying the efforts of the government to reduce the rate of population growth has been its basic commitment to eradicate poverty; yet, the performance of both poverty alleviation and family planning programmes have met with very little success. We

Table 1: *Population in India—1901–1981*

Census Year	Total Population (in millions)	Geometric Growth Rate	Net Additions (in millions)
1901	238.4	–	–
1911	252.0	+0.56	13.6
1921	251.3	−.003	−0.7
1931	279.01	+1.06	27.8
1941	319.7	+1.34	40.6
1951	361.1	+1.26	41.4
1961	439.2	+1.98	78.1
1971	548.2	+2.24	109.0
1981	685.2	+2.28	137.0
1991	843.9*	+2.11	158.7

Source: Government of India (1985). *Family Welfare Programme in India: Year Book, 1984–85*. Ministry of Health and Family Welfare: New Delhi.
    * Provisional figure.

argue here that while the persistence of poverty owes quite a lot, if not exclusively, to rapid population growth, family planning efforts have not been imaginative enough to fully understand the factors behind population growth. Paradoxically, the Sixth Plan document itself recognised that mere birth control programmes pursued in the country, under the circumstances, might not be able to deliver the goods but that there is need for a broader framework to tackle the problem of a growing population. It suggested the need to provide better health care, water supply, literacy and higher social-economic status to women, factors which can make a dent in the birth rate (GOI 1979). If the family planning programme, which the country is pursuing since 1952, has never been able to achieve the set targets, it is necessary to know why people are averse to it. Although research on family planning in India has grown into an industry in itself, most of the studies are superfluous and descriptive in nature.

The family planning programme has been severely criticised by many for its failure to reach the desired demographic goals.[3] But

[3] For a brief review of the programme and the major issues involved in its success see Kanbargi and Kanbargi (1989). This research is based on an on-going study 'Indian Family Planning Programme: Promising Path or Blind Alley?' by the same authors at the Population Research Centre, Institute for Social and Economic Change, Bangalore.

the question whether even an ideal family planning programme in India—a programme totally flawless—would have delivered the goods still remains unanswered. A few researchers have pointed out that for successful population planning, the social and economic conditions prevailing in the society are as important as the manner in which the family planning programme is implemented. For example, Mauldin and Berelson examined this issue, drawing data from ninety-four less developed countries, to assess the role of societal and family planning programme-related factors in the observed level of the performance of the family planning programme. (Their study placed the efforts of the Indian programme in the 'moderate' category and societal factors in the 'lower middle' category.) The study found that during the decade 1965 to 1975, greater declines in crude birth rates (CBR) observed were closely associated with 'substantial' family planning programme efforts and a 'high' social setting.[4] More recently, Lapham and Mauldin (1985) developed more robust indices of social setting and programme inputs to explain the differential performance of family planning programmes among countries which had adopted them. This exercise also placed the Indian family planning programme in the 'moderate' category while the programmes of countries like China and Indonesia were placed in the 'strong' category. The socio-economic conditions in India were placed in the 'lower middle' category as against the 'upper middle' category in which the Chinese social setting was placed. This study once again confirms the findings of previous studies that a combination of improved socio-economic setting and strong programme efforts leads to better performance in family planning.

POVERTY AND HIGH ECONOMIC VALUE OF CHILDREN

The failure of the family planning programme in India to reach the set demographic goals brings us to the issue of 'poverty' which these studies have measured in terms of an 'index' of social setting.

[4] For details on the construction of 'social setting' and 'programme efforts' indices see Mauldin and Berelson (1978). See also Freedman and Berelson (1976) for a similar exercise which found that social setting and programme-related factors have independent and equal importance in explaining the performance of the programme.

Why is it that couples of lower socio-economic status do not accept contraception and prefer larger families while macro-economic models justify the anti-natalist policies pursued by many less developed countries? What are the factors that determine the persistence of higher fertility values? Answers to these questions have to be sought in the theoretical formulations of Notestein (1953). Notestein holds that populations tend to move through three distinct phases, starting with high fertility-mortality and stationary populations, followed by declining mortality leading to growing populations, and finally, low fertility-mortality that would again re-establish stationary populations. This theory, known as the demographic transition theory based on the experience of European countries, assumes industrialisation and urbanisation as preconditions for bringing about this demographic change. Industrialisation and urbanisation would bring changes in the social and economic structure which in turn would bring about a decline in fertility. In backward agricultural societies, for example, children start working early and are a potential security for their parents in times of illness and in their old age (Kanbargi 1987, 1988). Hence they are considered assets by their parents. Because children are gainfully employed from a very young age, they carry high economic value and cost less as they do not attend school, both factors contributing to the persistence of higher fertility.[5] Caldwell (1978) reports that the observed fertility decline in Europe was due to the quite sudden rise in the cost of raising children and a decline in their input in household production. Kasarda (1971), based on his cross-sectional time series data came to the conclusion that child labour has an important bearing on fertility.

There is also other evidence to support the hypothesis that high economic value of children causes high fertility in India—the chief value being their work input in household production and agriculture. Mamadani (1972) illustrated with examples that children in village Manupur in Punjab perform a variety of tasks which are

---

[5] An intensive study recently conducted in rural Karnataka showed that parents who sent their children to school had to forego about four hours of their work daily. While child work was found to be positively associated with fertility, child schooling showed a negative association. The study based on a year's survey in forty-five villages spread over ten districts shows that the economic value of children in rural Karnataka is high and makes high fertility a rational proposition. For details see Kanbargi and Kulkarni (1986).

beneficial to parents. Nadkarni's study (1976) in Marathawada region in Maharashtra shows that children in poor households do considerable work both within and outside the house. At the macro level an econometric analysis of district-level data of the 1961 Census showed that variables positively related with fertility— such as size of landholdings, agricultural productivity and child wage rates—were also positively related with child labour and negatively with child schooling (Rosenzweig and Evenson 1977). Parents' preference for children's work participation over school-ing in fact demonstrates the perceived high economic value of children in most of the poor countries. To make children attend school and not work from a very young age is a formidable task. However, it may be noted that efforts by the state and central governments have hardly had an impact on either the incidence of child labour or on the rate of school drop-outs.[6] Under the circum-stances, the Karnataka study rightly highlighted the need to make several child activities redundant through the intervention of appropriate rural development programmes. The study suggested the need to eliminate the drudgery in rural life, particularly in food preparation, fetching water and fuel, tending cattle, etc., which, more than any direct attack, would go a long way in reducing child labour (Kanbargi and Kulkarni 1986).

POVERTY AND HIGH INFANT AND CHILDHOOD MORTALITY

High infant and childhood mortality in India also add to high fertility as parents want to ensure a minimum number of children. The major causes of deaths among children are the direct outcome of the poor living conditions existing in the country. The three leading causes of infant and childhood deaths are tetanus, diarrhoea and prematurity, which arise because of malnutrition among mothers, poor health care and the absence or scarcity of safe drinking water. Although over time infant and childhood mortality has shown a decline, the infant mortality rate (IMR) is conceded to be very high, at around 100 per 1,000 live births.[7] Nutritional

[6] For more details on child labour and its effect on schooling, fertility and overall development see Kanbargi (1991).

[7] For a comprehensive review of research on infant mortality in India, see Visaria and Jain (1988).

deficiencies account for most of the deaths among children below 5 years, and the girl child is more prone to such deficiencies as shown by the National Nutrition Monitoring Bureau (NNMB). About 85 per cent of children in India suffer from various degrees of undernutrition (Gopalan 1985). The nutritional level would rise slowly and follow the overall development that takes place in the society.[x]

SON PREFERENCE

Apart from the high economic value attached to children and high infant and child mortality that support a larger family size, another important factor that aggravates this problem is the very strong preference for sons observed in India and many other less developed countries. Son preference affects the family planning programme in two ways: most of the acceptors—as the service statistics show—have accepted family planning only after they have had at least one or two sons, thus reducing the demographic impact of contraception. Since son preference is so strong in society it results in a large number of mothers having only daughters or many having only one son. In both cases they resist contraception, which reduces the proportion of acceptors, and both these contribute to population growth. Though son preference is deeply ingrained in Indian culture, effective policy interventions are lacking in India while China could effectively counteract this with imaginative policy interventions.[y]

RAPID POPULATION GROWTH AND POVERTY

We have briefly examined how poverty-related factors lead to higher fertility and a faster population growth rate. How does a

[x] For more details see Rao and Gowrinath Shastry (1985).

[y] The reason why fertility declined in China so rapidly, apart from the rigorous implementation of the family planning programme, is the remarkable way the Chinese families responded to the changed environment brought about by several policy interventions. Expanded education and occupational opportunities that gave distinct advantages to daughters changed the strong son preference which existed in Chinese society. For details see Greenhalgh (1988).

growing population affect poverty? A rapidly growing population means there are more children, more children in a society means greater demand for primary education and health care services that need larger continuing investments. This would inevitably result in reducing the limited resources for other productive purposes. Under the circumstances, both the state and central governments find it extremely difficult to maintain even a minimum level of efficiency in providing health and educational facilities. The number of primary schools in India increased from 2,09,671 in 1950–51 to 5,03,741 in 1982–83, but the quality of schooling has remained perceptibly low. Primary schools without blackboards, single-teacher schools and schools run on the verandahs of temples and old dilapidated houses in the rural areas clearly bring out this fact.[10] Similarly, lack of medicines, buildings to house rural health centres, etc., also highlight the growing demands for primary health care services on the one hand, and the problem they create on the limited resources on the other. This is reflected in the lack-lustre health services the state governments in India are able to provide.[11]

Rapid population growth also creates enormous pressure on natural resources, particularly land. While the number of rural households in India has increased by 66 per cent, the increase in cultivated land has been only 2 per cent. As a result, during the last two decades the number of small and marginal holdings rose from 15.4 million to 35.6 million. The average size of landholdings fell from 0.27 acres to 0.14 acres during the same period (IBRD 1984). Fragmentation of landholdings often leads to greater dependency on family labour and reduces employment opportunities, which aggravates the poverty situation.

According to the demographic transition theory, industrialisation

---

[10] Scarcity of resources for education is also associated with distorted priorities in allocation within the education sector. For example, universalisation of primary education is a national goal and our Constitution stipulated that it should be achieved within ten years of its being framed. This has not yet been achieved. But allocation of resources within the education sector is more favourable to higher education, which in turn may be held responsible for the growing number of illiterates. For more on this see Jain (1981).

[11] A recent study carried out in Karnataka pointed out how the resource crunch on the one hand and faster expansion of health services on the other, pursued by the state government, has resulted in bringing down the credibility of health services at lower levels and how, in turn, it adversely affects the sterilisation programme. For details see Kanbargi (1990).

and urbanisation are the key predeterminants of rural–urban migration and increase in the acceptance of contraception. This would lead to a fall in fertility levels, as was observed in more developed countries. But the Indian situation seems to be far removed from this expectation. During the period 1960 to 1980, the shift observed in the proportion of labour force from the agricultural to the non-agricultural sector was very small and almost negligible.[12] It also signifies a fall in relative income per worker in agriculture. Rural–urban migration—which is significant in absolute terms—particularly to metropolitan cities, has meant appalling living conditions for most of the migrants. For several years to come strong population pressure on land will continue to exist and have an adverse effect on the number of days of wage labour available per labourer per year. The low level of employment potential in Indian agriculture has been pointed out by many researchers (Dandekar and Rath 1971: 25–48 and 106–46; Mitra 1976: 1041–45). Labour use as a percentage of labour supply available varied from 32 to 34 per cent during April–May to 94 per cent in December (Clark and Haswell 1970). A more recent analysis, however, reports a year-round surplus of labour in rural India (Rudra 1973: 277–80).

RAPID POPULATION GROWTH AND EMPLOYMENT

A growing population leads to a greater demand on employment opportunities. Employment is the chief source of income and is closely related with poverty status. One analysis points out that unemployment rates decline from high levels for very poor households, to moderate levels among households falling just below the poverty line, and low levels among better-off households (Krishnamurthy 1988). According to another analysis:

> the rates of unemployment are distinctly higher for the set of poor households than for the non-poor under weekly-status but much more so under the daily-status. The association between

---

[12] For more details on changes in the Indian labour force see Krishnamurthy (1984) based on census and NSS data; see also Sinha (1982).

poverty and unemployment is also reflected in the fact that the contribution to the unemployed person-weeks and unemployed person-days originating in the poor households is higher than their share in the economically active population of persons aged 5 and above (Sundaram and Tendulkar 1988).

The generation of employment opportunities is directly linked with the growth in capital stock and its efficient allocation. If the urban production system is tailored to absorb more and more labour generated by population growth, if more investment in fertilisers, irrigation, etc., is made in agriculture, the unemployment problem can be eased to a large extent. While unemployment is considered to be a cause of poverty, its greater incidence among the poor, as seen, has resulted in the government pursuing policies to reduce it in the form of employment-generation programmes like the Jawahar Rozgar Yojana, which have become a major component of the anti-poverty programme.

It should also be noted here that a fast-growing labour force may lead to its underutilisation. The enormous increase in government and public sector employment is associated with this phenomenon. A study points out 'typists in government offices playing cards during office hours, members of large families labouring at a snail's pace on tiny plots of land and the countless loitering peons and messengers, [are] all expressions of the phenomenon—an under-utilised labour supply' (Basu 1984). Krishan (1984) examined the contribution of population growth to unemployment in India by decomposing its various components to show that during 1959 to 1978, population growth was responsible for increasing unemployment (weekly status) by 42 per cent per annum. However, it should be noted that there are several constraints in data, concept, definition and measurement of unemployment. But we agree that unemployment, particularly of educated urban residents in India, has shown a continuing increase. For example, one estimate shows that as on December 1988, there were 30,050,000 applicants on the live registers of 759 employment exchanges in India, a figure which was only 3,29,000 in 1951 in 126 employment exchanges. According to the NSS data of the 38th round, twenty-one persons per 1,000 were unemployed in the rural areas as against 100 in urban areas. There has been an increase as shown by the 43rd round of the NSS—to forty-two in rural, and 114 in urban areas (usual status adjusted) (see *Facts For You* 1990: 32).

CONCLUSION

The type of poverty that existed in India prior to Independence when the country had an almost stable population is no doubt a thing of the past. The decade 1911 to 1921, for instance, saw 20 million influenza deaths that reduced the total population of the country. During the last years of British rule, the Bengal famine took a toll of 3.5 million persons and precious little is known about the extent of starvation deaths in India that were common at the time. Independence and the developmental programmes pursued have indeed brought several improvements in the lives of the people. Plague and small pox have been totally eradicated and malaria deaths have come down to a few thousand from millions. Droughts have a much less adverse impact on the lives of the people now and famines are a thing of the past. Yet, poverty of a less acute form has persisted and defied development efforts.

This brief overview indicates that the empirical studies that have tried to examine the interrelationship between population growth and economic development have come up with conflicting findings because of several factors. Despite this, there is substantial and growing evidence to show that poverty and rapid population growth reinforce each other. In order to derive greater benefits from development programmes, it is absolutely necessary to reduce the rate of population growth. More than the direct efforts at family planning, indirect methods could achieve better results. We have tried to highlight the need to reduce the economic value of children by making primary schooling compulsory and also by improving the probability of survival of children to bring the desired decline in population in the years to come. Needless to add that achieving high rates of literacy, particularly among women, would contribute to improving the quality of life of people and also in reducing population growth. Planning would be hardly meaningful and relevant if these issues are not accorded highest priority.

REFERENCES

Basu, Kaushik (1984). *The Less Developed Economy: A Critique of Contemporary Theory*. Oxford University Press: New Delhi.

Birdsall, Nancy (1977). 'Analytical Approaches to the Relationship of Population Growth and Development', *Population and Development Review*, vol. 3, nos. 1 and 2: 63–102, March–June.

Boserup, Easter (1965). *The Conditions of Agricultural Growth*. Allen and Unwin: London.

Caldwell, J.C. (1978). 'A Theory of Fertility: From High Plateau to Destabilisation', *Population and Development Review*, vol. 4, no. 4: 553–78.

Clark, Colin and M. Haswell (1970). *The Economics of Subsistence Agriculture*. St. Martins Press: London.

Coale, Ansley and Edgar Hoover (1958). *Population Growth and Economic Development in Low Income Countries*. Princeton University Press: Princeton.

Dandekar, V.M. and N. Rath (1971). 'Poverty in India', *Economic and Political Weekly*, vol. 6, nos. 1 and 2. Also published by the Indian School of Political Economy, Lonavala, 1971.

Demeny, Paul (1961). 'Investment Allocation and Population Growth', *Demography*, vol. 2: 203–33.

Enke, Stephen (1967). *Raising Per capita Income Through Fewer Births*: General Electric, TEMPO: Santa Barbara.

Facts For You (June 1990). Vol. 11, no. 12: 31–32. Annual Number, New Delhi.

Freedman, R. and B. Berelson (1976). 'The Record of Family Planning Programme', *Studies in Family Planning*, vol. 7, no. 1.

Glover, Donald R. and Julian Simon (1975). 'The Effect of Population Density on Infrastructure: The Case of Road Building', *Economic Development and Cultural Change*, vol. 23, no. 3: 453–68, April.

Gopalan, C. (1985). 'The Mother and Child in India', *Economic and Political Weekly*, vol. 20, no. 4; 159–66, 26 January.

Government of India (1979). *Draft Sixth Five-Year Plan 1978–1983*. Planning Commission: New Delhi.

Greenhalgh, Susan (1988). 'Fertility as Mobility: Sinic Transition', *Population and Development Review*, vol. 14, no. 4: 629–74.

Hirshman, Albert O. (1958). *The Strategy of Economic Development*. Yale University Press: New Haven.

IBRD (1984). *World Development Report 1984*. Oxford University Press: London.

Jain, A.K. (1981). 'Education Sector Approaches, Attainment and Fertility: An Illustrative Case Study for India', Working Paper No. 14, May. The Population Council: New York.

Jones, Gavin (1975a). 'Educational Planning and Population Growth', in Warren C.Robinson (ed.), *Population and Development Planning*. The Population Council: New York.

———. (1975b). 'Population Growth and Health and Family Planning', in Warren C. Robinson (ed.), *Population and Development Planning*. The Population Council: New York.

Jung, Woo S. and Munir Quddus (1984). Economic Development and Population Growth: International Evidence Based on Causality Tests', Working Paper No. 84–3, Department of Economics and Business Administration, Vanderbilt University: Nashville, Tennessee.

Kanbargi, Ramesh (1987). 'Oldage Security and Fertility Behaviour: Some Research Issues', in S.K. Biswas (ed.), *Aging in Contemporary India*. Indian Anthropological Society: Calcutta.

——— (1988). 'Child Labour in India: Carpet Industry of Varanasi', in Bequelle Assefa and Jo Boyden (eds.), *Combating Child Labour*. International Labour Organisation: Geneva.

——— (1990). 'Health and Family Planning Services in Two Primary Health Centres in Karnataka: An Evaluation'. Institute for Social and Economic Change: Bangalore (mimeo.).

———. (1991). *Child Labour in the Indian Subcontinent: Dimensions and Implications*. Sage Publications: New Delhi.

Kanbargi, Ramesh and P.M. Kulkarni (1986). 'Child Labour, Schooling and Fertility in Rural Karnataka—South India', in John Stoeckel and A.K. Jain (eds.), *Fertility in Asia: Assessing Development Impacts*. Frances Pinters Publishers: London.

Kanbargi, Ramesh and Shanta Kanbargi (1989). 'Indian Family Planning Programme: Some Issues', *Facts For You*, vol. 10, no. 12: 15–18, July, Annual Number.

Karve, D.G. (1936). 'Poverty and Population in India' as quoted in *India: Country Profile*. The Population Council: New York, May 1976.

Kasarda, John D. (1971). 'Economic Structure and Fertility: A Comparative Analysis', *Demography*, vol. 8, no. 3: 307–10.

Krishnamurthy, J. (1984). 'Changes in Indian Workforce', *Economic and Political Weekly*, vol. 19, no. 50: 2121–28, 15 December.

——— (1988). 'Unemployment in India: The Broad Magnitudes and Characteristics', in T.N. Srinivasan and P.K. Baradan (eds.), *Rural Poverty in South Asia*. Oxford University Press: Delhi.

Krishna, Raj (1984). *The Growth of Aggregate Unemployment in India:* World Bank Staff Working Paper No. 638.

Kuznets, Simon (1966). *Modern Economic Growth*. Yale University Press: New Haven.

Lapham, Robert and W. Parker Mauldin (1984). 'Family Planning Programme Effort and Birth Rate Decline in Developing Countries', *International Family Planning Perspectives*, vol. 10: 109–18.

Leibenstein, Harvey (1954). *A Theory of Economic Demographic Development*. Princeton University Press: Princeton.

——— (1985). 'The World Development Report 1984: A Review Symposium', *Population and Development Review*, vol. 11, no. 1: 135–37, March.

Malthus, Thomas (1798). *Essays on the Principles of Population as it Affects Future Improvements of Society*. London.

Mamadani, M. (1972). *The Myth of Population Control: Family, Caste and Class in an Indian Village*. Monthly Review Press: New York.

Mauldin, Parker and B. Berelson (1978). 'Conditions of Fertility Decline in Developing Countries', *Studies in Family Planning Programme*, vol. 9, no. 5: 91–147.

Mitra, A.K. (1976). 'Surplus Labour in Agriculture: Some Estimates', *Economic and Political Weekly*, vol. 11, no. 28: 1041–45.

Nadkarni, M.V. (1976). 'Over Population and the Rural Poor', vol. 11, nos. 31–33: 1163–72, August.

Nelson, Richard R. (1956). 'A Theory of Low Level Equilibrium Trap in Underdeveloped Economies', *American Economic Review*, vol. 46: 894–908.

Notestein, Frank (1953). 'Economic Problem of Population Change', in *Eighth International Conference of Agricultural Economists*. Oxford University Press: London.

Rao, N. Prahlad and J. Gowrinath Shastry (1985). 'Nutritional Profile in India Over a Decade', paper presented at the National Seminar on 'The Implementation of a Nutritional Policy in India', Srinagar, 28–30 October. National Institute of Nutrition: Hyderabad.

Rosenzweig, Mark and R. Evenson (1977). 'Fertility, Schooling and Economic Contribution of Children in Rural India: An Econometric Analysis', *Econometrica*, vol. 45, no. 5: 1065–79.

Rudra, Ashok (1973). 'Direct Estimates of Surplus Labour in Agriculture', *Economic and Political Weekly*, vol. 8: 277–80, Annual Number.

Shah, K.T. (1949). *Population: Report of the Sub-Committee, National Planning Committee*. Vora: Bombay.

Sinha, J.N. (1982). '1981 Census Economic Data: A Note', *Economic and Political Weekly*, vol. 17, no. 6: 195–202, February.

Sundaram, K. and S.D. Tendulkar (1988). 'Toward an Explanation of Interregional Variations in Poverty and Unemployment in India', in T.N. Srinivasan and P.K. Baradan (eds.), *Rural Poverty in South Asia*. Oxford University Press: Delhi.

Thomas, P.J. (1934–35). 'Population and Production', *Indian Journal of Economics*, vol. 15.

Visaria, P. and A.K. Jain (eds.) (1988). *Infant Mortality in India: Differentials and Determinants*. Sage Publications: New Delhi.

Wadia, P.A. and K.T. Merchant (1943). *Our Economic Problem*. New Book Co.: Bombay.

Zaiden, George (1968). 'The Foregone Benefits and Costs of a Prevented Birth: Conceptual Problem and an Application to the UAR'. IBRD Working Paper No. 11, January.

9

Land Reforms: The Next Phase

V.M. RAO

INTRODUCTION

The Gandhian perspective of the struggle for Independence and the restructuring of Indian society attached great importance to the elimination of rural oppression, exploitation and poverty arising from iniquitous land distribution and relations. Considerable thinking on land reforms took place prior to Independence, leading to the crystallisation of ideas on the strategy, priorities and programmes regarding land reforms. Gandhi visualised villages characterised by harmonious relations and collective efforts to promote development and welfare for all, beginning with the poorest among the poor (*antyodaya*), in which all sections of the population participated including the rich; in fact, the rich were expected to see themsleves as trustees safeguarding the interests of the poor.

The 1950s and the early 1960s until Nehru's death were marked by ambitious legislations for land reforms, comprising abolition of intermediaries, security of tenure and fair rents for tenants, transfer of ownership of leased lands to tenants, and enforcement of ceiling on onwership with a view of bringing about redistribution of land and consolidation of holdings. Some of the states went to the extent of legislating for the complete abolition of tenancy and for making the tillers the owners of land cultivated by them. The fervour which prevailed then for the structural reforms in Indian society could be gauged from the fact that cooperative farming— and even cooperative management of villages by the villagers themselves—was seriously proposed and discussed as a model for the reorganisation of rural society.

Even before Nehru's death, the food crisis had begun to assume menacing proportions in India. The closing years of the Nehru era witnessed a determined attempt to modernise agriculture and to place it on a secure trajectory of growth. By the mid-1960s it was realised by the political leadership and the policy-maker that the structural reforms would be of little avail by themselves and would not even be effectively implemented unless they formed part of a development strategy focused on healthy, growing and technologically resurgent agriculture. By a combination of favourable circumstances—but primarily through the innate qualities of patience, hard work and receptivity to change among peasants—India achieved a credible 'Green Revolution' during the late 1960s, an achievement which demonstrated the hollowness of myths about the hold of traditionalism over Indian agriculture and peasants.

The Green Revolution provided India some respite from the immediate pressures of food crisis and kindled new hope about the growth potential of Indian agriculture. This relief and stimulus came at an opportune moment since, by then, many in India and abroad—particularly some articulate, and even vociferous, foreign observers—had begun to despair about India's capacity to feed its growing population. And, yet, the Green Revolution did not spread like wildfire across the expanse of Indian agriculture; it was noticeably selective in its coverage of areas, crops and farmers. It held an important lesson for the policy-maker, viz., that growth in agriculture cannot be switched on by generating new technologies, rather, growth needs large investments, building up of farmers' skills, modernisation of supporting institutions and, above all, a government deeply committed to the goal of agricultural development but which, at the same time, is anxious to help farmers to acquire the capacity to stand on their own without dependence on others.

Unfortunately, once the food crisis passed, the agricultural policies seemed to have lost their thrust and the process of modernisation of agriculture could not gather the necessary momentum to spread beyond the few oases of growth generated by the Green Revolution. The end of the 1970s and the beginning of the 1980s witnessed another spell of stagnation in agriculture and a recurrence of acute anxiety among the top political leadership on this score.

The enhanced priority now proposed to be assigned to agricultural growth and modernisation has the effect of once again bringing to the fore the unfinished programme of land reforms which was sidelined in the wake of the Green Revolution in agriculture. Land reforms are gaining fresh relevance and urgency in the emerging changes in the development strategy for the following reasons: First, it is now recognised that without a minimal programme for land reforms, it will not be possible to establish the necessary preconditions for growth in the areas which have stagnated so far. Certain parts of eastern India—Orissa and Bihar for example—are often mentioned as important examples of such areas (Rao and Deshpande 1986). It is necessary to note that while in the earlier post-Independence decades agricultural growth was a precondition for effective land reforms, the changing agricultural scenario in India seems to have now reversed the direction of dependence. Second, as the Economic Advisory Council has stressed in its Interim Report, agriculture has to make a major contribution in absorbing the labour available in the rural economy in productive activities (GOI 1990). This again, depends on land reforms as, in their absence, the rural poor and landless may benefit little from employment opportunities arising in agriculture (Rao 1988). Third, the working of the poverty alleviation programmes shows that those with some land base, however modest, find it easier to participate in these programmes than those totally landless (Rao 1988). In a word, in the emerging situation in rural India, land reforms have to play an integrative role of bringing together the programmes for growth and those for poverty alleviation to form a comprehensive strategy for the development of the rural economy.

The purpose of this paper is to identify the priority objectives and tasks in the area of land reforms which could provide the integrative links between agricultural growth, modernisation and poverty alleviation. The next section presents a brief review of the current status of land reforms and their implementation. The intention is not to go into all historical details but take note of only the salient features relevant for the next phase in land reforms. In the light of this discussion, the next section outlines a perspective which is of help in identifying priority objectives and tasks which could enable land reforms to play the critical role expected of them in the rural economy.

CURRENT STATUS OF LAND REFORMS

There is a broad consensus among scholars of land reform that the legislation for the abolition of intermediary tenures like *zamindari* was implemented with a fair measure of effectiveness. It could also be said that, partly owing to land reforms but mainly due to growing economic pressures, there has been a progressive erosion in the ownership of land by the urban dwellers who have permanently migrated out of villages to settle down in towns and cities in non-agricultural (often white collar) occupations. Thus, the objectives of removing the non-functional interests between the tiller and the government has been achieved to some extent but the larger goal of land reforms to establish a system of land-ownership and cultivation which could ensure both equity and productivity in agriculture is still far from being reached.

This becomes clear when we look at the performance of ceiling and tenancy legislations. These legislations assume importance because the emerging confrontation in rural India is between the cultivating strata residing in villages who own the large proportion of agricultural lands, and the lower strata who provide labour as casual wage earners and as tenants working under informal arrangements. While there are considerable variations in this respect across the country, it is useful at the level of broad generalisation to assume that the main problem to be addressed by land reforms in the coming decades is to lay the foundation for establishing harmony and community of interest between the large and medium cultivators who own most of the land on the one hand and, on the other, the small and marginal cultivators and the landless labourers who lack adequate and assured access to land.

The ceiling and tenancy legislations have been able to achieve very little in this direction so far. As regards the ceiling legislation, it is instructive to take a look at the changing distribution of operational holdings in the recent years. Table 1 presents the distribution of operational holdings over the period 1970–71 to 1985–86. It brings out strikingly the process of marginalisation of holdings. The operational holdings below 1 hectare in size, which accounted for 51 per cent of all holdings in 1970–71, were 58 per cent of all holdings in 1985–86, an increase of 7 percentage points

Table 1: Operational Holdings in India—Agriculture Census

Category and Size	Number of Operational Holdings (Millions)				Area Operated (Million hectares)				Average Size of Holdings 1985–86
	1970–71	1976–77	1980–81	1985–86	1970–71	1976–77	1980–81	1985–86	
(1) (2)	(3)	(4)	(5)	(6)	(7)	(8)	(9)	(10)	(11)
1. Marginal (below 1 ha)	36.20 (51.0)	44.52 (54.6)	50.12 (56.4)	56.75 (58.1)	14.56 (9.0)	17.51 (10.7)	19.74 (12.1)	21.60 (13.2)	0.38
2. Small (1 to 2 ha)	13.43 (18.9)	14.73 (18.1)	16.07 (18.1)	17.88 (18.3)	19.28 (11.9)	20.90 (12.8)	23.16 (14.1)	25.53 (15.6)	1.43
3. Semi-medium (2 to 4 ha)	10.68 (15.0)	11.67 (14.3)	12.45 (14.0)	13.25 (13.5)	30.00 (18.5)	32.43 (19.9)	34.65 (21.2)	36.58 (22.3)	2.76
4. Medium (4 to 10 ha)	7.93 (11.2)	8.21 (10.0)	8.07 (9.1)	7.92 (8.1)	48.24 (29.7)	49.63 (30.4)	48.54 (29.6)	47.01 (28.7)	5.94
5. Large (10 ha and above)	2.77 (3.9)	2.44 (3.0)	2.17 (2.4)	1.93 (2.0)	50.06 (30.9)	42.87 (26.2)	37.71 (23.0)	33.19 (20.2)	17.20
All categories	71.01 (100.0)	81.57 (100.0)	88.88 (100.0)	97.73 (100.0)	162.14 (100.0)	163.34 (100.0)	163.80 (100.0)	163.91 (100.0)	1.68

Notes: 1. The figures in brackets are percentages of totals in the respective columns.
2. The figures for 1985–86 are provisional.

in a period of just fifteen years. It should also be noted that over
this period all other sizes of holdings (small, semi-medium, medium
and large) had diminishing shares in total holdings. Regarding the
shares of these size-groups in operated area, the first three had
increasing shares while the medium and large holdings, particularly
the large, experienced a decrease in their shares in the total
operated area. A significant point about the farm structure in
1985–86 is that a little over 51 per cent of total operated area was
cultivated by holdings less than 4 hectares in size (i.e., marginal,
small and semi-medium holdings). Thus, the process of marginalisation of operational holdings has been seen to be moving ahead
unchecked in recent years and might even gain in momentum in
the coming decades.

The ceiling legislation has been unable to check the process of
marginalisation for two reasons. The basic reason is that the surplus
land taken over for redistribution has been meagre and, out of
that, the land actually redistributed was even less (see Table 2).
For India as a whole, until June 1989, 7.3 million acres of land
were declared as surplus, of which 4.6 million acres were actually
allotted to the beneficiaries. As on 30 June 1989, the area available
for further distribution was only 4 lakh acres. It needs to be noted
that the area redistributed along with a small balance still to be
distributed (about 5 million acres in all) is only around 2 per cent
of the total cultivated area in the country. What is more important,
however, is that it has been estimated, in a recent exercise based
on the data for the year 1985–86, that even with a fairly low ceiling
of 10 hectares of non-standardised land, the surplus would just be
enough to increase the average size of marginal holdings from 0.38
hectares to 0.64 hectares (Rao 1990). It should be mentioned here
that the exercise was done using the data on *operational holdings*
and not on *ownership holdings*: the former data is likely to be
affected much less by defective land records than the latter. Thus,
even the potential capacity of ceiling legislation to help redistribution of land appears to be rapidly vanishing.

The second reason for the failure of ceiling legislation is that the
redistribution of surplus covered heterogeneous groups of cultivators
instead of being made available to only the landless or to the
marginal cultivators (see Table 3). The surplus received by the
marginal beneficiaries was not enough to make them viable cultivators. Further, the beneficiaries receiving surplus land obtained

Table 2: *Summary Statement Showing Progress under Implementation of Land Ceiling Laws (Cumulative) for Quarter Ending June 1989 (First Quarter)*
(Area in Acres)

Item 1	Pre-revised 2	Revised 3	Total 4
1. *Returns:*			
(i) No. of returns filed	96602	1460998	1557600
(ii) No. of returns disposed of	96056	1445292	1541348
(iii) No. of returns pending	546	15706	16252
2. Area declared surplus	2723818	4559310	7283128
3. Area taken possession	2500551	3624605	6125156
4. *Area distributed:*	1854077	2751164	4605241
(i) SC	518094	1097862	1615956
(ii) ST	188949	435058	624007
(iii) Others	1147034	1218244	2365278
5. *No. of beneficiaries:*	2066136	2151126	4217262
(i) SC	603914	891211	1495125
(ii) ST	283660	298978	582638
(iii) Others	1178562	960937	2139499
6. Area declared surplus but not distributed (S. Nos. 2 to 4)	–	–	2677898
7. *Total area not available for distribution due to:*			
(i) Litigation	–	–	1300438
(ii) Reserved for public purposes	–	–	344018
(iii) Unfit for cultivation	–	–	459480
(iv) Miscellaneous reasons	–	–	179713
Total (i) to (iv)			2283649
8. Not area available for distribution (6 – 7)	–	–	394249

Source: Department of Rural Development (Land Reforms Division), Government of India.

meagre supportive assistance like inputs, credit and extension guidance. For example, an official evaluation in Karnataka of the schemes specially introduced to help the allottees of surplus land found them to be 'inadequate considering the number of prospective beneficiaries and the actual cost of land development' (Government of Karnataka 1987).

This failure of ceiling legislation and its limited potential to help redistribution of land have some significant implications for the

Table 3: *Land Gained by Different Size Class of Farmers Under Tenancy Provision in Karnataka*

Size Class of Farmers	Land Gained Per House (in Acres)
0 acres of land held	–
0–2.5	2.49
2.5–5.0	3.02
5.0–10.0	2.99
10.0–15.0	3.00
15.0 and above	9.00

Source: V.S. Satyapriya and S. Erappa (1984). 'Land Reforms in India: Some Field Evidences', in A.R. Rajapurohit (ed.), *Land Reforms in India*. Ashish: New Delhi.

policy approach to the question of tenancy. If we cannot realistically plan to achieve a structure of operational holdings with much less inequality than at present with the consequence that a large proportion of operational holdings remain marginal with no hope of increase in size through addition to owned land, the tenancy system could provide a two-fold flexibility to overcome the constraint of limited scope for redistribution. First, large holdings facing a labour-cum-supervision problem will have the alternative of leasing part of their land to small and marginal cultivators who have a labour surplus. If adequate measures are taken to build up the entrepreneurial capabilities and skill of the small and marginal cultivators, leasing-in of land by them from the large holders would be consistent with the promotion of both equity and productivity. In the absence of an open and recognised tenancy system, the large cultivators could be tempted—as is already happening in some parts of India—to divert land from agricultural crops to tree crops requiring less labour and supervision. Second, in the reverse direction, an open tenancy system would also make it easier for the cultivators with tiny holdings to lease out their land and take up other remunerative occupations. A common form taken by the poverty trap is a situation where a cultivator remains tied to his tiny holding in the absence of alternative occupation. Ineffective use of *both* land and labour is the characteristic feature of this situation. It is needless to point out that with the increasing marginalisation now occurring in Indian agriculture, more and more cultivators would run the risk of being caught in such a poverty trap.

Unfortunately, the legislation for tenancy reform has not been able to establish a system meeting the criteria of equity and productivity. The provisions made in the legislation for security of tenure and fair rents, i.e., the provisions which could provide incentives to tenants and make the tenancy arrangement equitable to both the parties to the transaction, remained largely unimplemented (GOI 1988). In fact, such provisions could even be regarded as unimplementable in the typical rural situation where dominant landlords lease out land to small and unorganised tenants. The limitations of our legal system in helping the weak against the strong are too well-known to be repeated here.

As the tenancy was difficult to regulate, some of the states, Karnataka in the early 1970s, for example, sought to abolish the tenancy system altogether. This phase of tenancy legislation had mixed results:

(*i*) The provisions for resumption of land for personal cultivation and for voluntary surrender of land by the tenant were extensively misused by the large holders to take back the lands from the tenants.

(*ii*) Where the tenancy was based on oral agreement, the legislation was helpless in restoring the lands to the tenants.

(*iii*) The tenants who benefited from the legislation were middle or large owners who had leased in land to enlarge their operational holdings. While the full documentation of the impact of the legislation for transfer of lands to tenants would need elaborate analysis of large statistical materials, a glimpse can be obtained from Table 4 that the legislation, irrespective of the intention of the policy-maker, acquired a bias in favour of the tenants who had land of their own, particularly the large owners, in the course of implementation.

A widespread effect of the attempt to abolish tenancy through legislation was to drive it underground. A recent report on tenancy prepared by the National Sample Survey Organisation finds evidence of the substantial and growing extent of 'informal' tenancies (NSSO 1989). The document reports that 'the estimates of leased in area operated was of the order of 2.2 million hectares according to the Agricultural Census, 1980–81 (which was) only one-fourth

Table 4: *Land Gained by Different Size Class of Farmers Under Ceilings Provision in Karnataka*

Size Class of Farmers	Land Gained Per House (in Acres)
0 acres of land held	2.30
0–2.5	2.25
2.5–5.0	1.73
5.0–10.0	4.48
10.0–15.0	Nil
15.0 and above	Nil

Source: V.S. Satyapriya and S. Erappa (1984). 'Land Reforms in India: Some Field Evidences', in A.R. Rajapurohit (ed.), *Land Reforms in India*. Ashish: New Delhi.

of the corresponding estimate of 8.9 million hectares thrown up by the National Sample Survey of 1981–82. This difference is mainly because the Agricultural Census, being record-based, could not take into account the tenancy which was contracted orally.' A recent seminar on 'Land Reforms—A Retrospective and Prospect', organised by the Planning Commission, mentions a much higher estimate of 'one-third of land (being) under concealed and informal tenancy' (Planning Commission 1989). More interesting, an assessment of land reforms made by the Government of India itself refers to concealed and informal tenancy as the most pressing prevalent problem calling for urgent attention in the policies for reforms (GOI 1988).

A factor which could have contributed to the failure of land reforms is that they stressed the equity aspect of the reforms but neglected the productivity aspect. As a result, the reform created and intensified conflicts among the rural groups but failed to stress the common interest of all groups in bringing about an increase in productivity. Recent researches on the Indian rural economy have presented in great detail the neglect of agricultural and rural sectors, leading to low and declining relative incomes in these sectors and a widening of disparities between them and the urban sector (Rao 1986). Two indicators are mentioned here to suggest that the policies for land reform have also been distorted by insufficient attention to the objective of raising productivity in agriculture. First, compared to the prominence in reforms received by the ceiling and the tenancy legislations, the programmes for consolidation of holdings—which is important for efficient use of land, cost-effective cultivation and adoption of improved methods and technologies—has made negligible progress in the last four decades, except in a few states, owing to the very low priority accorded to the programme. For example, a recent study of the programme in Bihar brought out the disturbing finding that over the period 1958 to 1985, 'out of 168.72 lakh hectares of agricultural area [consolidation work] has been completed only in 11 lakh hectares and it was frankly admitted that, out of this land, in about two-thirds of the area the cultivators have not shifted to their newly allotted *chaks*.' The study attributes the dismal performance of the programme to lack of interest on the part of policy-makers, faulty implementation, dilatory completion and lack of publicity (University of Lucknow 1988). Second, and more interesting, an assessment of the situation of land reforms in Kerala and West Bengal—states which have been in the forefront in the implementation of strong and effective reform measures with the help of highly politicised groups of rural poor—came to the conclusion that the agricultural economies of these states have not benefited much from the reforms because of the constraint posed by lack of adequate agricultural growth in these states (Ghose 1983). Significantly, the lowest levels of rural poverty among the states in India prevail not in Kerala and West Bengal but in Punjab and Haryana—areas with remarkable and sustained agricultural growth for more than two decades past.

The limited capability of even radical land reforms to help a rural economy handicapped by a slow growth of agriculture is reflected well in the following assessments of reforms in Kerala and West Bengal. K.N. Raj, eminent scholar and proponent of strong land reforms, sums up the Kerala experience thus:

Evidently, it is the improvement in the terms of trade [of its export products] and the large-scale inflow of remittances from migrants abroad that have maintained some semblance of prosperity in the state in recent years. This cannot last very long, unless the opportunity is used for strengthening the technological basis for more rapid agricultural growth in the future: the land reforms that have been implemented provide a sound institutional framework for such strengthening but cannot obviously be a substitute for it . . . . It should be evident from [our] analysis that nothing definitive can be said about the impact of agrarian reform on poverty in Kerala (see his paper in Ghose 1983).

As regards West Bengal, A.K. Ghose, who has looked at the land reforms from a perspective focused on 'the imperatives of growth, technological change and reduction in poverty and unemployment within the agrarian sector', finds that,

> the agrarian reform programme, currently being implemented by the Government of West Bengal, does address itself to the fundamental problems facing the agrarian economy (viz., land-lordism, usury, landlessness of rural poor and their need for more employment and higher wages). In the short run, these measures are both necessary and desirable. However [their] concrete achievements so far have been inadequate . . . . If the benefits of [these] measures are to be consolidated and built upon in the longer run, conscious efforts must be made to develop cooperative or joint farming at the next stage. This is necessary not only for pre-empting a renewed process of polar-isation of income and wealth, but also for facilitating the adoption of modern technology which is essential for growth (Ghose 1983).

A PERSPECTIVE FOR THE NEXT PHASE IN LAND REFORMS

The content and priorities of the next phase in land reforms need to be formulated as a part of an integrated policy framework for agriculture and rural development. It is assumed that the following would be the principal components in the policy framework now being evolved in the country. The attempt here is to outline a perspective on land reforms which is consistent with and comple-mentary to these components.

(*i*) A strong set of policies to focus research, extension, in-vestments, credit and institutional support on growth and modernisation of agriculture in certain areas (like dry land areas) and farmer strata (like small and marginal cultivators) which have remained stagnant so far.

(*ii*) Activation of planning systems at the zonal and district levels to formulate comprehensive land use programmes (including *both* cultivated lands *and* common property lands) and to identify optimum composition of crops, combination of ancillary activities and feasible packages of enterprises to make small and marginal farmers viable and growth-oriented.

(*iii*) Effective programmes for the poor—assets/skills, employment guarantee, minimum wages and minimum needs schemes—to provide relief and support to the poor, to reduce their dependence on the rural rich and to improve the local environment (good roads, schools, fair price shops) affecting their efficiency and welfare.

These components are important for the next phase in land reforms for the following reasons. If these components are weak and ineffective, land reforms would remain only a symbolic gesture as in the past. On the other hand, if they are strong, land reforms would have a good impact and, also, provide support to and complement the other components in the policy framework.

The next phase in land reforms should focus on the following objectives:

(*i*) Provide access and incentives to as many rural poor as possible to earn their livelihood from land, subject to land use being efficient and consistent with planning norms.

(*ii*) In pursuance of this objective, aim at a distribution of operational holdings with reasonable lower and upper limits on the size of holdings. In effect, this means rationing of scarce land. But, it needs to be emphasised that an upper limit on the size of holding need not mean ceiling on the incomes of cultivators since they can use the land more intensively and/or take up remunerative ancillary and other activities.

(*iii*) Prevent emergence of dominant landowners. Where the power structure in rural communities is based on large land-ownership, the objective should be to curb their influence.

(*iv*) Disincentives against ownership of land *primarily* for rent income, speculative income and security against risks and uncertainty.

(*v*) Adequate flexibility, permitting people to move in and out of cultivation as an occupation so that land remains in the hands of willing and enterprising farmers who are prepared to invest and modernise farming.

The realisation of these objectives needs quick and substantial progress in accomplishing the following tasks.

1. Improvements in Land Records

(*a*) Urgent attention to problems caused by lack of accuracy and reliability.
(*b*) Updating of information on the availability of categories of land suitable for different major uses.
(*c*) Identification of covert ownership of land by large holders, informal tenancy, encroachment of common lands, breach of land use rules, etc., by taking the help of well-informed people and leaders/representatives of target groups in the village.
(*d*) Easy accessibility to records for the owners/cultivators. Facilities for giving them pass books so that they have with them authenticated information. Working out a feasible programme for the computerisation of land records would be a major step towards achieving these conditions.

2. Clarity Regarding Critical Concepts

(*a*) Unambiguous definition of 'personal cultivation' to include only those who *take decisions, participate in the labour and supervision, and bear the major part of the risks of cultivation*.
(*b*) Determination of two limits on *farm size*. An *upper limit* to ensure careful and effective land use capable of promoting labour absorption, and a *lower limit* to make the farm viable. The upper limit can serve as the ceiling on ownership of land by a cultivating household. The lower limit does not mean that the cultivators with holdings less than the lower limit would be barred from cultivation. Rather, the idea is to monitor the number of non-viable holdings—just as the poverty line is used to determine the extent of poverty—with a view to devising special programmes for

them, as also to prevent the sale, sub-division or fragmentation giving rise to holdings below the limit.

(c) Definition of tenants in such a manner that all those parti-
cipating in cultivation as *de facto* tenants, irrespective of the
nomenclature used, would be eligible to receive the protection and privileges given to the tenants by the legislation.

3. Incentives and Disincentives for Holding Land

(a) Punitive measures against the households concealing ownership of land above the ceiling and/or concealing leasing out
of land.

(b) Punitive tax on the holders deliberately keeping the land
idle or putting it to improper use.

(c) Since abolition of tenancy would close a source of flexibility
in the system, tenancy may be permitted with more liberal
protection to tenants. For example, land remaining under
tenancy (with the same or changing tenants) for a specified
number of years could be made non-resumable by the owner.

(d) Measures and pressures against those owning land for purposes other than personal cultivation—for rental income,
gains from escalating land values, and as an asset serving as
a protection against risks. In each of these cases, it should
be possible to provide a substitute to land to meet the
desired purpose.

(e) Special assistance to holdings below the lower limit mentioned above to combine cultivation with other enterprises,
join group farming or leave cultivation altogether. In the
latter case, their lands should revert to the government and
not to their tenants, if any. This will check the phenomenon
of 'reverse' tenancy where the owner is a small holder and
the tenant a large holder.

(f) Checking the formation of new holdings below the lower
limit.

(g) Scrutiny of all cases of 'voluntary surrender' of lands by
tenants by a committee consisting of leaders/representatives
of target groups.

To conclude, land reforms focused on the objectives and tasks
enumerated above need to be part of a comprehensive planning-
cum-programme framework to make optimum and sustainable use

of our land resources. Consolidation of holdings, speedy development of common lands for the benefit of the rural poor, shifting of marginal lands now under plough to more appropriate non-arable uses, and diversification of the rural economy should receive as much emphasis in this framework as measures to promote equity. Land reforms should be viewed as a component which enables the framework to harmonise the basic goals of development planning in India, viz., growth, equity and the provision of viable livelihood opportunities for the poor.

REFERENCES

Ghose, A.K. (1983). *Agrarian Reform in Contemporary Developing Countries.* Croom Helm: London.

Government of India (1988). 'Land Reforms', in Occasional Papers (First Series). Department of Rural Development: New Delhi.

———— (1990). *Interim Report on Employment-oriented Strategy of Development.* Economic Advisory Council: New Delhi.

Government of Karnataka (1987). *Report on the Working of Land Reforms Act Follow-up Measures.* Bangalore.

National Sample Survey Organisation (1989). *Status of Tenancy and Land Holdings in India.* New Delhi.

Planning Commission (1989). *Land Reforms: Retrospect and Prospect.* New Delhi.

Rao, V.M. (1988). 'Interventions for the Poor', *Economic and Political Weekly* (Special Number), November, pp. 2409–20.

———— (1990). 'Land for the Poor', paper prepared for the National Commission on Rural Labour.

Rao, V.M. and R.S. Deshpande (1986). 'Agricultural Growth in India', *Economic and Political Weekly*, vol. 21, nos. 38 and 39: A101–12, 20–27 September.

University of Lucknow (1988). *Consolidation of Agricultural Holdings: A Case Study of Bihar and Orissa.* Lucknow.

10

Food, Nutrition and Prices: Some Macro Issues

R. RADHAKRISHNA and C. RAVI

INTRODUCTION

It is by now well-documented that with the introduction of new technology in the mid-1960s, India could avert famines, reverse the upward trend in the relative price of foodgrains, and, by the mid-1970s, achieve self-sufficiency in foodgrains. However, these desirable goals were achieved at a cost. The new technology, limited as it was to well-endowed regions, sharpened regional disparities and did not result in significant improvements in food availability nor in its entitlement for the poor in the less developed regions. In order to promote the new technology, India allowed the price of foodgrains to be higher than the market clearing price by stocking foodgrains and incurring huge subsidies. What is worse, the per capita consumption of foodgrains levelled-off even before much improvement could be made in the nutritional status of the poor. The weakening relationship between foodgrain consumption and income at the macro level poses a dilemma. The low expansion of foodgrain demand may provide temporary relief from bouts of price inflation in wage goods but, certainly, would aggravate the problem of malnutrition.

This paper attempts to highlight the various dimensions of the food problem from the demand perspective. It seeks to quantify the relationships between food, nutrition and prices, utilising the parameter estimates of demand models provided by Radhakrishna and Ravi (1990). The following section outlines the main features of the food situation during 1986–87, including the cost of calories obtained from alternative sources. It also brings out the variations in the levels of food intake among different expenditure strata and also between rural and urban areas. Shifts in consumption patterns have also been analysed. The next section presents demand elasticities evaluated from the demand models. It also examines the proposition that substitution of non-food items for food items has weakened the relationship between food and income. The prediction model given in Radhakrishna and Ravi (1990) has been simulated by changing the values of exogenous variables. Comparisons between the base year and simulated predictions are made in the last but one section to answer the following questions: What would have been the consumption of various food items in 1986–87 had there been no change in tastes? What is the effect of relative price change on food consumption? What are the nutritional consequences of redistribution?

FEATURES OF INDIA'S FOOD SITUATION

Consumption Levels

With annual total expenditure at Rs. 1,558 billion and population at 797 million, per capita monthly expenditure worked out to Rs. 163 in 1986–87 (Table 1). The rural–urban difference in per capita expenditure was fairly large. The rural areas had a per capita expenditure of Rs. 141 per month, with two-thirds of it devoted to food, whereas the figure for urban areas was Rs. 226 per month with slightly more than half devoted to food. Although the share of food in total expenditure was lower, the urban areas had a higher per capita expenditure of 39 per cent on food because of their higher level of per capita expenditure. Further, the urban areas displayed significantly higher levels of expenditure on milk and milk products, fruits and vegetables, and other foods, and a lower level of per capita expenditure on cereals. The share of the former category in food expenditure was 46 per cent in the urban and 32 per cent in the rural areas. On the other hand, the share of cereals was as low as 28 per cent in the urban against 44 per cent in the rural areas, which pushed the expenditure on cereals in urban

Table 1: Expenditure and Population Distribution in 1986–87
(Per capita Expenditure Rs 0.00/30 days)

Commodity Groups	Rural Expenditure Groups					Urban Expenditure Groups					All India
	I	II	III	IV	All Rural Groups	I	II	III	IV	All Urban Groups	
1. Rice	15.31	22.92	26.87	30.09	23.70	14.53	18.90	20.76	22.39	20.27	22.81
2. Wheat	6.96	8.43	10.44	13.70	9.85	8.77	10.94	12.34	14.47	12.53	10.55
3. Other cereals	6.88	7.05	6.80	6.72	6.85	4.19	3.03	2.59	2.14	2.70	5.78
Total cereals	29.15	38.40	44.11	50.51	40.40	27.49	32.87	35.69	39.00	35.50	39.14
4. Pulses	3.03	5.59	6.98	10.03	6.35	3.86	5.83	7.68	9.94	7.83	6.73
Total foodgrains	32.18	43.99	51.09	60.54	46.75	31.35	38.70	43.37	48.94	43.33	45.87
5. Milk and milk products	2.98	7.34	13.52	26.78	12.54	4.81	10.60	18.07	34.49	22.17	15.03
6. Edible oils	3.27	5.14	6.88	10.06	6.30	4.76	7.57	10.61	16.13	11.70	7.70
7. Meat, egg and fish	1.84	3.36	5.34	8.89	4.83	3.02	4.97	7.23	13.07	8.82	5.86
8. Sugar and *gur*	1.75	3.09	4.65	7.20	4.15	2.65	4.07	5.42	7.70	5.81	4.58
9. Fruits and vegetables	4.53	6.09	8.96	13.49	8.25	5.72	9.23	13.07	21.61	15.41	10.04
10. Other foods	4.08	6.53	8.86	16.14	8.81	6.57	9.85	14.25	32.83	20.58	11.86
11. Total foods	50.65	75.55	99.28	143.09	91.62	58.88	84.99	112.04	174.78	127.55	100.92
Non-food items	16.35	28.52	46.44	108.48	49.31	20.77	37.28	60.69	168.59	98.47	62.04
12. Total	67.00	104.07	145.72	251.57	140.93	79.65	122.27	172.73	343.37	226.02	162.96
Total expenditure (billion)	128.28	151.44	296.64	421.98	998.34	29.76	43.68	114.36	371.52	559.32	1557.66
13. Share in rural/urban expenditure	0.1285	0.1517	0.2971	0.4226	1.0000	0.0532	0.0781	0.2045	0.6642	1.0000	–
14. Population (millions)	159.62	121.31	169.66	139.73	590.32	31.12	29.76	55.18	90.16	206.22	796.54
15. Share in rural/urban population	0.2704	0.2055	0.2874	0.2367	1.0000	0.1509	0.1443	0.2676	0.4372	1.0000	–

Note: I—Very poor; II—Moderately poor; III—Lower non-poor and IV—Higher non-poor.

areas lower than in the rural areas. Overall, the urban areas exhibited higher levels of food consumption, except for cereals, with a more diversified food basket.

Expenditure Distribution and Consumption Patterns

Total expenditure and the consumption of various items by expenditure groups are shown in Table 1. The expenditure groups were formed on the basis of the Planning Commission's 'poverty line', treating households below 75 per cent of the poverty line as very poor, between the poverty line and 150 per cent of the poverty line as lower non-poor, and above 150 per cent of the poverty line as higher non-poor.[1] As expected, consumption of food items increased as we moved from lower to higher expenditure groups and the relationship between consumption and total expenditure was stronger for milk and milk products. The higher non-poor group's per capita expenditure on milk and milk products was six times and on food three times that among the very poor group. The composition of the consumption basket varied between groups. The very poor groups of both rural and urban areas devoted as high as three-fourths of their expenditure to food while the non-poor groups devoted only about half. Foodgrains (cereals and pulses) accounted for a major part of the food expenditure among the very poor groups: 64 per cent in the rural and 53 per cent in the urban areas. On the other hand, milk and milk products, fruits and vegetables, and other food items figured prominently in the consumption of the upper expenditure groups: the share of these items of food was more than one-third. These findings suggest that the demand for foodgrains would depend on the incomes of the poor whereas the demand for milk and milk products, fruits and vegetables, and other foods would depend proportionately more on the incomes of the rich.

The rural–urban difference in the share of food in total expenditure between comparable expenditure groups varied only narrowly. But, because of higher urban inequality, the share of food in total expenditure was lower at the aggregate level in the urban areas. With respect to specific food items, their budget shares varied between comparable rural–urban expenditure groups. The rural

---

[1] This study employed the poverty line of the Planning Commission given for the year 1983–84. Price adjustments were made while arriving at the poverty lines for other periods by using appropriate price deflators.

areas exhibited a larger share of foodgrains, whereas the share of other food groups was higher in the urban areas. These findings suggest that given the inequalities within rural and urban and aggregate expenditure, an increase in urban share in income would reduce the demand for foodgrains and total food and also result in considerable substitution within the foodgrain group in favour of wheat and pulses at the cost of coarse cereals.

Foodgrain Intake vs. Norms

The quantities of foodgrains consumed by the expenditure groups in 1986–87 are given in Table 2. The per capita monthly consumption of cereals at 15.32 kg in the rural and 11.67 kg in the urban areas was more than the Indian Council of Medical Research's (ICMR) consumption norm of 386 gm/day (11.58 kg/month). More significantly, no expenditure group, except the urban very poor suffered from cereal deficiency; this group suffered a deficiency of 22 per cent. These results suggest that although cereal availability was sufficient to provide an adequate diet to an average Indian at the aggregate level, inequality affected about 4 per cent of the population. The consumption of pulses which averaged 1.44 kg/month in the rural areas was slightly lower than the ICMR norm of 50 gm/day (1.5 kg/month). On the other hand, the per capita consumption of pulses in the urban areas at 1.77 kg/month was nutritionally adequate. However, severe deficiency of pulses existed among the poor groups in both rural and urban areas. The consumption of pulses among the rural very poor was deficient by 55 per cent, and among the urban very poor by 42 per cent. The corresponding deficiency in pulses among the moderately poor was 16 per cent and 12 per cent, respectively, in rural and urban areas. On the whole, as much as 43 per cent of the population suffered from deficiency in pulses.

Calorie Intake

Calories derived from a rupee spent on a food item in 1986–87 are shown in Table 3. As expected, cereals were the cheapest source of calories. Hence, the lower expenditure groups derived more calories from a rupee because of their higher budget share on cereals. Within the category of cereals, rice was the most expensive source of calories: a rupee spent on rice would provide nearly

Table 2: *Foodgrain Consumption in Quantity in 1986–87*
(Kg/per capital/30 days)

Commodity Groups	Rural					Urban					
	Expenditure Groups				All Rural Groups	Expenditure Groups				All Urban Groups	All India
	I	II	III	IV		I	II	III	IV		
1. Rice	4.72	7.07	8.28	9.28	7.31	3.90	5.08	5.58	6.02	5.63	6.88
2. Wheat	3.26	3.95	4.90	6.43	4.62	3.49	4.36	4.92	5.77	4.99	4.72
3. Other cereals	3.40	3.49	3.37	3.33	3.39	1.63	1.18	1.01	0.83	1.05	2.78
Total cereals	11.38	14.51	16.55	19.04	15.32	9.02	10.62	11.51	12.62	11.67	14.38
4. Pulses	0.68	1.26	1.58	2.27	1.44	0.87	1.32	1.74	2.25	1.77	1.52
Total foodgrains	12.06	15.77	18.13	21.31	16.76	9.89	11.94	13.25	14.87	13.44	15.90

Table 3: Calories Contained in One Rupee Expenditure on Food Items in 1986–87
(Kcal/rupee)

Commodity Groups	Rural Expenditure Groups				Urban Expenditure Groups			
	I	II	III	IV	I	II	III	IV
1. Rice	1048	1048	1048	1048	913	913	913	913
2. Wheat	1623	1623	1623	1623	1379	1379	1379	1379
3. Other cereals	1675	1670	1562	1229	1471	1367	1307	1110
4. Milk and milk products	225	225	220	219	175	174	174	176
5. Edible oils	411	419	416	408	457	455	452	450
6. Meat, egg and fish	58	60	57	56	46	49	48	56
7. Sugar and gur	810	782	765	733	662	649	646	638
8. Other foods	366	358	356	343	310	293	293	271

Notes: 1. Calories contained in one rupee expenditure on a commodity group are evaluated from the NSS quantity and expenditure data on items contained in the group using the calorie values of food items given in the NSS Report No. 238, volume 1.

2. The estimates for rice, wheat and other cereals are based on the 42nd round NSS data and for the other items on une 17th round NSS data. In the case of the latter, appropriate commodity price indices have been used for deflation.

3. Quantity figures are not available for all the items included in 'other foods'. Hence, those items for which quantity figures are available are considered. This implies that calories contained in one rupee expenditure on the included items will approximate the calories contained in a rupee expenditure on the commodity group.

60 per cent lower energy as compared to wheat and coarse cereals. This suggests that the market prices of cereals did not reflect their nutritional value. Rural–urban comparisons of the calorie costs indicate that the calories derived from a rupee spent on cereals was higher in the rural areas, which was due to the lower price of cereals in these areas.

Calorie intake levels by source in 1986–87 for various expenditure groups are presented in Table 4. Cereals were the most important source of calorie supply accounting for 72 per cent of the total calorie intake in the rural areas and 59 per cent in the urban. More significantly, the very poor group derived almost its entire calorie intake from cereals: 83 per cent in the rural and 76 per cent in the urban areas. How do calorie intake levels of the various groups compare with the norms? The Planning Commission recommended 2,400 Kcal/day/person for the rural and 2,100 Kcal/day/person for the urban areas. If we adopt these norms, the calorie intake level was lower than the norm by 5 per cent in the rural areas and just met the requirement in the urban areas. It is worth observing that calorie deficiency was severe among the poor groups: the calorie intake was deficient by 35 per cent among the very poor and 13 per cent among the moderately poor group in the rural areas, and by 34 per cent and 17 per cent among the very poor and moderately poor groups, respectively, in the urban areas. The urban lower non-poor group suffered a marginal deficiency which can be ignored. The higher non-poor groups were characterised by overnutrition: calorie intake levels were higher by about 25 per cent over the nutritional norms. Clearly, redistribution would have improved the nutritional status of all the groups by simultaneously increasing the nutritional level of the lower expenditure groups and reducing overnutrition among higher expenditure groups.

The above analysis does suggest that although all the groups, except the urban very poor, consumed an adequate amount of cereals, all the poor groups suffered from calorie deficiency. It appears that the calorie deficiency was due to the shortfall in the consumption of milk and milk products, meat, egg, fish, etc., as compared to the recommended levels of the ICMR.[2] One might

[2] The ICMR norms were based on a least-cost diet exercise carried out for given prices. Needless to say, the composition of the optimum food basket varies with prices. Hence, one has to be cautious in using the commodity specific norms when the prices differ from those used in the least-cost exercise.

Table 4: Calorie Intake by Source in 1986–87
(Kcal/per capita/day)

Commodity Groups	Rural					Urban				
	Expenditure Groups				All Rural Groups	Expenditure Groups				All Urban Groups
	I	II	III	IV		I	II	III	IV	
1. Rice	535	801	939	1051	828	442	575	631	681	616
2. Wheat	377	456	565	741	534	403	503	567	665	576
3. Other cereals	383	392	354	275	351	205	138	113	79	116
4. Milk and milk products	22	55	99	195	92	28	61	104	202	129
5. Edible oils	45	72	95	137	86	73	115	160	242	176
6. Meat, egg and fish	4	7	10	17	10	5	8	12	24	16
7. Sugar and gur	47	80	119	176	105	58	88	117	164	124
8. Other foods	142	217	294	453	275	167	247	314	582	399
Total	1555	2080	2475	3045	2281	1381	1735	2018	2638	2152

Note: The calorie intake estimates are derived by multiplying the expenditure on a commodity with the calories contained in one rupee of expenditure on it given in Table 3. These should be taken as very approximate. The expenditure on commodities is predicted from a model discussed later.

argue that the consumption patterns of the poor groups were unbalanced in favour of cereals and their nutrition levels can be improved by substituting such food items as milk or meat for cereals. However, Table 3 provides evidence contrary to the above presumption. It can be seen that cereals are by far the least expensive source of calories.

Shifts in Consumption Patterns

Recent evidence reveals shifts in consumption patterns. We have analysed these shifts using the time series data on consumer expenditure. The data reveals a shift in consumption patterns since 1973–74. As the changes are similar for all the groups, we have illustrated the shifts in consumption patterns by considering the budget proportions of the rural very poor group as shown in Table 5. The proportion of total expenditure spent on cereals fluctuated between 56 and 60 per cent without showing any trend till 1973–74, after which it registered a declining trend. Correspondingly, there has been an increase in the proportion spent on non-food items and on some of the other food items. The proportion spent on non-food items increased from 18 to 25 per cent, and on milk and milk products from 3 to 5 per cent. Shifts in consumption patterns have also taken place within the cereal group; wheat seems to be replacing coarse cereals (Radhakrishna and Ravi 1990). For instance, the share of coarse cereals in the cereal expenditure of the rural very poor group declined from 33 per cent in 1973–74 to 17 per cent in 1986–87, while the proportion spent on wheat increased from 16 to 25 per cent. Price and taste factors must have contributed to such changes in consumption patterns. It appears that these shifts offset the positive effect of the recent decline in the price of cereals.

FOOD DEMAND FUNCTIONS

Piece-wise Linear Expenditure System

Recently, Radhakrishna and Ravi (1990) estimated the piece-wise Linear Expenditure System (LES) for seven and eleven commodity

Table 5: Trends in Budget Shares at Constant Prices for the Rural Very Poor Group

Year	Cereals	Milk and Milk Products	Edible Oils	Meat, Egg and Fish	Sugar and gur	Other Foods	Non-Food Items
1964–65	0.594	0.034	0.035	0.021	0.017	0.134	0.165
1965–66	0.602	0.033	0.032	0.017	0.019	0.137	0.161
1969–70	0.564	0.034	0.034	0.022	0.022	0.145	0.179
1970–71	0.572	0.035	0.032	0.021	0.021	0.145	0.174
1972–73	0.584	0.025	0.032	0.019	0.014	0.141	0.186
1973–74	0.587	0.031	0.031	0.020	0.018	0.132	0.180
1977–78	0.558	0.035	0.033	0.019	0.022	0.125	0.208
1983	0.505	0.039	0.036	0.015	0.026	0.141	0.237
1986–87	0.475	0.051	0.042	0.017	0.024	0.137	0.254

Note: Budget shares are expressed at 1969–70 prices.

groups.[3] Their estimates are based on nine NSS rounds from 1964–65 to 1986–87. In order to allow for possible shifts in taste in the mid-1970s, they have specified the LES as:

$$p_{it} \, q_{it} = C_i \, p_{it} + (b_i + b_i{}^* \, D) \, (y_t - \Sigma_j \, C_j \, p_{jt}) + E_{it}$$

$$\Sigma_i \, b_i = 1 \qquad \Sigma_i \, b_i{}^* = 0$$

D = 0 for 1964–65, 1965–66, 1969–70, 1970–71, 1972–73, 1973–74
D = 1 for 1977–78, 1983, 1986–87
where q_i denotes the per capita monthly consumption of the ith item, p_i the price of the ith item, y the per capita monthly expenditure, b and C the parameters and E is the random disturbance term. In the above specification, the C parameters are assumed to remain constant between the two periods but the b parameters are assumed to vary. The parameter estimates along with measures of goodness of fit are given in Radhakrishna and Ravi (1990). The LES gives extremely good fit to the data and is consistent with all theoretical restrictions. We shall utilise the estimates of seven commodity LES for our analysis.

Marginal Budget Shares

The marginal budget shares for period I (1964–65 to 1973–74) given by b and period II (1977–78) to 1986–87) given by b + b* are provided in Table 6. The results suggest shift in tastes: the marginal budget share of cereals declined and that of non-food items increased in period II for all expenditure groups. For instance, for the rural very poor group the marginal budget share of cereals was estimated to be 0.53 in period I and 0.39 in period II, the marginal budget share of non-food items to be 0.17 in period I and 0.25 in period II. The marginal budget shares of other food items increased in period II. However, the marginal share of food declined. The preceding analysis clearly brings out the weakening relationship between foodgrains/food consumption and total expenditure due to change in tastes.

We see clear patterns in the behaviour of marginal budget shares across the expenditure groups. Since the patterns are similar

---

[3] For the use of piece-wise LES in demand studies see Radhakrishna and Murthy (1980) and Ahmed and Ludlow (1988).

Table 6: Marginal Budget Shares (bs) of the LES for Seven Commodity Groups

Commodity Groups	Very Poor		Moderately Poor		Lower Non-Poor		Higher Non-Poor	
	Period I	Period II	Period I	Period II	Period I	Period II	Period I	Period II
(Rural)								
Cereals	0.533	0.387	0.348	0.227	0.222	0.096	0.073	0.030
Milk and milk products	0.060	0.073	0.119	0.125	0.135	0.143	0.065	0.062
Edible oils	0.037	0.052	0.025	0.038	0.024	0.036	0.021	0.022
Meat, egg and fish	0.028	0.033	0.033	0.038	0.033	0.040	0.017	0.018
Sugar and *gur*	0.030	0.033	0.034	0.037	0.037	0.034	0.035	0.022
Other foods	0.145	0.174	0.141	0.162	0.137	0.158	0.075	0.074
Non-food items	0.167	0.247	0.300	0.373	0.411	0.492	0.715	0.772
(Urban)								
Cereals	0.390	0.287	0.177	0.096	0.085	0.040	0.008	0.007
Milk and milk products	0.082	0.092	0.140	0.146	0.143	0.147	0.069	0.062
Edible oils	0.055	0.066	0.039	0.063	0.047	0.051	0.015	0.015
Meat, egg and fish	0.040	0.045	0.039	0.040	0.047	0.050	0.026	0.021
Sugar and *gur*	0.040	0.038	0.037	0.033	0.026	0.023	0.010	0.008
Other foods	0.189	0.198	0.185	0.189	0.213	0.206	0.183	0.128
Non-food items	0.204	0.274	0.363	0.433	0.440	0.484	0.689	0.759

Note: Period I includes 1964–65, 1965–66, 1969–70, 1970–71, 1972–73, 1973–74.
Period II includes 1977–78, 1983, 1986–87.

Source: R. Radhakrishna and C. Ravi (1990). *Food Demand Projections for India*. Centre for Economic and Social Studies: Hyderabad (monograph).

for both periods, we confine our discussion to the estimates pertaining to the latter period. Table 6 shows that the marginal budget share of cereals fell from 0.39 to 0.03 between the very poor and non-poor higher groups in the rural areas, and from 0.29 to 0.01 in the urban areas. In contrast, the marginal budget share of non-food items rose from 0.25 to 0.77 in the rural areas and from 0.27 to 0.76 in the urban areas. Clearly, while the cereal group dominates the budgets of the poor, non-food items dominate the budgets of the rich. These patterns imply that changes in income distribution will affect demand. It is worth observing that in terms of patterns in marginal budget shares across the strata, the higher non-poor group stands out distinctly both in rural and urban areas. The marginal budget shares of milk and milk products, meat, egg and fish, etc., follow a pattern as one moves from the very poor to the lower non-poor, and the pattern changes between the lower non-poor and higher non-poor. The marginal budget shares of milk and milk products and of edible oils increase; those of meat, egg and fish, sugar and *gur* and other food items remain more or less constant as one moves from very poor to non-poor lower groups, and, in contrast, they *all* decline between the lower and higher non-poor groups. In general, a rupee transferred from the higher to lower group would reduce the demand for non-food items and increase the demand for food items.

Propensity to Consume Calories

We have computed the average and marginal propensities to consume calories using the calories contained in one rupee of expenditure given in Table 3, and the demand models of Radhakrishna and Ravi (1990).[4] The results shown in Table 7 refer to 1986–87 prices, based on the parameter estimates of the two periods. It should be stressed that propensities computed from period II LES are 1986–87 estimates and are historical in nature, while those computed from period I LES are contrafactual as they have been evaluated at 1986–87 prices from period I LES.

What is the effect of changed taste on propensities to consume calories? Table 7 clearly shows that changed tastes had a depressing

---

[4] For the derivations of calorie demand function from the LES, see Radhakrishna (1984).

Table 7: *Marginal and Average Propensity to Consume Calories at 1986–87 Prices*

Expenditure Groups	Period I		Period II	
	Marginal Propensity	Average Propensity	Marginal Propensity	Average Propensity
Rural				
1. Very poor	805	. 851	624	696
2. Moderately poor	571	733	408	599
3. Lower non-poor	416	618	254	509
4. Higher non-poor	171	438	106	363
Urban				
1. Very poor	575	569	456	520
2. Moderately poor	335	476	240	426
3. Lower non-poor	225	395	171	350
4. Higher non-poor	84	244	66	230

effect on calorie intake uniformly across all the expenditure groups. For instance, for a rupee value of consumption, the effect of change in tastes was a decline of 155 calories in the case of the rural very poor and 49 calories in the case of the urban very poor. What would be the implication of this finding on the poverty line defined as the expenditure corresponding to a given calorie intake level? The answer is obvious: it would raise the poverty line.

Demand Elasticities

Expenditure elasticities for 1986–87 for various groups evaluated at their mean expenditures are presented in Table 8. As one would expect, expenditure elasticities vary between groups and conform to the inference drawn on the basis of marginal budget shares. As we move from lower to higher groups, expenditure elasticities for food items (including calorie elasticity) decline and the elasticity for non-food items increases. It is notable that calorie elasticity is lower than food elasticity. This is because rising expenditure is associated with a shift in food consumption away from calorie-intensive commodities.

The own-price elasticities given in Table 9 possess correct signs and display the expected pattern across expenditure groups. The effect of a 10 per cent increase in prices on calorie consumption is shown in Table 10. The conclusions suggested by the price effects

Table 8: Expenditure Elasticities at 1986–87 Prices Computed from the LES for Seven Commodity Groups

Commodity Groups	Rural Expenditure Groups					Urban Expenditure Groups				
	Very Poor	Moderately Poor	Lower Non-Poor	Higher Non-Poor	Rural Aggregate	Very Poor	Moderately Poor	Lower Non-Poor	Higher Non-Poor	Urban Aggregate
Cereals	0.886	0.608	0.318	0.151	0.447	0.839	0.363	0.194	0.059	0.255
Milk and milk products	1.644	1.797	1.544	0.580	1.094	1.517	1.671	1.403	0.619	0.892
Edible oils	1.076	0.774	0.755	0.545	0.724	1.102	1.029	0.825	0.325	0.560
Meat, egg and fish	1.218	1.205	1.089	0.509	0.866	1.168	0.983	1.182	0.555	0.759
Sugar and gur	1.254	1.172	1.084	0.779	0.992	1.142	0.980	0.726	0.364	0.570
Other foods	1.003	0.934	0.928	0.470	0.757	0.974	0.925	1.019	0.682	0.797
Food	0.994	0.863	0.745	0.401	0.681	0.983	0.816	0.796	0.475	0.628
Non-food items	1.018	1.374	1.543	1.793	1.606	1.044	1.411	1.375	1.549	1.496
Calories	0.926	0.703	0.496	0.282	0.547	0.897	0.566	0.471	0.288	0.442

Note: These elasticities are evaluated from the period II LES at the mean total expenditure levels of the expenditure groups.

Table 9: Uncompensated Price Elasticities at 1986–87 Prices

Commodity Groups	Rural Expenditure Groups					Urban Expenditure Groups				
	Very Poor	Moderately Poor	Lower Non-Poor	Higher Non-Poor	Rural Aggregate	Very Poor	Moderately Poor	Lower Non-Poor	Higher Non-Poor	Urban Aggregate
Cereals	−0.832	−0.581	−0.279	−0.194	−0.431	−0.633	−0.289	−0.171	−0.051	−0.203
Milk and milk products	−1.323	−1.311	−0.988	−0.670	−0.888	−0.887	−0.989	−0.984	−0.491	−0.646
Edible oils	−0.889	−0.599	−0.500	−0.618	−0.616	−0.660	−0.633	−0.598	−0.252	−0.396
Meat, egg and fish	−0.998	−0.913	−0.708	−0.577	−0.710	−0.689	−0.597	−0.835	−0.422	−0.541
Sugar and *gur*	−1.027	−0.888	−0.703	−0.875	−0.839	−0.672	−0.593	−0.518	−0.275	−0.395
Other foods	−0.853	−0.752	−0.657	−0.561	−0.660	−0.649	−0.632	−0.772	−0.567	−0.624
Non-food items	−0.865	−1.022	−0.992	−1.229	−1.109	−0.712	−0.906	−0.980	−1.034	−1.008

Note: These elasticities are evaluated from the period II LES at the mean expenditure levels of the expenditure groups. Aggregate elasticity of an item is computed from the groups' elasticities by averaging them, using their shares in the consumption of the item as weights.

Table 10: Percentage Change in Calorie Consumption Due to a 10 per cent Rise in Prices

Price of Commodity Groups	Rural					Urban				
	Expenditure Groups				All Groups	Expenditure Groups				All Groups
	I	II	III	IV		I	II	III	IV	
1. Cereals	-7.16	-5.06	-2.72	-1.62	-3.66	-5.27	-2.68	-1.73	-0.56	-1.66
2. Milk and milk products	-0.05	-0.18	-0.40	-0.52	-0.33	-0.25	-0.35	-0.52	-0.51	-0.47
3. Edible oils	-0.31	-0.35	-0.31	-0.32	-0.32	-0.53	-0.54	-0.58	-0.32	-0.43
4. Meat, egg and fish	-0.03	-0.05	-0.08	-0.08	-0.06	-0.14	-0.12	-0.08	-0.10	-0.11
5. Sugar and gur	-0.30	-0.36	-0.38	-0.51	-0.41	-0.38	-0.37	-0.37	-0.21	-0.29
6. Other foods	-1.04	-1.10	-1.05	-1.00	-1.03	-1.48	-1.30	-1.38	-1.38	-1.42
All food prices	-8.89	-7.10	-4.94	-4.05	-5.81	-8.04	-5.37	-4.66	-3.08	-4.90
7. Non-food items	-0.37	-0.07	-0.02	-1.22	-0.33	-0.93	-0.29	-0.06	-0.20	-0.48
All prices	-9.26	-7.03	-4.96	-2.83	-5.48	-8.97	-5.66	-4.72	-2.88	-4.42

are obvious. The effect of the price of cereals is very large in magnitude and other price effects are almost insignificant, except for the higher non-poor group. The price effects weaken as we move from lower to higher groups. For instance, a 10 per cent increase in the price of all food items reduces the calorie consumption of the very poor group by 8.9 per cent in the rural areas and 8.0 per cent in the urban areas, while for higher non-poor groups the corresponding reductions are 4.1 per cent and 3.1 per cent, respectively.

EFFECTS OF TASTES, REDISTRIBUTION AND RELATIVE PRICES

Radhakrishna and Ravi (1990) have provided a prediction model which uses the log-normal specification for expenditure distribution and the LES for consumer demand. Predictions for the base year, i.e., 1986–87, have been made by using the actual values of the exogenous variables in the prediction model (columns 2 and 6 in Table 11). The model has been simulated by replacing the period II LES parameter estimates with those of period I (columns 3 and 7 in Table 11). The difference between the simulated predictions and base year predictions would give the effect of changed taste between periods I and II. In the second experiment, the model has been simulated by replacing the relative prices in 1986–87 with those in 1969–70 (columns 4 and 8 in Table 11). In order to examine the effect of redistribution, the model has been simulated by reducing the Gini coefficients of the expenditure distribution of rural and urban areas by 30 per cent (columns 5 and 9 in Table 11). Of the three simulation experiments, the first two deal with historical changes and the last deals with a hypothetical situation. It is important to note that the results of the simulation experiment dealing with change in tastes are only approximations since it is unlikely that the dummy variable used in the specification of the LES can represent the complex taste phenomenon adequately. In fact, the specification implies that tastes are invariant within a period but vary between periods. Hence, these results are more illustrative than final.

Taste Effect

Taste effect can be inferred from a comparison of columns 2 and 3 (for rural areas) and 6 and 7 (for urban areas) in Table 11. The results confirm the finding in the previous section that change in tastes had an unfavourable effect on food consumption. For instance, in the absence of a change in tastes per capita food consumption would have been higher by 9.2 per cent in the rural and 8.0 per cent in the urban areas. Further, cereal consumption would have been higher by 26.7 per cent in the rural and 9.1 per cent in the urban areas.

On the basis of the calorie norms of the Planning Commission, the bottom 30 per cent of the population had a per capita calorie deficiency by 794 Kcal/day in the rural areas and 563 Kcal/day in the urban areas. In the absence of taste changes the deficiency would have been only 446 Kcal/day in the rural and 374 Kcal/day in the urban areas. Thus, changed tastes aggravated the calorie deficiency of the bottom 30 per cent of the population by 348 Kcal/day in the rural areas and 189 Kcal/day in the urban areas. The estimates need to be qualified since the modelling of the taste effect is not perfect. Nevertheless, the direction of change does not require any such qualification. The findings clearly highlight the adverse effect of taste changes on the calorie intake of the poor.

Relative Price Changes

The effect of the relative price change between 1969–70 and 1986–87 can be read by comparing columns 2 and 4 (for the rural areas) and 6 and 8 (for the urban areas) in Table 11. The relative price change had a favourable effect on food consumption. For instance, it increased the per capita food consumption by 6.3 per cent and 3.9 per cent, and cereal consumption by 6 and 2.7 per cent in rural and urban areas, respectively. This stands to reason because cereal prices increased at a lower rate between 1969–70 and 1986–87. It is important to note that the positive relative price effect could not offset the negative effect of the change in tastes on food consumption.

More interesting is the effect of the relative price change on the calorie intake of the bottom groups; the results suggest that the

Table 11: Base Year Predictions and Simulation Results

Commodity Groups	Rural				Urban			
	Base Year Predictions	Simulation Results Based On			Base Year Predictions	Simulation Results Based On		
		Period I LES	69–70 Relative Price	30% Reduction in the Gini Coefficient		Period I LES	69–70 Relative Price	30% Reduction in the Gini Coefficient
Bottom 30%								
(Per capita consumption: Rs/month)								
1. Cereals	30.08	38.48	27.00	37.19	29.82	34.62	28.25	34.90
2. Other foods	22.39	18.62	27.95	29.10	42.04	41.12	45.27	56.41
Total food	52.47	57.11	54.95	66.29	71.86	75.74	73.52	91.31
3. Non-food items	16.95	12.31	16.15	21.49	29.26	25.38	28.65	41.04
Total expenditure	69.42	69.42	71.10	87.78	101.12	101.12	102.17	132.35
(Per capita consumption: Kcal/day)								
Calorie intake	1606	1954	1473	1988	1537	?1726	1483	1865
Middle 40%								
(Per capita consumption: Rs/month)								
1. Cereals	41.47	52.05	39.49	43.06	36.52	40.77	35.64	37.12
2. Other foods	45.97	42.03	52.62	49.24	87.17	89.71	92.70	94.44
Total food	87.45	.94.08	92.11	92.31	123.68	130.48	128.34	131.56
3. Non-food items	37.06	30.43	34.04	40.33	70.00	63.20	66.86	77.99
Total expenditure	124.51	124.51	126.15	132.64	193.68	193.68	195.20	209.55
(Per capita consumption: Kcal/day)								
Calorie intake	2285	2749	2241	2385	2162	2356	2148	2249

Top 30%

(Per capita consumption: Rs/month)							
1. Cereals	49.57	47.72	48.54	39.36	39.60	39.02	39.00
2. Other foods	85.79	98.17	79.56	147.64	168.42	156.64	135.37
Total food	135.36	145.89	128.10	187.00	208.01	195.65	174.36
3. Non-food items	98.98	90.89	77.04	207.04	186.03	200.20	167.28
Total expenditure	234.34	236.78	205.14	394.04	394.04	395.86	341.65
(Per capita consumption: Kcal/day)							
Calorie intake	2967	3613	2854	2752	2934	2785	2636

All Groups

(Per capita consumption: Rs/month)							
1. Cereals	40.49	38.21	42.94	35.36	38.57	34.44	37.02
2. Other foods	50.84	58.88	52.29	91.77	98.75	97.65	95.31
Total food	91.33	97.04	95.24	127.13	137.32	132.09	132.33
3. Non-food items	49.60	45.73	45.69	98.89	88.70	95.40	93.69
Total expenditure	140.93	142.82	140.93	226.02	226.02	227.49	226.02
(Per capita consumption: Kcal/day)							
Calorie intake	2286	2243	2407	2152	2341	2139	2250

Note: Expenditure is expressed at 1986–87 prices.

relative price change augmented the calorie intake levels of these groups. The increase in per capita calorie intake of the bottom group due to the relative price change was 133 Kcal/day in the rural areas and 54 Kcal/day in the urban areas. This suggests that there is ample room for policy-makers to influence the level of calorie intake among the poor by changing the relative price.

Redistribution Effect

What will be the consequences of redistribution? Table 11 suggests that redistribution (30 per cent reduction in the Gini ratio) increases food consumption at the cost of non-food items at the aggregate level. It increased the per capita food consumption of the rural areas by 4.3 per cent and the urban areas by 4.1 per cent, and cereal consumption of the former by 6.1 per cent and the latter by 4.7 per cent.

Redistribution had a sharp effect on the calorie intake of the poor. For example, it increased the per capita per day calorie intake of the lowest 30 per cent by 382 Kcal in the rural areas and 328 Kcal in the urban areas. Had there been no change in tastes, the gains of redistribution would have solved the calorie deficiency problem. However, the relative price and redistribution measures can make a substantial dent in the problem of calorie deficiency. Clearly, food-linked income transfers would be very effective.

CONCLUDING OBSERVATIONS

The shift in tastes has aggravated the calorie deficiency of the lowest 30 per cent of the population and weakened the relationship between calorie consumption and income. The causes of the change in tastes are little researched. If the acceleration in the economic growth experienced by India in the recent past projects into the future, it is likely that poverty in terms of income may decline, but poverty in terms of food consumption might persist. Though the decline in the relative price of cereals increased cereal consumption and calorie intake, these gains could not compensate for the decrease in calorie intake due to change in tastes.

Even though the deficiency in calorie intake was marginal at the aggregate level, the poor experienced severe calorie deficiency because of inequality. If one considers the ICMR norm of cereal consumption, the poor did not suffer from cereal deficiency. Hence, calorie deficiency can be attributed to their low consumption of non-cereal foods. It should also be stressed that the ICMR norms should be used with caution since its concept of a balanced diet was based on past prices and its recommended food basket is sensitive to prices. Since cereals are the cheapest source of calories for the poor, any shift in tastes away from cereals makes calories more expensive. An important question is whether to increase the calorie consumption by concentration on price factors only, or consider non-price factors such as tastes as well

Historical experience suggests that growth would increase the incomes of the poor, but the process would be slow. Hence, significant improvements in the nutritional status of the poor cannot be achieved in the near future directly through growth. In this regard two policy interventions should be considered: (*i*) redistribution of income and (*ii*) increasing the consumption of specific food items by lowering their prices for the poor through subsidies. It should be stressed that the prevailing structural conditions may limit the scope of the former and the fiscal crisis may rule out the latter. Needless to say, there are no soft policy options for improving the nutritional status of the poor.

REFERENCES

Ahmed, E. and S. Ludlow (1988). *Aggregate and Regional Demand Response Pattern in Pakistan*, DEP no. 12. The Development Economics Research Programme, London School of Economics: London.

Radhakrishna, R. (1984). 'Distributional Aspects of Calorie Consumption: Implications for Food Policy', in K.T. Achaya (ed.), *Interface between Agriculture, Nutrition and Food Science*. The United Nations University: Tokyo.

Radhakrishna, R. and K.N. Murthy (1980). *Models of Complete Expenditure System for India*, Working Paper 80–98. International Institute of Applied Systems Analysis: Austria.

Radhakrishna, R. and C. Ravi (1990). *Food Demand Projections for India*. Centre for Economic and Social Studies: Hyderabad (monograph).

11

Three Epochs of Technology–
Extension Nexus in Karnataka
Agriculture: Some Policy Issues

S. BISALIAH

INTRODUCTION

$\mathbf{E}$conomic research on the sources of differences in agricultural productivity across countries has led to the major inference that these sources could be classified into three broad groups: resource endowments (e.g., land), technical inputs (e.g., seeds and fertilisers), and human capital (comprising education, skills and knowledge embodied in a country's population). It is in this perspective that the development of technology through research and technology transfer through extension has been recognised as the key knowledge input indispensable for generating and sustaining productivity-led agricultural development.

In the emergence of the technology-extension nexus to support agricultural development in Karnataka, three epochs are identifiable: old technology and old extension epoch (E_1) spanning the years 1955–56 to 1967–68[1], new technology and old extension epoch (E_2) spanning the years 1968–69 to 1978–79, and a new technology and new extension epoch (E_3) spanning the years 1979–80 to 1987–88. One could develop various means of delineating epochs with appropriate methodological moulds to define structural breaks in agricultural development. But the present study is based on a

[1] Data availability has been the major consideration in defining the first epoch with the year 1955–56 as the beginning.

simple version of epoch delineation, focusing on the 'availability' of crop varieties and cultural practices, and on the type of extension system built up to reach farmers at the field level.

Since the theme of old and new technologies is familiar in terms of traditional and new crop varieties along with their associated cultural practices, a brief exposition of the new system of extension, viz, Training and Visit System (known as the Agricultural Extension Project in Karnataka) is in order to extract policy issues, if any, from the implementation of this new system. Under the Community Development Programme, the concept of the multipurpose extension worker was implemented in 1952. Dissatisfaction with the effectiveness of the multipurpose extension worker in increasing agricultural production led to the formulation and implementation of a variety of special programmes focusing on crops, techniques, or regions (Bisaliah 1983). The Training and Visit (T & V) system is one in a long line of innovations in the area of extension service to promote agricultural development. The World Bank-aided new model of extension has been implemented in Karnataka since October 1978 in a phased manner. Since the transition from the multipurpose extension system to the new model of extension has been the most striking development in agricultural extension, a brief reference to the premises governing the new model is warranted. The model places its focus on: (*i*) technical advice to raise crop production by emphasising dominant crops and key practices; (*ii*) two-step flow communication system, i.e., communication of the technical messages by the village-level extension worker to the contact (master) farmers, and by the contact farmers to fellow (pupil) farmers; and (*iii*) a closer link between research and extension to increase the professional competence of the extension worker. Added to these is the main premise of the model that the major constraint in increasing agricultural production is insufficient knowledge of improved technology. Hence, 'knowledge transfer alone' has been the watchword of the new model.

Keeping the three epochs of technology-extension nexus in view, there are five issues which form the theme of this paper. First, what have been the major trends in the extent as well as the nature of technology spread during these three epochs? Second, what have been the shifts in the patterns of agricultural output growth? Third, have the productivity trends been distinctly different during these three epochs? Fourth, what has been the magnitude of resource-saving and resource-loss averted effects that have emerged in Karnataka's agriculture? Fifth, what agricultural policy issues could one derive from the development experience during the three epochs?

TECHNOLOGY SPREAD: SOME BROAD TRENDS

One of the approaches in assessing the performance of the technology-extension nexus during different epochs is to examine trends in technology spread in terms of area under high yielding varieties (HYVs), and the use of chemical fertilisers, certified seeds and pesticides. Coupled with these components of biochemical technology[2] are trends in irrigated area. Table 1 presents details on these broad trends. These results show that: (i) area under HYVs had increased manyfold, (ii) total fertiliser use had increased from a meagre 0.10 lakh tonnes during E_1 to 2.03 lakh tonnes during E_2, and to 4.73 lakh tonnes during E_3; (iii) the quantity of certified seeds and pesticides used experienced a quantum jump from one epoch to another; and (iv) there was a considerable increase in area under irrigation.

The results presented in Table 1 lead to one major conclusion which is relevant for deriving policy implications: the annual rate of growth of technology spread was greater during E_2, and during E_3 the increase in technology spread took place at a decreasing rate. Added to this overall result on technology spread, one could also examine crop-wise and farming system-wise results on fertiliser use in Karnataka. The micro-level result (Table 1) that fertiliser use per hectare had increased from about 3 kg during E_1 to 19 kg during E_2, and to 42 kg during E_3, conceals more than it reveals. A recent study (with macro-level data of the year 1984–85) showed that: (i) paddy, sugarcane and cotton, with an area share of 35 per cent in the state of Karnataka, accounted for 86 per cent of total fertiliser use in the state; (ii) about 89 per cent of total fertiliser use was for irrigated areas/crops, and the remaining 11 per cent for

---

[2] No attempt is made in this paper to document the spread of the components of mechanical technology.

Table 1: *Technology Spread: Some Broad Tends*
(Averages for Epochs)

Particulars	E_1	E_2	E_3
1. Area under HYVs (lakh ha)	0.66	24	29
	(1966–67)	(1977–78)	(1987–88)
2. Irrigated area as per cent to gross cropped area	9.15	14.26	17.13
3. Total fertiliser use (lakh tonnes)	0.10	2.03	4.73
4. Fertiliser used per ha (kg)	2.8	18.80	41.50
5. Certified seeds (qntls in lakhs)	0.7	1.64	3.44
	(1972–73 to 1974–75)	(1978–79 to 1980–81)	(1986–87 to 1987–88)
6. Pesticides (technical grade materials in metric tonnes)	2288	2674	4486
	(1972–73 to 1974–75)	(1978–79 to 1980–81)	(1987–88)

rain-fed areas/crops; and (*iii*) fertiliser use per hectare was 227 kg under irrigated farming and 41 kg under rain-fed farming. Further, the quantity of fertiliser used per hectare was 415 kg for irrigated sugarcane, 320 kg for cotton, 216 kg for groundnut and 202 kg for paddy. More on the policy implications of this later (Govindaraju 1989).

PERFORMANCE OF PRODUCTION AND PRODUCTIVITY GROWTH

One of the issues outlined for examination here is whether the patterns of output growth have shifted over a period of time. Table 2 provides results on compound growth rates of production, area and productivity of major crops in Karnataka during two periods— pre-Green Revolution Period (P-I) and Green Revolution Period (P-II). From these results, two broad conclusions about shifts in the growth rates of output of different crops as well as the patterns of output growth could be made. First, *ragi*, *bajra*, pulses and cotton had experienced higher rates of output growth during P-II, whereas rice, sorghum, oil-seeds and sugarcane could be rated as crops which had experienced low rates of output growth during the same period. Second, there was a considerable shift in the patterns

Table 2: *Compound Growth Rates of Production Area and Productivity of Major Crops in Karnataka*

Crops	Production Growth Rate		Area Growth Rate		Productivity Growth Rate	
	P-I	P-II	P-I	P-II	P-I	P-II
1. Total cereals	4.45	3.65	1.75	−0.90	2.66	4.58
Rice	5.67	1.89	2.99	−0.76	2.60	2.66
Sorghum	3.27	1.14	1.80	−3.09	1.44	4.66
Ragi	6.28	6.47	3.04	−0.61	3.24	6.89
Bajra	0.88	6.73	0.36	2.52	0.52	4.11
2. Total pulses	1.74	3.09	0.60	0.37	1.13	2.76
3. Total oil-seeds	0.68	−0.05	1.54	1.03	−0.87	−1.07
4. Other crops:						
Cotton	2.78	8.91	0.77	0.05	1.99	9.26
Sugarcane	6.03	2.38	4.79	4.38	2.29	−1.91

Source: Mruthyunjaya, S. Bisaliah and V.R. Srinivasan (1982). *Pace and Pattern of Agricultural Output Growth in Karnataka.* University of Agricultural Sciences: Bangalore.
P-I: 1951–52 to 1964–65, P-II: 1966–67 to 1977–78.

of output growth of different crops. Oil-seeds and sugarcane had experienced area-led output growth patterns, cotton a productivity-led growth pattern, and pulses area-cum-productivity-led growth pattern during both periods. Crops such as sorghum, *ragi*, rice and *bajra*, however, experienced a shift from an area-cum-productivity-led growth pattern during P-I to a productivity-led growth pattern during P-II.

Yet another possible approach to gauge the performance of agriculture in Karnataka over a period of time is to analyse trends in the productivity of major crops. These broad trends are shown in Table 3, from which one broad result that could be extracted is that productivity gains were more during E_2 in the case of all crops, with the exception of oil-seeds and sugarcane, and productivity gains were more only in the case of oil-seeds during E_3. As shown in Table 4, crop innovations have been much more visible in the case of oil-seeds during E_3. An increase in area under sunflower from 0.76 lakh hectares in 1980–81 to 11.39 lakh hectares in 1987–88, and in safflower from 0.12 lakh to 1.32 lakh hectares during the same period has been an encouraging trend in the case of oil-seeds which have been labelled laggards in growth performance. The transformation of a single crop *rabi* tract in the state into

Table 3: *Percentage Change in Productivity of Major Crops*

Crops	Percentage Change During		
	E_2 over E_1	E_3 over E_2	E_3 over E_1
1. Total cereals	47	11	62
Rice	40	11	56
Ragi	31	17	53
Sorghum	73	3	78
Bajra	57	14	80
2. Total pulses	34	−9	22
3. Total oil-seeds	No change	15	15
Groundnut	5	24	30
4. Sugarcane	5	−11	−7

Table 4: *Crop Innovations During E_3*
(Area in lakh hectares)

Crops	1980–81	1984–85	1987–88
1. Sunflower	0.76	4.80	11.39
2. Safflower	0.12	1.28	1.32
3. *Kharif* pulses in *Rabi* tracts	0.60	2.79	2.98
4. High yielding red gram in southern districts	0.10	–	0.90
5. Groundnut in rice fallows of coastal areas	0.04	–	0.39

a double crop economy by growing pulses during the *kharif* season, the introduction of high yielding red gram in the southern districts of the state, and motivating farmers to grow groundnut in rice fallows of the coastal areas could be rated as important dimensions of agricultural development in the state during E_3.

RESOURCE SAVING EFFECTS OF PRODUCTIVITY CHANGE

The effectiveness of the technology-extension nexus in agriculture could be gauged in terms of resource-saving effects due to efficiency gains in production. Some of the micro-level studies conducted in Karnataka provide a quantitative assessment of resource-saving effects (Bisaliah 1984; Gundu Rao, et al. 1985a and 1985b): (*i*)

About 23 per cent of increased productivity in paddy could be attributed to efficiency gains (due to an upward shift in production function) from new varieties and associated cultural practices. In other words, with the same level of input used under traditional varieties, 23 per cent more output per acre could be obtained under new varieties. (*ii*) About 72 per cent of increased sorghum output per farm could be attributed to the efficiency gain effects of new varieties. (*iii*) In the case of *ragi*, about 33 per cent of increased yield per unit of cultivated area could be ascribed to efficiency gains made possible with the introduction of improved varieties. Further, an average farm transplanted with an improved variety of *ragi* yielded about 65 per cent more output per unit area than an average farm using the local variety and the broadcasting method. Of this total change in productivity, about 53 per cent could be attributed to efficiency gains, i.e., shifts in technological parameters due to new techniques of planting and improved varieties of *ragi*.

Another approach in assessing efficiency gains would be to focus on estimating both the amount of complementary input (non-land input) saved with the availability of new technologies and of the amount of input loss averted—the loss which could have taken place in the absence of new varieties and their associated cultural practices. It is estimated that the resources (i.e., capital, fertilisers and labour) saved in the production of old-technology level of output with the use of new methods of planting and improved varieties of *ragi* would be worth Rs. 220 per hectare. Further, the estimated amount of resource loss averted due to the availability of new technologies for producing new technology-level of output would be about Rs. 363 per hectare (Gundu Rao, et al. 1985a). During the year 1987–88, out of about 11.16 lakh hectares of land under *ragi*, 10.97 (about 98 per cent) lakh hectares of land was under improved varieties. At the estimated rate of Rs. 220 per hectare, the estimated amount of resource saving would be Rs. 241 million per annum. The estimated resource loss averted at the rate of Rs. 363 per hectare would be Rs. 398 million. The major knowledge inputs that have contributed to this magnitude of resource saving effected and resource loss averted are obviously from the technology-extension nexus[3]. The nexus has shifted the production

---

[3] The magnitude of estimates arrived at needs to be read with qualification, since estimates from micro-level studies have been extended to the entire state.

function upwards and the cost function downwards, giving rise to resource-saving and resource-loss averted effects.

Yet another approach in assessing the agricultural development experience of the state is to estimate the land-saving effects that have emerged during E_2 and E_3, the results of which are presented in Table 5. During E_2, the average quantity of cereals produced was 56.26 lakh tonnes per annum, using 59.72 lakh hectares of land at a productivity level of 942 kg per hectare. If 56.26 lakh tonnes per annum were to be produced during E_2 at the E_1 yield level (643 kg per ha), Karnataka would have required 87.50 lakh hectares of land. This shows that Karnataka could save land to the extent of 27.78 lakh hectares due to the availability of higher productivity level technology for cereals. Similarly, land-saving effects have been estimated for other crops and crop groups. It can be seen from Table 5 that during E_2, with the exception of oil-seeds and sugarcane, all other important crops and crop groups had given rise to productivity-led positive land-saving effects. During E_3, barring pulses and sugarcane, the land-saving effects were positive. But the magnitude of land-saving effects declined during E_3, with the exception of oil-seeds, where land-saving effects were found to have been perceptible.

POLICY ISSUES AND IMPLICATIONS

The main concern of this section is to recapitulate the major findings of the analysis, formulate policy issues and derive implications of these issues.

First, Karnataka agriculture has experienced considerable increase in the use of high pay-off inputs such as HYVs, fertilisers, pesticides and certified seeds during a span of over two decades. However, the annual rate of technology spread was greater during second epoch (the period of old extension and new technology) than during third epoch (the period of new technology and new extension). Added to this uneven rate of technology spread as between two epochs was the uneven use of chemical fertilisers across farming systems and crop enterprises. Out of the total quantity of fertiliser used, 89 per cent was for irrigated areas/crops and 11 per cent was for rain-fed areas/crops. Per hectare use of

Table 5: *Land-Saving Effects of Productivity Change*
(Lakh hectares)

Crops	Land Saved During	
	E_2	E_3
1. Total cereals	27.78	6.16
Rice	4.59	1.30
Ragi	3.29	1.92
Sorghum	16.31	0.65
Bajra	3.47	0.76
2. Total pulses	4.87	−1.43
3. Total oil-seeds	−0.02	2.56
4. Sugarcane	0.06	−0.19

fertiliser was about 227 kg under irrigated farming and only 41 kg under rain-fed farming. About 86 per cent of total fertiliser use was for only three crops viz., paddy, sugarcane and cotton.

As a result of considerable technology spread of Karnataka's agriculture during the last two decades, there has been a tendency towards transition to industrial agriculture, i.e., dependence of agriculture on the industrial sector for its key inputs. In this context, the issue that warrants attention is whether a country which is deficient in energy and capital should not think of an alternative technological path instead of an import-intensive, energy-intensive and capital-intensive technology. Further, the rate of diffusion of new technology slowed down during the third epoch. It is in this perspective of the needed search for alternative technological paths that the concept of organic farming assumes importance. In its developed form, organic farming is not a throw back to a primitive era, but an alternative modern system of production which seeks to rely solely on biological processes to obtain high quality and yields which are at least as good as those achieved under fossil- fuel-based industrial agriculture. This requires the evolution of more efficient varieties of crops which can harvest energy from the sun and nitrogen from the air. It is understandable that these research avenues are difficult to pursue, but they are suggestive of the challenges as well as the opportunities for agricultural scientists and those in charge of the formulation of agricultural research policy.

Second, an analysis of the pattern of output growth in the state suggests that sorghum, *ragi*, rice and *bajra* had experienced a structural break with a shift from an area-cum-productivity-led growth pattern during the first period to a productivity-led growth pattern during the second period. Cotton continued to be under the productivity-led pattern, oil-seeds and sugarcane under area-led, and pulses under area-cum-productivity-led patterns of output growth during both periods. Further, results on trends in the productivity of major crops are suggestive of one major conclusion, i.e., productivity gains were more in the case of all major crops, except oil-seeds and sugarcane, during E_2, and productivity gains were perceptible in the case of oil-seeds alone during E_3. These results on the patterns of output growth and productivity trends suggest a host of issues relating to agricultural development policies, programmes and strategies. How much of the slow-down in productivity increase as well as yield plateaus during E_3 could be explained in terms of inadequacies of research efforts and of the new extension system, problems of 'drafting' the laggards into a productivity-led output growth strategy, and lack of adequate development support? The present exercise is not an attempt to disentangle the effects of these and many other factors which have a bearing on productivity, but to indicate the issues and their implications.

A positive relationship between agricultural research and productivity change in agriculture is a familiar theme. One exercise suggests that: (*i*) cereal crops which have experienced high rates of productivity growth are the ones which have received a major share of the research investment made in Karnataka; (*ii*) in the case of oil-seeds, low productivity and low research investment are found to have taken place; (*iii*) cotton had recorded high productivity growth along with high research investment; (*iv*) low research investment and negative productivity growth were observed in the case of sugarcane, (UAS 1980). These broad results suggest the need to increase investment in agricultural research.[4] In fact, one of the major challenges facing Indian agricultural universities is inadequate funds for agricultural research. The share of the ICAR in the central government's research and development expenditure decreased from 22 per cent in 1980–81 to 13 per cent in 1984–85. Total expenditure on agricultural research in India was only 0.3

---

[4] For details see the report of ICAR (1988) and William K. Easter, et al. (1989).

per cent of the value of agricultural production during the first half of the 1980s and it has been nearly constant in real terms since then.

In addition to gearing up efforts in the area of 'yield increasing research', there is a need to recognise the importance of investment in 'yield maintenance' research (UAS 1980). One of the critical issues in the area of agricultural research is technology depreciation or obsolescence. If the new varieties of seeds were to become subject to disease and other problems after a few years of production, their yields would decline. Studies of technology development in sugarcane, wheat and rice improvement show that the technology potential in a given research area can be exhausted, leading to a very slow rate of technology development. This would warrant 'yield maintenance research' to replenish technology potential. Our agricultural research policy appears to have accorded almost no emphasis to this dimension of research.

The general observation usually made is that agricultural research is stagnant with no continuous flow of technological breakthrough. However, we fail to realise that the rate of progress of technology will be limited by the advancement of basic knowledge. Basic knowledge establishes the boundaries within which technological innovations are possible. If basic knowledge is static, applied research is subject to the principle of diminishing returns and will eventually come to a halt. Further, since basic knowledge does not expand continuously or smoothly, technological breakthroughs can be expected to move in cycles or spurts. A breakthrough in basic research (e.g., in the areas of plant genetics, microbiology and plant physiology) leads to an initial rapid harvest of technological innovations, followed by a slowing-down of innovative activities. In the absence of emphasis on basic research, applied research efforts are likely to end up with the 'rediscovery of the wheel'. This would warrant an agricultural research policy, placing emphasis on a proper mix between basic and applied research in agricultural sciences, the dimension of which should form part of productive research management.

Third, in addition to examining the critical issues in the area of agricultural research policy, there is a need to identify the inadequacies of the new extension system introduced in Karnataka since 1978 (see Bisaliah 1983). It may be recalled that the new extension system focusing on 'knowledge transfer alone' has the potential of educating the farmers about the finer aspects of new technology, viz., the 'how' and 'when' dimensions. These finer dimensions of new technology could be powerful sources of non-cash inputs and a force for preventing stagnant/downward trends in agricultural productivity. Further, the new system has helped us realise how well prepared or unprepared the agricultural development support system is in technology generation and technology transfer, in providing complementary agricultural services such as credit, inputs and marketing infrastructure, and in sorting out a 'fair' input–output price policy.

A brief exposition of the inadequacies of the new extension system and the possible directions in which the system could be made more productive is in order.

As discussed earlier, the two-step flow communication system forms one of the building blocks of the new system. The contact farmers are expected to act as multiplicators by spreading technical messages to fellow farmers. The institution of contact farmers has the potential for reinforcing the local privileges at the expense of helping the more disadvantaged farmers. This is likely to be so when the contact farmers fail to play their role in the onward transmission of technical messages to fellow farmers. With the breakdown of the second-step flow of communication, the knowledge input distribution system would bypass 90 per cent of the farming community. Skewed distribution of the ownership of assets (especially of land), coupled with a skewed distribution of material and knowledge inputs would intensify the development dualism between contact and fellow farmers. This would warrant the need to develop appropriate criteria for selecting contact farmers, evaluating the possibility of using contact farmers primarily as organisers of groups seeking technical information, and the possibility of field-level extension workers working directly with the entire group, instead of clinging to the concept of the progressive farmer syndrome (see Bisaliah 1983). Recently (1989–90), the T & V system of extension was modified as the Training, Visit and Demonstration Approach in Karnataka, and has been introduced in some selected *taluks* (Government of Karnataka 1990). The basic approach of the modified version is to couple demonstration with visit, focusing on the contact group instead of the contact farmers. This new extension methodology consists essentially of a diagnostic approach of constraint identification at the field level, group approach and demonstration. Preliminary results indicate improvements in the levels of technology adoption and crop yields (ibid.).

It is claimed that significant gains in productivity can be achieved by using available resources more efficiently without significant increase in investment or in purchased inputs. The initial emphasis should, in fact, be on such management practices rather than on increased use of purchased inputs. This requires tremendous effort to transform our 'material input'-focused extension strategy to 'knowledge input' strategy. The extension system appears to be more comfortable in reaching the farmers with new varieties of seeds rather than with non-cash inputs alone. This obviously requires concerted efforts to reinforce the importance of non-cash inputs at the time of training, visit and demonstration.

The productivity of extension service depends very much on the flow of new research findings and other forms of development support. To feed the communication pool, the flow of new research findings should be continuous. The research support is required not merely to break yield barriers, but also to prevent agricultural productivity from declining. For the reasons discussed earlier, continuous technological breakthrough is difficult to realise. However, this line of reasoning is not meant to defend the inadequacies of the research management system, but to indicate the difficulties in providing a continuous flow of new research findings to support the knowledge transfer system. In the absence of new research information relay activity, why do we fail to recognise that the training recipients might be bored and the trainers embarrassed at having nothing new to interest their audience?

It is within this perspective that there is a need to examine the issue whether the 'selectivity' and 'top soil development syndrome' should continue to draw more of our development support or whether extension of support to laggards in the development process should be the main consideration from the angle of both equity and growth, using the 'available' technological base. If the country is looking for policies to tap the production potential in agriculture and for ensuring equity, the main policy challenge appears to be that of the development of laggards. In the absence of a proper policy focus on the development of laggards in agriculture, stagnation and even decline in agricultural productivity observed during the third epoch is likely to persist. Development policies and programmes directed towards this group are likely to give rise to more incremental gains in productivity and production from the agricultural sector. Both in supply and demand management (especially for inferior grains and simple industrial products), this numerically dominant group may play an effective role.

Finally, it might be recapitulated that gains in productivity of crops have given rise to considerable resource- (non-land) saving effects, resource-loss averted effects and land-saving effects in Karnataka's agriculture. The land-owning class is the direct beneficiary of these gains, in addition to 'gains' from input subsidy (particularly so when the key input like fertiliser use is concentrated mainly in irrigated areas/crops, and that too, in the case of only three crops), output–price support, and easy access to other development support facilities. The accrual of all these 'development gains' varies almost linearly with the amount of land owned. The major challenge confronting policy-makers today is how to mobilise part of the development gains accruing to those with large holdings made possible by resource investment by society at large, to evolve new technologies and take these to farmers through the extension service, and by devoting resources to extend all other forms of development support. In other words, is there a case for mobilising part of the 'windfall' development gains accruing to farmers?

In this regard, two important measures for the mobilisation of these gains could be considered—re-examination of the agricultural tax base as well as the tax rate, and land ceilings (for details see Bisaliah 1984). But the research base for indicating policy directions in these two areas is far from adequate. Is the agricultural sector inadequately taxed at present? What has been the extent of increase in the taxable capacity of the agricultural sector due to support from the technology-extension nexus and other development measures? How wide is the scope for imposing additional tax burden without seriously affecting investment and agricultural production? If left untaxed, how is the 'surplus' income likely to be used? Further, effective supply of land has increased due to productivity-led land-saving effects, as also due to increased cropping intensity. This may provide a case for downward revision of land ceilings. But a strong empirical base is required to answer some of the questions which are pertinent in this regard. Are small farms as efficient as large farms so that efficiency in production is not adversely affected? Would a further reduction in holding size through the policy of land ceilings increase total employment and output in the short-run, but slow down the growth of employment and output in the long-run owing to possible reduction in savings and investment? What special development policy–programme mix is required to sustain the productivity of a small-farm rural economy? Perhaps opinion, intentions and judgements are likely to gain an upper hand in resolving these issues in the absence of adequate research-based inferences.

REFERENCES

Bisaliah, S. (1977). 'Decomposition Analysis of Output Change Under New Production Technology in Wheat Farming: Some Implications to Returns on Research Investment', *Indian Journal of Agricultural Economics*, vol. 32, no. 3: 193–201, July–September.

———— (1983). New System of Technology Transfer and Agricultural Development in Karnataka (unpublished). University of Agricultural Science: Bangalore.

———— (1984). 'Land Substitutes and Yield-led Agricultural Output Growth: Some Implications to Distribution of Development Gains', in S.B. Chakrabarti et al. (eds.), *Agrarian Situation in India*, vol. 1, Anthropological Survey of India, Government of India: Calcutta.

Govindaraju, K.V. (1989). *Economic and Agronomic Factors Influencing the Use of Chemical Fertilizers—Cropwise and Regionwise in Karnataka*. Institute for Social and Economic Change: Bangalore, August.

Gundu Rao, D.S., S. Bisaliah and H.S. Krishnaswamy (1985a). 'Technical Change and Efficiency Gain in Dryland Agriculture: An Econometric Study', *Margin*, vol. 17, no. 4: 37–47, July, NCAER.

Gundu Rao, D.S., S. Bisaliah and H. Chandrasekhar (1985b). 'Accounting for Productivity Differential in Dryland Agriculture: An Econometric Exercise', *Indian Journal of Agricultural Economics*, vol. 40, no. 4: 536–44, October–December.

ICAR (1988). *Report of the ICAR Review Committee*. ICAR: New Delhi.

Government of Karnataka (1990). *Training, Visit and Demonstration Approaches*, Special Study Report No. 19, Monitoring and Evaluation Unit, Department of Agriculture: Bangalore.

Mruthyunjaya, S. Bisaliah and V.R. Srinivasan (1982). *Pace and Pattern of Agricultural Output Growth in Karnataka*, University of Agricultural Sciences: Bangalore.

UAS (1980). *Performance Appraisal*. Misc. Series No. 29, University of Agricultural Sciences: Bangalore.

William Easter, K., S. Bisaliah and John O. Dunbar (1989). 'After Twenty-Five Years of Institution Building, the State Agricultural Universities in India Face new Challenges', *American Journal of Agricultural Economics*, vol. 71, no. 5: 1200–05, December.

global economy. With the softening of prices, the burden of energy import which weighed heavily, especially on the oil-importing countries, has eased considerably. Indeed, it has led to energy issues fading into the background and the spread of a euphoric feeling that the energy crunch was well behind us and that the global economy (which has become heavily oil-dependent in the present century) could carry on as before.

The respite may in fact be short-lived. With the Iran-Iraq conflict drawing itself to a weary end, there was a revival in the global economy and the world oil demand once again started rising, even if slowly. The Middle East has once again been the scene of a major conflict affecting supplies from Iraq and Kuwait. A temporary remedy was found by stepping up production in countries such as Saudi Arabia and Venezuela and by the United States releasing oil from its strategic reserves. But the long-term problem remains. The non-OPEC oil production is expected to level-off in the 1990s. It is not that the world is fast running out of energy resources, but with the bulk of the balance oil reserves being held by the countries in the Middle East and with the lessons they have learnt in the past, an inevitable upward movement of prices is to be expected. According to a recent study of the possible OPEC strategy of closely regulating the production level, crude oil prices may hover around a base figure of US $29 barrel (in 1989 prices) by the year 2000 (Fesharaki 1990). This is certainly not a comforting prospect for oil-importing countries like India, which are struggling to maintain a resonable rate of economic growth.

Energy and Economic Growth

Parallel with the steady growth in overall energy consumption all over the world in the last few decades, there has been a change in the mix of fuels: modern or commercial forms of energy, namely, coal, hydrocarbons and electricity have steadily replaced traditional fuels (firewood, animal dung and crop residues). Convenience in handling, transport and storage and higher efficiency of utilisation have been the main factors accounting for the growing importance of the commercial forms of energy. The nexus between energy consumption and the level of economic development has been well-established not only over time but across countries; this has been documented in several studies. Based on a comprehensive analysis of the global trends in energy output, trade and consumption between 1929 and 1968, Dormstadter observed:

> A prominent characteristic of per capita consumption of commercial energy forms is its systematic and quantitatively close association with indicators of general economic development, measured here by per capita GNP—that is, an area's production of all goods and services per person. This relationship between GNP and energy holds both cross-sectionally and historically: the higher the nation's income or output on the current international scale, the higher in general its level of energy consumption; as its GNP rises over time, so does its energy consumption—in close, even if not proportionate, conformity (Dormstadter et al. 1971).

Inter-country comparisons, however, bring out the fact that the energy–economy elasticity of the developing countries is markedly higher than that of the developed countries. For instance, the Dormstadter study estimates the energy–GNP elasticity coefficient (i.e., ratio of growth rate of energy consumption to the growth rate of GNP) of the developed regions at 0.85 for the period 1950 to 1965, whereas it is as high as 1.67 for the developing regions. According to a more recent study, during the period 1973 to 1985, the OECD countries, which represent the bulk of the industrial market economies, were able to limit the growth of primary energy consumption to 6 per cent, even though their economy grew by 32 per cent during this period (Steeg 1986). It has therefore become commonplace to say that in the advanced economies, energy consumption and economic growth have become delinked from each other. But this has not yet happened in the developing countries, where the energy–GDP elasticity coefficient still remains well above unity.

The above statement, it should be remembered, pertains to commercial energy only. In the industrial economies, where the consumption of traditional fuels is negligible, data on commercial energy almost fully reflects the total energy consumption. This is not the case in the developing countries where traditional fuels continue to be used in large quantities. On account of limitations of data with respect to such fuels, recorded statistics generally pertain to commercial fuels only, but this gives a partial picture.

As far as these modern fuels are concerned, the growth rate of consumption still remains well above that of the economy.

The situation in India is not different from that of other developing countries. Traditional fuels still play a dominant role in the household sector and account for around 45 per cent of the total energy consumption. The Advisory Board on Energy (ABE 1985) estimated the elasticity coefficients for different periods which is shown in Table 1.

Table 1: *Energy–GDP Elasticity*

Period	I	II	III
1953–61	1.04	0.83	1.51
1961–71	0.81	0.79	1.32
1971–78	0.97	0.83	1.24

Notes: I. Primary energy to GDP.
II. Total energy (commercial + non-commercial) to GDP.
III. Commercial energy to GDP.

As seen from the above figures, the total energy–GNP elasticity coefficient does not show a substantial change between 1953 and 1978. The commercial energy–GDP elasticity coefficient has declined but remains high. A similar conclusion can be drawn from a more recent analysis by Sengupta (1989). Table 2 shows GDP and energy consumption during the period 1953–54 to 1987–88.

It is clear that there is a close correlation between GDP and energy consumption. Taking commercial and non-commercial energy together, the elasticity is less than 1. But the elasticity of commercial energy with reference to GDP is still a high 1.46.

A similar pattern emerges from an analysis in terms of growth rates and elasticity coefficients. Between 1953 and 1978, the average annual GDP growth rate was 3.77 per cent. In comparison, the growth rate of total energy consumed was 3.26 per cent, indicating an energy–GDP elasticity coefficient of 0.86. The growth rates of commercial and non-commercial energy consumption were 5.64 per cent and 1.71 per cent per year, respectively, giving an elasticity coefficient of 1.49 for commercial energy and 0.47 for non-commercial energy.

Taking commercial and non-commercial consumption together, the Indian scenario is not dissimilar to that of the Western countries

Table 2: *GDP and Energy Consumption in India*

Year	GDP at 1980–81 Prices (Rs crores)	Energy Consumption in Peta Calories		
		Commercial	Non-Commercial	Total
1953–54	47863	218.069	632.165	850.234
1960–61	62904	318.640	732.707	1051.347
1965–66	72122	484.838	804.055	1288.893
1970–71	90426	582.269	867.525	1449.794
1975–76	104968	787.447	979.625	1767.072
1980–81	122226	967.285	1058.400	2025.685
1984–85	150542	1172.914	1058.400	2231.314
1987–88	170363	1407.808	1125.750	2533.558

The above data fits into the following equations:

$$\text{Log } E_1 = -10.30469 + 1.46268 \text{ log } Y \qquad R^2 = 0.9837$$
$$(19.018)$$
$$\text{Log } E_2 = 1.56641 + 0.45636 \text{ log } Y \qquad R^2 = 0.9673$$
$$(13.326)$$
$$\text{Log } E_3 = -2.52881 + 0.86246 \text{ log } Y \qquad R^2 = 0.9900$$
$$(24.340)$$

(Figures in brackets are t values)

E_1 = commercial energy
E_2 = non-commercial energy
E_3 = total energy
Y = GDP

in that the energy consumption is growing slower than the economy. This does not mean, however, that energy is no longer an issue to be concerned about. The real problem lies in the high commercial energy–GDP elasticity, a contributory factor being the steady replacement of traditional fuels by commercial forms of energy. While the elasticity is bound to decline over time, the growth rate of commercial energy consumption will continue to remain higher than the overall economic growth rate for many years to come. In other words, we are still far from rupturing the link between commercial energy consumption and the growth of the GDP. This indeed represents the crux of the energy problem facing the country.

Growing Role of Electricity

A feature which calls for special notice is the growing role of electricity in the energy spectrum. This phenomenon is global in nature. Being high quality energy, it is easily convertible into other forms of energy such as heat or motive power. It is readily transportable over long distances. It is versatile in its applications and can be used with a high degree of efficiency. Yet other factors in its favour are the convenience of use and feasibility of generating electricity from a variety of sources. For all these reasons, in the developed and developing countries alike, electricity consumption has consistently registered a faster growth rate than either coal or oil. Table 3 shows the position of the OECD countries (UNIPEDE 1983).

Table 3: *Share of Electricity in Energy Consumption in OECD Europe (in percentages)*

	1960	1965	1970	1975	1980	1985	1990
Iron and steel	16.9	20.4	22.7	24.3	29.0	31	32
Industry (other than iron and steel)	31.7	33.5	34.1	35.6	38.7	42	45
Transport	5.4	5.0	4.6	4.2	4.2	4.4	4.5
Residential, commercial and agricultural	19.6	24.5	27.8	32.2	36.5	45	50
Total	20.8	23.7	25.4	27.6	30.4	34	37

Notes: 1. Electricity converted to primary energy equivalent taking 4500 Kwh = 1 toe (tonne of oil equivalent).
2. 1985 and 1990 estimates based on International Energy Agency (IEA) forecasts (same conversion principle).

Except in the transport sector, where viable technologies to replace the internal combustion engine are not yet available, electricity has made inroads in all the sectors of the economy.

The trend in India is similar. Electricity consumption rose from 7.6 Twh in 1953–54 to 159.29 Twh in 1987–88, giving an average annual growth rate of 9.63 per cent. The electricity–GDP elasticity coefficient was as high as 2.55. This has however declined over time and is about 1.76 in the current decade, which is still significantly higher than that of other forms of energy.

The change in the sectoral consumption is also interesting as seen in Table 4.

What is interesting is the fact that among the different consumption sectors, the highest elasticity is shown by the agricultural sector, followed by the household sector. This is an encouraging

Table 4: *Sectoral Consumption of Electricity (Utilities)*
(in percentages)

Year	Domestic	Com-mercial	Industry	Railways	Agri-culture	Others
1970–71	8.8	5.9	67.6	3.2	10.2	4.3
1975–76	9.7	5.8	62.4	3.1	14.5	4.5
1980–81	11.2	5.7	58.4	2.7	17.6	4.4
1985–86	14.0	5.9	54.5	2.5	19.1	4.0
1987–88	14.7	6.0	48.8	2.5	23.8	4.8

Source: CMIE (1989). 'Current Energy Scene in India', July.

sign as it reflects greater use of electricity for productive agriculture and is also a pointer towards some improvement in the quality of life. In the coming years as well, we have to gear up not only to meet sharp increases in demand for commercial energy, but an even steeper rise in the requirement of electricity.

OUTCOME OF ENERGY PLANNING

A brief look at the outcome of energy planning in the last few years from certain broad economic aspects is in order here. In every Five-Year Plan, the energy sector has been accorded high priority and the financial allocation to this sector has grown steadily over the years, as seen in Table 5.

In physical terms also, commercial energy production has registered impressive increases, particularly in the last two decades. The installed capacity for electricity generation has increased fourfold since 1970–71. Coal production has gone up three times in the last twenty years. Starting from 6.8 million tons in 1970–71, the domestic oil industry has crossed the 30 million ton mark, though the growth has levelled-off in the last three years.

The Eighth Five-Year Plan, which had been under preparation for a long time, recently received the approval of the National Development Council. Although the complete picture of the sectoral allocations is not available, it is clear that, given the acute resource situation in the country, the share of the energy sector in total public investment is unlikely to go up. In fact, the private

Table 5: *Plan Allocation for Energy*
(percentage)

Plans	Total Plan Outlay (Rs crore)	Share of Energy Sector in Plan Outlay				Total
		Power	Petroleum and Gas	Coal and Lignite	Non-Conventional Energy	
First	1960	19.7	–	–	–	19.7
Second	4672	9.7	0.8	1.9	–	11.8
Third	8577	14.6	2.6	1.3	–	18.5
Annual	6625	14.1	2.7	1.1	–	17.9
Fourth	15779	18.6	1.9	0.7	–	21.2
Fifth	39426	18.7	3.6	2.9	–	25.2
Annual	12177	18.4	4.2	0.2	–	22.8
Sixth	109292	16.7	7.8	3.5	0.1	28.1
Seventh	180000	19.0	7.2	4.1	0.3	30.6

Source: K. Sengupta (1989). 'Pace of Economic Development and Long Run Requirement of Commercial Energy in India', *Urja*, vol. 26, no. 6.

sector is being encouraged to make a substantial contribution to the creation of new capacity in power and petroleum, and possibly coal.

Has energy proved a constraint to economic growth? Ignoring for the moment the shortcomings in distribution and the none-too-free access of the rural people to commercial forms of energy, the problem in recent years has essentially been that of shortage in electricity supply. In the 1970s, there used to be acute shortage of coal, but this has been overcome. Questionable as the policy may be, supplies of petroleum products have been maintained with liberal imports to supplement domestic crude oil production. Electricity being a non-tradeable commodity, the country's requirements have to be met from domestic sources only. In most parts of the country, availability has remained short of requirements and on account of under-investment in the Sixth and Seventh Five-Year Plans, the gap has widened. There are several estimates of the loss of production consequent on electricity shortages, but these are mostly rough exercises and too much reliance cannot be placed on the calculations. There can be no doubt, however, that with heavy power cuts imposed from time to time, there is loss of production, apart from other consequences such as underutilisation of capacity and lay-off of labour.

We may examine another aspect, namely, how far the energy consumption pattern reflects the other major goal of development, that of equity. Unfortunately, not enough data is available to enable us to identify a trend. The 18th round of the National Sample Survey (1963–64), which was virtually the first effort to obtain a nation-wide picture, showed that there was a high income elasticity of consumption of energy. The 28th round of National Sample Survey (1973–74) did not reveal any perceptible change. The manner in which energy consumption shows a skewed distribution across income levels as brought out by this round is depicted in Table 6.

Table 6: *Index of Income-wise Energy Consumption in the Household Sector*

Expenditure class Rs. per month per capita		Index of Total per capita energy consumption in	
		Rural	Urban
All expenditure classes together		100	100
(i) 0–21	..	66	48
(ii) 21–28	..	80	61
(iii) 28–43	..	90	82
(iv) 43–75	..	101	96
(v) Above 75	..	138	125

Source: Government of India (1979). *Report of the Working Group on Energy Policy*. Planning Commission: New Delhi.

The latest picture available on an all-India basis is from the Domestic Fuel Survey conducted by the NCAER (Natarajan 1985), for which the reference priod was 1978–79. The tables drawn from this survey give us an idea of the interrelationship between energy consumption and household income with respect to two modern fuels, namely, LPG and electricity.

The data presented in Tables 7 and 8 shows a definte correlation between energy consumption and per capita income with regard to LPG and electricity. As regards kerosene, the NCAER study showed that about 94 per cent households in India used kerosene, 40 per cent of the consumption located in urban areas. Over 80 per cent of the kerosene consumed in the rural areas was for lighting; in contrast, heating claimed a share of 75 per cent in the cities and

Table 7: *Consumption of LPG in Urban Areas by Household Income*

Income Class (Rs.)	Consumption (% Share)	Per capita (kg)	% LPG Users
Up to 3,000	2.3	0.3	1.0
3,001–6,000	21.4	1.1	5.3
6,001–12,000	43.5	3.8	18.0
12,001–18,000	15.2	9.3	42.1
Above 18,000	18.1	11.1	56.3
All	100.0	2.2	9.1

Table 8: *Consumption of Electricity by Income*

Income Class (Rs)	Per Capita (kwh)		
	Rural	Urban	Total
Up to 3,000	2.4	12.1	3.6
3,001–6,000	5.5	29.2	11.4
6,001–12,000	9.9	52.0	24.3
12,001–18,000	15.3	78.6	37.2
Over 18,000	17.3	107.9	53.7

towns. Though the proportion of families using kerosene for heating was correlated with income, there was a sharp fall in its use for lighting, which resulted in an overall negative correlation with income. The obvious explanation is that the wealthier families switch over to more convenient fuels. When the analysis is carried out in terms of useful energy, the iniquitous distribution of per capita energy consumption stands out more prominently. The relatively well-to-do families use more efficient energy conversion devices and fuels of higher 'quality'.

It is a moot point whether the degree of inequality in energy consumption vis-à-vis income has undergone any change in the last forty years. As already mentioned, comparable data is not available. One can only surmise that inasmuch as income inequalities in our society have not reduced, similar inequalities in energy consumption remain.

Another aspect which requires attention is the energy intensity of the Indian ecnomy. Table 9 sets out the position.

It is but natural that the pattern seen earlier with regard to

Table 9: *Energy Intensity of the Indian Economy*

Year	Energy Intensity of the GDP (Kcal/Re)		Total
	Commercial	Non-Commercial	
1953–54	455.61	1320.78	1776.39
1960–61	506.55	1164.80	1671.35
1965–66	672.25	1114.85	1787.10
1970–71	643.92	959.38	1603.30
1975–76	750.18	933.26	1683.44
1980–81	791.39	865.94	1657.33
1984–85	779.13	703.06	1482.19
1987–88	826.36	660.79	1487.15

Source: Ramprasad Sengupta (1989). 'Pace of Economic Development and Long Run Requirement of Commercial Energy in India', *Urja*, vol. 26, no. 6, December.

energy–GDP elasticity should be repeated here. Viewed overall, the Indian economy is not growing more energy-intensive and there is a secular decline, mainly because of the reducing share of non-commercial fuels. Replacement of traditional fuels by modern forms of energy which can be used with greater efficiency has brought down the energy intensity. But, significantly, in terms of commercial energy use, the economy is showing a trend of rising energy intensity.

From the cursory picture presented above, one sees that planning for energy, as it has been implemented over the last four decades, has neither succeeded in ensuring adequate availability, nor has it subserved the goal of reducing economic inequalities. In terms of commercial fuels which, as mentioned earlier, are at the base of our energy problem, the economy is becoming more and more intensive in the use of energy.

System of Energy Planning in India

In a planned economy, energy demand and supply should match. Why then are there persistent and growing electricity shortages? Clearly, this is a reflection of the shortcomings in the planning process. Let us therefore look at the system of energy planning in India.

The development of an energy plan must have the following sequence:

   (*i*) estimate of future demand;
   (*ii*) evaluation of the potential of domestic energy resources;
   (*iii*) definition of policy objectives;
   (*iv*) formulation of individual projects; and
   (*v*) estimation of capital requirements.

Having regard for the close interconnection between energy and economic development, planning for energy cannot be autonomous: it must necessarily be integrated into the national development plan. As the prime planning agency in the country, the Planning Commission plays a major role in energy planning for India, as it does for all the sectors of the national economy. State governments also carry out planning exercises, but their range and depth are limited. The various organisations engaged in energy supply, such as State Electricity Boards, the Oil and Natural Gas Commission and Coal India, have their own planning units which provide valuable input to the national planning process. Besides, ad hoc studies at the macro, meso and micro levels carried out by institutions (e.g., NSSO, CSO and NCAER) and research scholars provide insights to planners.

The methodology developed by the Planning Commission to give a theoretical underpinning to the plan is well-known and does not require elaboration here. From the point of view of energy planning, what is relevant is the fact that the input–output model which is used to derive the sectoral output profiles, is one of the core models and in this model, electricity, coal and lignite, and crude oil and natural gas figure as distinct sectors. The input–output model is supplemented by the material balance approach which helps to assess the capacity and output to be generated in specific sectors at a disaggregated level, sometimes even to the level of individual projects. The iterative process between the macro economic, input–output and investment models is carried out until convergent results are obtained in line with the socio-economic goals determined by the government. With the considerable experience acquired during the last forty years, a fair amount of sophistication has developed in the process of planning for commercial energy. The input–output methodology is expected to ensure inter-sectoral consistency. The question naturally arises as to why, despite elaborate preparations and methodological refinements which go into the preparation of a Five-Year Plan, there should be energy shortages?

The answer lies in the fact that there are inherent weaknesses in the national planning process. Even while finalising a Five-Year Plan, distortions are introduced because of perceptions at the political level which result in over-optimistic plans not fully supported by resources. As a result, during the course of implementation, certain sectors do not receive requisite financial support. This has in fact happened to the power sector in the Sixth and Seventh Five-Year Plans. Even to begin with, the financial allocation for this sector was patently inadequate in relation to the physical targets. Available resources were spread too thinly over different projects, resulting in an all-round slippage in the dates of commissioning. In the energy sector where lead times are long, beginnings on new projects have to be made well in advance to synchronise with the growth of demand. On account of the insufficiency in plan allocation, sufficient beginnings are not being made. In such a situation, there can be no hope of bridging the gap between power supply and demand. The problem of resource shortfalls is most pronounced in state plans and since the bulk of the power utilities are in the states, the consequences are serious. Even in the central sector, inadequacy of resources made its appearance in the Seventh Plan. An attempt has been made to narrow the resource gap by flotation of public bonds. While this may provide some immediate relief, it cannot be resorted to in the long-run as it is imprudent to finance infrastructure development with high cost capital. The problem of resource availiability is compounded by the fact that in the state plans, allocations to the irrigation and power sectors appear prominently, and when a state government faces a difficult financial situation, the tendency is to divert available funds to sectors which have high public visibility and appreciation. The instruments available to the Planning Commission to maintain plan discipline are very limited.

In effect, planning for energy in India is confined to commercial fuels alone. Though the importance of traditional fuels in the Indian economy is well-recognised, even today there are serious data limitations. There are methodological problems in assessing non-commercial energy consumption which is mostly in the household sector. The production of traditional fuels is in the hands of millions of individuals. A good part of such production is consumed within the households of the producers themselves. Many rural families still depend heavily on fuel collected free of cost by the members of the family. Only a fraction of the output enters the market. Therefore, for purposes of all-India estimation, reliance has been placed heavily on National Sample Surveys, in some rounds of which data on energy consumption is collected as a part of the estimation of household expenditure. Possibly because of the pressing demand for data on other important economic parameters such as poverty and employment, there is no regular periodicity in the collection of energy data in the NSS rounds. And, even when information has been collected, analysis and publication of results take a long time. To establish the time trend and also for cross-sectional studies, it is necessary that once in every five rounds or so, energy data is compiled on a comparable basis. Some scholars have been critical of both the definitions and the methodology of the NSS. For instance, the data on kerosene consumption generated through the National Sample Surveys substantially differs from the figures of distribution and supply available with the oil companies. Nevertheless, this is the only mechanism available to collect data on a nation-wide scale. It is always possible to introduce methodological refinements based on past experience so as to improve the reliability of the data. Such mega-surveys should be supplemented by regional- and village-level surveys, which not only provide a countercheck of the data collected through larger surveys, but also provide deeper insights into the changing energy patterns and help in the formulation of appropriate policies.

While we have some knowledge of energy consumption in households, we know very little about the situation in the non-household sector. The unorganised sector plays an important part in the national economy, accounting for a good proportion of the non-agricultural NDP (Net Domestic Product), as may be seen from Table 10.

This sector, large though it is, does not receive explicit attention in energy planning exercises; some segments are left out altogether.

The Annual Survey of Industry (ASI) encompasses the organised sector of manufacturing industry, as well as certain categories of establishments covered by the Factories Act (1948) and its statistical coverage includes energy consumption. Therefore, the ASI provides fairly extensive information regarding the energy situation in organised industry. But it is only recently that some attempt is being made to collect information regarding enterprises which are not registered under the Factories Act. Here, the responsibility for the collection of data is divided between the National Sample

Table 10: *Estimation of Unorganised Sector in NDP*

Section as per National Industrial Classification (NIC) 1970	Major Head of Industrial Activity	Per cent Share in NDP		
		Organised Sector	Unorganised Sector	Total
0	*Agriculture, Hunting, Forestry and Fishing*	1.8	38.1	39.9
1.	Mining and quarrying	1.1	0.1	1.2
2 and 3.	Manufacturing	10.3	6.0	16.3
4.	Electricity, gas and water	1.5	–	1.5
5.	Construction	2.5	2.9	5.4
6.	Wholesale, retail trade: Restaurants and hotels	1.4	12.4	13.8
7.	Transport, storage and communication	3.1	2.6	5.7
8.	Finance, insurance, real estate and business service	3.1	2.9	6.0
9.	Community, social and personal services	8.5	1.7	10.2
	Total	33.3	66.7	100.0
	Total (excluding agriculture, etc.)	31.5 (52.4%)	28.6 (47.6%)	60.1 (100.0%)

Source: National Accounts Statistics, January 1987 (CSO).

Survey Organisation and the Central Statistical Organisation (CSO). The NSSO is expected to cover own-account manufacturing enterprises (which do not hire labour) and non-directory establishments (enterprises employing five persons or less, of whom at least one is hired). The CSO is expected to cover directory establishments (enterprises employing not less than six persons, of whom at least one is hired). The results of the 40th round of the NSS covering own-account and non-directory manufacturing establishments are not yet available. Summary tables of the CSO's directory manufacturing enterprises survey (1984–85) have been published, but they do not give quantitative data on energy assumption. As a result, we remain ignorant of the energy supply and consumption patterns in this important segment of the economy. Efforts will have to be made in future to bridge this gap in information.

While our knowledge of patterns of non-commercial energy consumption is limited, we know even less regarding the sources of supply. A striking feature of the fairly large number of village studies which are now available is the enormous variation from village to village with respect to both the mix of fuels consumed and the manner in which these fuels were procured. The paucity of data is felt acutely in the case of the most important traditional fuel, namely, fuelwood. We do not know how much of the fuelwood consumed in India originates from the forests, how much from government or village common lands, and how much from private holdings. The data of recorded production maintained by the forest authorities accounts for only a very small fraction of the estimated consumption. The National Commission on Agriculture placed the forest share at 10 per cent. It is well-known that while the estimates of consumption cover the total biomass used as fuel (i.e., including twigs, leaves, etc.), it has been the traditional practice in the forest departments to keep account of only the volume under bark. The Working Group on Energy Policy (GOI 1979) had pointed out how, even with respect to the forest areas, dependable figures were not available on either the capital stock or the annual increment. Though it is more than a decade since the Working Group gave its report, there is no improvement in data availability.

Even with regard to commercial energy, where the data base is relatively stronger, systematic planning efforts have remained confined to the national level. In a vast and diversified country like India, this needs to be supplemented by disaggregated planning at the regional level. This calls for systematic collection of data and building up of regional/state-wise data bases.

While the input–output technique is considered to be useful for medium-term planning, its limitations for long-term planning are well-recognised. In the energy sector where both supply and consumption patterns change slowly, long-term planning is important. The general trend has therefore been to resort to energy modelling, which incorporates both economic and technological changes anticipated in the planning horizon. Because of lack of reliable data on such important parameters as income and price elasticities, it may be difficult at the present stage to formulate energy models which can be used for operational purposes in developing countries. It is encouraging, however, to see a start being made in this direction in our country. The Tata Energy Research Institute has developed a model based on the end-use approach. A number of scholars have developed models covering specific segments of the energy economy. A comprehensive and elaborate commercial energy modelling exercise has been carried out for the Planning Commission by Ramprasad Sengupta, but for no apparent reason the results of the exercise have not been released to the public. A problem faced by researchers is access to data, which is mostly confined to government and public sector organisations in Delhi and the state capitals. It is necessary that institutional arrangements be made for regular and wide dissemination of energy data.

The development of a comprehensive data base which covers all forms of energy must receive priority attention. Ministers of Coal, Petroleum and Power have developed information systems which are wide in their coverage, though there are some elements missing. With regard to non-commercial sources of energy where, as already pointed out, there are major gaps in data, nodal organisations have to be identified and entrusted with the responsibility of building up data bases in their areas. If, as it must, energy planning is to be carried out in an integrated manner, there has to be an agency in the Government of India assigned with the clear task of taking an overview of the energy scenario, examining policy options and developing a coherent energy policy. Such an agency will also be the appropriate location for a comprehensive energy data base which networks with 'sectoral' data bases. A weakness in the Indian planning system has been the absence of such a coordinating agency. The Department of Power, which had earlier been assigned this task, has not been effective in this regard. When the Advisory Board on Energy was established, expectations ran high that the Board, placed as it was outside the structure of the Ministers, would emerge as an agency which would evaluate alternative energy strategies and advise the government regarding the most desirable course of action. For reasons which need not be dealt with here, the Board did not prove effective and has been disbanded, its residual functions being taken over by the Planning Commission. One can well argue that the Planning Commission which continuously interacts with various Ministries and is the main agency for national economic planning is ideally suited for the coordination of energy policy. While this viewpoint has considerable validity, energy, being only one of the several areas of concern of the Planning Commission, is unlikely to receive full attention. Taking into account the structure and mores of the central government, it would be useful to create a Department of Energy as subunit of the Cabinet Secretariat. This department, while remaining compact in size, could include energy economists, system analysts and a few select technical personnel.

CURTAILING THE DEMAND FOR ENERGY

As we have seen in an earlier section of this paper, the challenge facing the country is to ensure adequate supplies of energy to sustain the desired rate of economic development. A question frequently asked is whether the process of economic growth cannot be less energy-intensive. The countries of the Third World, it is argued, should not regard the Western historical model of development as the only course available and should chart out a growth path which does not call for large additions to energy supply. Some scholars have argued (e.g., Goldemberg et al. 1988) that policy-makers have traditionally displayed excessive concern with issues of energy *supply* and have neglected the *end use* of energy. Consumption of energy is not an end in itself; what is important is the service that energy performs. One should look at the present and future human needs served by energy and the technological options of meeting such needs at minimum cost. It should be possible, through a combination of concerted measures for energy conservation and choice of appropriate technologies, to bring down future energy requirements. With a lower demand, the range of energy supply options become wider. This will facilitate a process of development which is enviornmentally more benign and sustainable in the long-run. It is also argued that energy policy should be a positive instrument to achieve the goal of a more equitable society and ensure that the basic needs of the poorer segments of the population are met.

What are the prospects of being able to bring about a reduction in the energy intensity of the economy? If, without compromising growth and other objectives, the rate of increase in the demand for commercial fuels can be arrested, it will undoubtedly ease both the problem of mobilising internal resources and managing the strain on balance of payments. Unfortunate as it may be, the prospects in this direction are none too bright. First, the rate of growth of population still remains high and has not declined as sharply as one had anticipated. Second, there is general agreement that the per capita consumption of energy, which is at an abnormally low level in India—reflecting pervasive poverty—must increase. This is necessary to raise productivity and improve incomes; equally, it is necessary to improve the quality of life by reducing human drudgery, specially for women. It is well-known, for instance, that rural families spend many hours each day in collecting water and fuel. Any solution inevitably entails the use of some energy.

Viewed from a macro perspective, the main contribution to economic growth has to be provided by the agricultural and industrial sectors of the economy in the next few decades. Extension of irrigation (particularly the exploitation of ground-water) and increased use of chemical fertilisers, together with the use of high yielding varieties of seeds, have contributed to the spurt in India's agricultural production in the last twenty-five years. In the process, agriculture has become more energy-intensive. As regards industry, it is generally accepted that Indian industry must undergo modernisation and technological upgradation in order to serve the domestic market in an efficient manner and to be competitive in international markets. We have to accept the fact that the pool of technology available is essentially Western technology which tends to be both capital- and energy-intensive. Even in the area of small-scale industry, one has already witnessed the decline of traditional industries and their replacement by modern units using commercial forms of energy. Parallel to the growth of the agricultural and industrial sectors, there has necessarily to be the expansion of the transport sector for the movement of raw materials and the products to the market. The transport sector, once again, is energy-intensive. These aspects apart, as pointed out earlier, commercial fuels are bound to replace traditional fuels in increasing measure. All these factors will keep the commercial energy intensity of the economy at a relatively high level. The rate of growth in the consumption of energy per unit of output will slow down, but a decline in absolute terms is unlikely for several decades to come.

In a situation of rising energy demand, the need to use energy efficiently does not require any elaboration. Energy conservation does not mean a slow-down in the process of development, but aims at achieving such development, reducing the energy demand at the same time through the adoption of energy-efficient technologies and other measures. Though there is a growing awareness among the consumers of energy that saving is more cost-effective than increasing energy supply, India's performance in energy conservation has been poor. A variety of factors have contributed to this unsatisfactory situation. First, there has been no rational energy price policy. Coal and electricity are under-priced and do not reflect their economic cost; subsidies are given to sections of consumers who do not deserve them. In the case of petroleum products, high prices are justified as a means of inhibiting consumption. But in reality, in the Indian situation, high prices only serve the purpose of raising revenues for the government, as there is hardly any scope for inter-fuel substitution. Indian industry, which accounts for the largest share of commercial energy consumption has not, with a few exceptions, taken determined steps to improve energy efficiency. Because of sheltered markets, the tendency has been to pass on increased energy prices to the consumers by simply raising the price of their products.

While it is not within the scope of this paper to go into energy policy issues, a facet of energy conservation which needs special mention is the containment of oil demand. India is and will remain deficit in petroleum products and international prices will soon start reflecting their scarcity value once again. The transport sector accounts for the largest share of oil consumption and presently, alternative technologies which avoid the use of petroleum fuels are not available. As the expansion of the transport sector is a prerequisite for economic growth, oil demand will maintain an upward trend in the next few decades. Clearly, if this demand is to be managed, systematic action has to be taken to keep the growth of demand to the minimum. Planning in our country over the last three plan periods which have elapsed since the oil crisis of 1973 has not reflected this concern. Continued neglect will place the country in a serious situation.

It is not that energy conservation can obviate an absolute rise in energy requirements. But keeping in view the high capital intensity of energy supply industries, rising energy costs and the need to keep oil consumption to the minimum, energy conservation has to figure prominently in future plans.

A new dimension, the importance of which is being appreciated only in recent years, is the impact of energy consumption on the ecology and environment. There is hardly any energy source which is totally enviornmentally benign, not even the new and renewable energy technologies which are under development. Every form of energy consumption carries with it some externalities. Social cost-benefit techniques cannot fully reflect environmental costs because of methodological limitations. Nevertheless, in the evolution of future planning for energy, the environmental aspects will have to be squarely taken into account.

CONCLUSION

To reiterate, energy planning is not an autonomous process and has to be related to the broader social and economic goals which underpin the formulation of national development plans. The demand for energy will depend not only on the projected rate of growth but on its content as well. If a high rate of growth is projected, this will correspondingly imply high growth rates of the agricultural and industrial sectors and, therefore, the growth in energy demand will also be high. On the other hand, if the main thrust is on employment generation in agriculture and labour-intensive industries, human resource development and provision of basic minimum needs, the requirement of energy will be relatively less. One has therefore to derive the profile of future energy requirements from the major objectives of national planning. Whatever be the energy requirement, it is important that plans embody financial and other measures needed to ensure its availability. In the same way, while energy policy can assist in achieving the redistributive goal to which the country stands committed, such a goal cannot be reached through energy planning alone; nor is it the most effective instrument. The major thrust has to be from fiscal and industrial policies and the orientation of the total plan strategy. These would have to provide the framework within which the pattern of energy consumption could be so directed as to buttress the broader goals.

Since 1973, there have been a number of high-level exercises in the formulation of energy policy in our country. Eminently acceptable policy statements are embodied in official documents such as the Five-Year Plans. But, in terms of action, energy management remains weak and inconsistent. Though the nature and magnitude of the problem are recognised, there is as yet no evidence of a determined effort at tackling the problem. There is a high degree of ad hocism in policy decisions and excessive concern with the immediate future to the neglect of long-term consequences. In the energy sector where both supply and consumption patterns can change only slowly, the absence of a long-term perspective can be disastrous. As the gravity of the energy crunch is now more serious than ever before, one hopes that both the formulation and implementation of future plans will embody a coherent energy policy.

REFERENCES

Advisory Board on Energy (1985). *Towards a Perspective on Energy Demand and Supply in India in 2004/5*. New Delhi.

Dormstadter, J., et al. (1971). *Energy in the World Economy: A Statistical Review of Trends in Output, Trade and Consumption since 1925*. Johns Hopkins Press: Baltimore.

Fesharaki, Fereidun (1990). 'Oil Prices in the Short, Medium and Long Term', *Energy Policy,* vol. 18, no. 1: 66–71, January/February.

Government of India (1979). *Report of the Working Group on Energy Policy*. Planning Commission, New Delhi.

Goldemberg, J., T.B. Johansson, A.K.N. Reddy and R.H. Williams (1988). *Energy for a Sustainable World*. Wiley Eastern, New Delhi.

Natarjan, I. (1985). *Domestic Fuel Survey with Special Reference to Kerosene*, vol. 1. National Council of Applied Economic Research: New Delhi.

Sengupta, R. (1989). 'Pace of Economic Development and Long Run Requirement of Commercial Energy in India', *Urja*, vol. 26, no. 6: 63–74.

Steeg, H. (1986). 'Energy Situation in IEA Countries—Evolution in the Past and Future Prospects', paper prepared for the 13th Congress of World Energy Conference, Cannes.

UNIPEDE (1983). 'Technological Innovations in the Energy Field', paper prepared for the 12th Congress of World Energy Conference, New Delhi.

13

Planning and Environmental Concerns

M.V. NADKARNI

$\mathbf{P}$lanning has come to be accepted in India and other developing countries as a major strategy of economic development and for achieving higher levels of human welfare, even in the context of a mixed economy dominated by market forces. Though the strategy has never been to supplant market forces, in fact, recent policies of liberalisation have given them a boost, it has nevertheless always been acknowledged that it is necessary to have broad targets of achieving economic development and improving human welfare, to ensure the resources to achieve such targets, and to formulate policies that help this task. Then it is left to the mixed economy, including its market forces, to implement the plan which expresses them all. Targets might not always be achieved, nor resources adequately raised. Yet, planning exercises and formulations from a long-term perspective have been very helpful in giving a certain direction to market forces, as also in monitoring economic development.

Since planning is not a matter of merely targeting certain growth rates and estimating incremental capital–output ratios, but essentially one of improving human welfare, environmental concerns require not only marginal or formal attention, but the incorporation of all aspects of economic development into planning. Environmental concern is not a concern for nature as against humans. It views human beings as a part of nature, which indeed they are. They can modify nature, but can never be independent of it and cannot afford to be indifferent to it, since their own welfare is dependent on the health of the natural environment in which they live. When environmentalists oppose certain development projects which have significant and adverse side-effects, they are essentially worried about the far-reaching and long-term consequences of such effects on human welfare. For example, if effluents into rivers affect fisheries and the quality of drinking water, it is human welfare which is directly affected. If a development project displaces hundreds of thousands of people for whom there is no effective and adequate resettlement plan, the reason for opposing such a project cannot be naively attributed to a fear of interfering with nature.

Unfortunately, the negative side-effects of unimaginative and short-sighted development projects could not receive due attention, mainly because of the overemphasis on growth rates. When the emphasis shifts from growth rates to providing livelihood and improving the quality of life, the concern for the environment is bound to receive greater prominence. By quality of life we do not mean only an aesthetic consideration of keeping the natural environment beautiful for outdoor picnics. It means essentially improving the level of human welfare, and ensuring basic human needs including adequate and healthy food, fuel, clean water and air, and decent housing. Insofar as short-sighted development projects adversely affect these determinants of human welfare, they actually retard economic development rather than promote it.

In India we are quite right in acknowledging another source of environmental deterioration apart from the negative side-effects of short-sighted development projects—that is poverty or lack of development itself, which is made clear in the plan documents themselves.[1] Driven by poverty and despair and lack of alternative means of livelihood, people incur the risk of illegally cutting trees for fuel or encroaching on forest lands for cultivation. Not being able to afford relatively pollution-free fuel, housewives cook their food on smoky *chulhas* with half-dried twigs in ill-ventilated cottages. Not having adequate toilet facilities, faecal diseases are common in India's villages and even towns. With no dependable sources of clean water, even quenching thirst is a hazard in many places. If development planning is worth its salt, it cannot be

[1] For example, both the Sixth Plan (GOI 1981: 343) and the Seventh Plan (GOI 1985: 385) mention that environmental problems in India arise due to poverty and underdevelopment on the one hand, as also the negative effects of badly planned or implemented development programmes on the other.

indifferent to these problems. However, though underdevelopment is a source of degradation of both the environment and quality of human life, it is equally clear that economic development, particularly economic growth, does not by itself prevent environmental damage any more than it can eradicate poverty.

For the same reason, planning—even central planning—for economic development too does not by itself ensure environmental concern. It is true that profit motive which spurs capitalist development, if left unregulated, tends to ignore all adverse side-effects inflicted on others and hence, environmental damage caused in the process of economic growth as well. It is also true that planning, especially socialist planning, insofar as it can take into account the totality of effects including such side-effects, can show environmental concern more naturally than free market forces. Such planning can also take into account the needs of future generations more than free market forces. Yet, in practice, socialist states hardly showed greater evidence of environmental concern than the market economies, though, of course, they showed much greater concern for meeting the basic needs of the population by pricing these at levels which the poor could afford. They also valued economic growth as a target as much as the market economies. Being almost perennially short of resources needed for investment, diverting some of it to prevent environment damage was not considered quite feasible, especially where it increased costs. After all, socialist planned economies were a part of the world economy dominated by capitalism and market forces, and they could not take the risk of adversely affecting their competitive position in the world market. Unless all countries of the world are committed to certain minimum environmental goals by signing an international environment charter and binding themselves to pursue policies consistent with it, this problem cannot be adequately solved.

The need for such a commitment by all governments arises within a country too, particularly in a federal or quasi-federal set-up. There is competition between different states within such countries to attract capital, which could lead to the 'liberalisation' of implementation of environmental and labour laws as an incentive! A certain commitment and political will to care for the environment and thereby human welfare is necessary on the part of all powers that be, even for incorporating environmental concern into planning and implementing such concern in practice. This is so both within a country and in the world at large. National planning, which incorporates state plans as well, can greatly facilitate general agreement on common goals and reduce such undesirable competition at the expense of environmental health and human welfare.

The fear that environmental concern in terms of strict pollution prevention or control may adversely affect economic growth seems to be highly exaggerated. Pollution control creates new openings for technological advance and employment opportunities, and cannot be considered as a national cost (see Royston 1979: esp. ch. 6). In fact, it is an expenditure to prevent or moderate costs imposed on the environment, which is worth incurring since greater damage can thereby be averted. We cannot save on environment costs by saving on pollution control. A study of pollution caused by the cement industry showed that costs incurred on pollution control were far less as compared to costs imposed by pollution by way of increased human and animal morbidity, and decreased agricultural productivity (Abubacker 1990). Moreover, costs of pollution control are generally marginal or moderate at the micro level, which most firms can easily afford. Even if these costs are passed on to consumers, the resulting price rise is not going to be significant, certainly not as steep as the hike in petroleum prices in 1973. If developing countries like India could absorb this hike without damaging the economy, a much less significant rise in the prices of consumer goods on account of pollution control can hardly be expected to harm the economy of either the firms or the country as a whole. A three-year study (1982–83 to 1984–85) of fifteen firms from different industries in Karnataka showed that for the bulk of observations, investment in pollution control was as low as around 1.7 per cent of total investment, and annualised pollution control costs (including depreciation and interest on fixed capital, and operating costs) were as low as around 0.2 per cent of annual turnover and around 2.1 per cent of total annualised costs (Ravichandran 1989: pp. 160–61).[2] This shows the relative magnitude involved for most of the firms. Even where the costs are likely to be significant, they can be reduced or completely

---

[2] These figures are median values in the modal quartile, the quartiles formed by dividing the entire range of values in respect of each indicator into four equal parts. The bulk of the observations (79 to 88 per cent) were located in the lowest quartiles for all the three indicators, which, therefore, turned out to be the modal quartiles.

covered by recycling wastes, or by converting pollutants into economic goods by recovering wastes in a usable form.[3]

Once anti-pollution legislation is brought into force, standards fixed and monitoring made effective, pollution control becomes an on-going process, and it may appear that planning does not have to consciously incorporate it. Yet, it is a fact of life that in India there are many firms which have not implemented pollution control measures, most of them in the small- and medium-scale sectors. Even the firms which have installed treatment plants prefer to keep them idle to save on scarce electricity. There has been some progress in the case of water pollution control, but not much in treating air pollution. Even in water pollution, the small-scale and cottage sector (such as tanneries) often find it feasible to adopt pollution control only when common or collective treatment plants are established. Treatment of municipal sewage is woefully inadequate. The disposal of solid waste and problems of noise pollution are hardly tackled. The technology for pollution treatment has to be imported in many cases, the cost of which can be brought down considerably if developed indigenously. It is particularly necessary to promote pollution prevention technologies which are built into project or plant design, instead of 'add-on' technologies which are introduced after the plants are installed. Built-in technologies are cheaper, but also require advance planning. All this can be solved only if these tasks are explicitly recognised in planning, and concrete programmes developed for effective implementation. There has been too much reliance on administrative or regulatory measures, and there is need to consider supplementary measures, such as developing economic instruments in the form of pollution charges. A use of economic instruments, whether in the form of pollution charges or environment-friendly pricing policy for natural resources, does not reduce the role of planning. A pricing policy is to be made to subserve planning goals and strategies.

Pollution control is only a small part of environmental management. In a wider context, environmental concern expresses itself in a sustainable use of all natural resources—land, water, minerals, forest, fisheries, and so on. If the rationale of planning is that economic development cannot be left completely to free market

[3] For example, see the case of GNFC (Karia 1987).

forces and should be subjected to certain broader economic, social and political values, the use of natural resources too cannot be left to free market forces and should be subjected to the same values. Only planning the use of natural resources can give expression to such values. The present use should be in the light of future needs and the costs that the present use can impose on future generations. For a rational allocation of resources, their pricing has to reflect their scarcity, both in the present and the future, or else scarce resources can be squandered. Costs of extraction and transportation to consuming centres do not reflect the scarcity of resources, certainly not *in situ* scarcity. The solution offered is to price resources which reflect not merely the direct marginal cost of production (including cost of regeneration, extraction, transport, etc.), but also marginal social costs (the costs imposed on others). In the case of exhaustible resources, apart from these two components, the price should also include marginal user cost—a measure of costs imposed on future generations by the present use of resources at the margin. The sum of these three components is called 'marginal opportunity cost' (Pearce, et al.: 167). Competitive market pricing does not ensure such prices where the marginal social costs and marginal user costs are significant, though to some extent perceived scarcity of a resource in future can influence current prices. It may be noted that marginal user cost allows for technological change that can replace scarce resources by new and relatively more abundant resources, and also the cost of developing such a technology.[4]

The concept of marginal opportunity cost (MOC) can be a useful aid in planning. Not only can it indicate the appropriate level of use of a particular resource, reconciling both economic and environmental interests, it can also be useful in evaluating development projects (Pearce and Markandya 1989: esp. 45). However, when policies or projects being evaluated involve large—and not just marginal in the sense of small—changes to the stocks of natural resources, a comparison between the value of total stock before and after the change is necessary. The word 'marginal'

[4] The formula for estimating marginal user cost (MUC) as given by Pearce et al. (1989: 171) is: $MUC = (P_B - C)/(1 + r)^T$ where P_B is the price of technology that would substitute for the resource eventually, C is the cost of extraction of the resource which will be substituted, r is the rate of discount and T is the time by which the backstop technology comes into play.

cannot therefore be rigidly interpreted only as 'small' (ibid.: 45–46). It indicates incremental changes, and the increments could be large.

Should this concept be used only for shadow-pricing in evaluating the use of resources, and not for actual pricing? No doubt, shadow-pricing of resources is normal in evaluating development projects. It could be used even in deciding whether or not the export of a particular commodity is desirable. For example, if the MOC of an exported commodity, such as mineral ore, exceeds its border price, it is clearly undesirable to export it, and its trade should be brought down to a level where its MOC and border price are equal. If, on the other hand, the border price is higher than the MOC, then exports could be stepped up (Pearce and Markandya 1989: 49). Even within a country, the same principle can be employed. If the MOC of producing the extra unit of a commodity is higher than its prevailing price, there is clearly no case for producing it. It is evident here that ecological considerations do not imply a blanket ban on further exploitation of natural resources, but the decision rests on how the MOC would compare with the price.

However, it may still be possible to produce the commodity or exploit the resource when the actual price is lower than the MOC, if the price can be raised to the level of the MOC. In this case, the MOC can serve as a basis for actual pricing. It is common knowledge now how forest wealth was squandered by pricing timber at lower than its regeneration cost so that nobody had an incentive for its regeneration. This does not mean that the 'producer' or contractor should be given a high price and be allowed to make a huge profit. The people of the country as a whole collectively are owners of natural resources, and are represented by the state in a democracy. The government should be within its right to levy high enough taxes or royalty rates, such as to absorb the difference between cost of extraction or production (including transport, marketing, etc.), and the MOC so as to discourage overexploitation of a resource. Of course, producers can be allowed to have higher prices where they regenerate resources, so that costs of regeneration are absorbed. No amount of planning for afforestation can succeed if there is an incentive for overexploitation and no incentive for regeneration. It shows how pricing policy can be used as a planning tool or as an instrument of achieving plan objectives.

We should, however, also be conscious of the limitations of

pricing policy in discouraging the consumption of precious natural resources. That a tax or levy may be passed on to consumers is not objectionable in itself if it induces them to curtail the consumption of the resource. However, this need not happen if the demand for the resource is price inelastic, or, if the price increase is only nominal or monetary and not real (relative to other prices), and/or if the incomes of consumers are increased in the meanwhile, making them absorb the price increase with ease. This is what happened in the case of petroleum prices, the increase in which was more nominal than real, considering the fact that oil prices have fallen in real terms to almost their pre-1974 levels (Newbery 1990: 80). It led to no curtailment of demand though it may have stimulated the development of fuel-saving cars. Even if fuel consumption per kilometre of vehicles may have declined, the total consumption has increased several times due to the manifold increase in the number of vehicles itself. Even the per capita consumption of petroleum increased, and not total consumption alone. In such cases a more basic policy change, even at the macro level, is necessary. No substantial economy in the use of petroleum can be expected as long as the emphasis is on private or individual transport, and not on mass or public transport. The relevance of planning should be obvious here, particularly insofar as it can overcome the limitations of price policy.

Even in other instances, it may appear that estimates of the MOC could be so high that few new investments which involve the natural environment could seem feasible. Worse still, it may be difficult even to estimate them in some cases. However, the costs imposed by negative externalities could be avoided or minimised by incorporating pollution treatment in plant design or by choosing an alternative development project which is environment-friendly. A moment's reflection will show that the cost of avoiding a negative externality such as pollution can itself be substituted for marginal external or social cost even if the former is lower. This is because once the project incorporates pollution treatment or is modified to avoid external cost, it is no longer the same project. The MOC of an environment-friendly project is expected to be lower than that of an environment-indifferent project and has a better chance of being selected in a comparative project appraisal. If, however, the former is higher in a certain case, then such a development project should not be undertaken in the present and future interests of both the environment and human welfare. Evidently, we have to search for alternatives, even alternative technologies, which make the choice of development projects with low MOC possible, and one of the tasks of planning is to promote such desirable alternatives. One point, however, should be very clear: we cannot reduce the cost of development projects by ignoring the marginal external costs or user costs or by underestimating them either internationally or otherwise. They can be reduced only by consciously taking note of all externalities and user costs, and taking steps to minimise them through due improvements or modifications in project design or devising alternatives which do so.

An example of how a development project need not be rejected in toto, and how desirable alternatives could be devised is provided by the report of a Working Group set up to assess the impact of a proposed tea plantation project in the Kodagu (Coorg) district of Karnataka (KSCST 1990).[5] The plantation was proposed on 1,800 hectares of C and D class lands which had no tree cover worth speaking of, and no adverse environmental consequences were expected by the project as originally formulated. Though no deforestation was involved directly on the lands proposed under tea, the Working Group felt that there was a distinct possibility of the deforestation of nearby *sholas* due to the influx of people who would need fuelwood. Unless there was provision to raise fuelwood to meet their needs as a part of the project, this danger could not be avoided. Second, the concerned land was used for grazing by the villagers, though the grass cover was of an inferior variety. The project had not provided for meeting the fodder needs of villagers and also the immigrant population resulting from the tea project. The Working Group, based on estimates of fodder and fuel requirements (calculated from the special studies made), recommended reducing the area proposed under tea plantation from 1,800 to 1,047 hectares, and also asked for the provision of a fuelwood plantation under 337 hectares and 416 hectares on which to raise fodder, apart from suggesting precautions against soil erosion and water pollution. At the time of writing this paper, the economic

[5] The Working Group consists of M.V. Nadkarni (Chairman), Cecil J. Saldanha, Madhav Gadgil, A.K.N. Reddy, Ramprasad, Vinod Vyasulu, Vanaja Ramprasad, S. Rajagoplan, and Ravi Puranik (Member-Secretary). It was set up by the KSCST at the instance of the Department of Ecology and Environment of the Government of Karnataka in 1989.

viability of the altered or the recommended alternative was being assessed by the plantation project in the light of prevailing tea prices and economies of scale. The point, however, is that merely to make the project economically viable we cannot ignore the environmental costs.

Incorporating environmental concern in planning has to be at both the project and policy levels. At the project level, it expresses itself in systematic environmental impact assessment (EIA) of all options involved, facilitating a choice on an informed basis. Such information is required at three distinct levels in the project design and planning process: '(a) The initial identification of potential sites and comparison of site options; (b) The evaluation of process design options; (c) The detailed assessment of the consequences of the development at the selected site' (Roberts and Roberts 1984: 280). Any EIA would require a detailed probe into all possible consequences, not only physical and biological, but also the social consequences on human welfare, both at the present time and in fufure, both near the site and elsewhere.

In project evaluation it is important to remember that a project cannot be passed merely because the estimated gain from it exceeds environmental costs. Environmental costs cannot be offset in this manner; they can be offset only by taking counter measures as a part of the project, such that the environment costs are reduced to zero or tolerable levels—measures for pollution abatement, rehabilitation and resettlement of displaced persons, etc. In other words, 'all projects yielding net benefits should be undertaken subject to the requirement that environmental damage should be zero or negative' (Pearce et al. 1990: 58).

Planning, however, does not end with EIA of projects in incorporating environmental concern. The long-term planning of policies and their implementation are equally necessary. One of the tasks of planning is to see what alternative growth strategies are feasible and what the requirements (costs) of each strategy are in terms of natural resources, particularly energy, compared with the gains expected (employment generation, poverty alleviation, growth of income, etc.). Some growth strategies may be more energy-intensive than others. There could also be alternative strategies of energy generation which may have different cost and feasibility implications. These costs should include indirect or external costs too, such as polluting effects of petrol from which lead is not removed. It is easier to control pollution generated by a factory with a definite location, but far more difficult to control dispersed pollution as in the case of leaded petrol, pesticides and fertilisers. Here again, we cannot ignore their environmental costs by ignoring them, and we have to seek and promote environment-friendly alternatives.

Another sphere where a clear policy is needed is in respect of land use. While on the one hand we bemoan deforestation, we freely permit, regularise and encourage encroachments on forests in the name of poverty alleviation and land for the poor. It is not often realised that even while intending to benefit some poor, other poor are deprived of the access to forests and the fruits thereof; besides, those who actually gain from encroachments may not even be the intended beneficiaries. Even after forty years of planning, we do not yet have a clear land use policy and planning.

There are several other spheres where policy planning in environmental interests is needed, but we do not have to go into great detail here. It should suffice to conclude with the observation that while it is hardly necessary or feasible to abandon economic growth, it is both necessary and feasible to make it meaningful and relevant to human welfare. Planning can play a crucial role in this task.

REFERENCES

Abubacker, M.H. (1990). 'Socio-Economic Impact of Pollution: A Case Study of Cement Factories in Tiruchirapalli District, Tamil Nadu,' Ph.D. Thesis submitted to Bharathidasan University, Tiruchirapalli.

Government of India (1981). *Sixth Five-Year Plan 1980–85*. Planning Commission: New Delhi.

——— (1985). *Seventh Five-Year Plan 1985–90*, vol. 2. Planning Commission: New Delhi.

Karia, V.K. (1987). 'Pollution Control', in Malcolm Adiseshiah (ed.), *Economics of Environment*, ch. 6. Lancer International; New Delhi.

KSCST (Karnataka State Council for Science and Technology) (1990). *Impact Assessment for Karnataka Tea Project*. Working Group Report (Chairman, M.V. Nadkarni) submitted to the Department of Ecology and Environment, Government of Karnataka, Bangalore.

Newbery, David (1990). 'Commodity Price Stabilisation', in Maurice Scott and Deepak Lal (eds.), *Public Policy and Economic Development: Essays in Honour of Ian Little*. Clarendon Press: Oxford.

Pearce, David and Anil Markandya (1989). 'Marginal Opportunity Cost as a Planning Concept in Natural Resource Management', in Gunter Schramm and J. Jeremy Warford, *Environmental Management and Economic Development*, Ch. 4. Published for the World Bank by Johns Hopkins University Press: Baltimore and London.

Pearce, David, Anil Markandya and Edward B. Barbier (1989). *Blue Print for a Green Economy*. Earthscan Publication: London.

Pearce, David, Edward Barbier and Anil Markandya (1990). *Sustainable Development: Economics and Environment in the Third World*. Edward Elgar, Hants: England.

Ravichandran, M. (1989). 'Economics of Pollution Prevention and Control—A Study of Industrial Pollution in Karnataka', Ph.D. Thesis at the Institute for Social and Economic Change, Bangalore, submitted to the University of Mysore.

Roberts, R.D. and T.M. Roberts (eds.) (1984). *Planning and Ecology*. Chapman and Hall: London and New York.

Royston, Michael G. (1979). *Pollution Prevention Pays*. Pergamon Press: Oxford.

14

Financing the Plans: Resource Crunch or Lack of Political Will?

ATUL SARMA

INTRODUCTION

$\mathbf{T}$he planned path of development in the framework of a mixed economy was adopted in India to pursue multiple goals. Both the public and private sectors were to function in unison to achieve a high rate of growth of the economy. Economic development in the planning process was expected to ensure better income and wealth distribution across different income classes and balanced growth across regions. The public sector was to be at a commanding height to set the right prices in the economy. Physical and financial controls were to be used to direct private sector investment consistent with macro goals and sectoral requirements. It appeared as though economic planning worked well in the country, and the size of the planned investment rose at an increasingly higher rate from plan to plan.

But the economy started reflecting an increasingly greater strain in the course of financing the successive plans. What is more, the economy displayed the severest strain in financing the plan during the period that it recorded the highest growth (i.e., in the 1980s). In the face of such a severe resource crunch, a smaller plan was favoured by some, even in official circles, restricting its scope to only the vital sectors and privatising many public enterprises which could as well be run by the private sector. Such thinking might have been inspired partly by the privatisation exercises carried out with success, at least for a while, and partly due to the rumblings in East European countries and the erstwhile Soviet Union.

Having accepted the inevitability of planning for economic development with distributive justice, this paper discusses three inter-related issues. The following section examines the changing role of different sources of financing the past plans and shows how, in the process, the economy is facing a resource crunch. In the last section the factors which have led to such a resource crunch have been discussed and an attempt made to understand the political economy that underlies the present problems of the economy.

SOURCES OF FINANCE: THEIR CHANGING ROLES

As is well-known, keeping in view the aggregate growth rate set, the total investment requirement during a plan period is worked out in a consistency frame. Although the investment that is to be made by the public and the private sectors is separately determined, the investment in the public sector is direct while the allocation in the private sector is indirect through policy instruments such as licensing, fiscal policies, monetary policies and import controls. Thus, resources have to be mobilised only to finance public sector plan outlay during a plan period.

The major sources from which public sector plan outlay is financed during a plan period are:

    (*i*) Balance from current revenue (BCR)
   (*ii*) Additional resource mobilisation (ARM)
  (*iii*) Contributions of public enterprises
  (*iv*) Market borrowings
   (*v*) Small savings
  (*vi*) Miscellaneous capital receipts
 (*vii*) External assistance
(*viii*) Deficit financing

Of these sources, the first three can be considered as own-resources of the government.

Table 1 shows the relative importance of these sources in financing public sector plan outlay during the last seven Five-Year Plans. It should be pointed out that the Table combines the first three sources under one category and treats them as own-resources,

Table 1: *Financing Pattern of Public Sector Plan Outlay Under the Five-Year Plans—Estimates (E) and Actuals (A)*
(Percentages to aggregate resources)

I. **Own-Resources** (*Balance from current revenues and contribution of public enterprises including additional resource mobilisation*)
II. **Domestic Capital Receipts**   III. **Net Inflow from Abroad**
IV. **Deficit Financing**   V. **Aggregate Resources**

		I	II	III	IV	V
First Plan	E	35.8	25.0	25.2	14.0	100
1951–52 to 1955–56	A	38.4	35.0	9.6	17.0	100
Second Plan	E	28.1	30.2	16.7	25.0	100
1956–57 to 1960–61	A	26.3	30.8	22.5	20.4	100
Third Plan	E	37.5	25.9	29.3	7.3	100
1961–62 to 1965–66	A	33.8	24.8	28.2	13.2	100
Fourth Plan	E	43.4	34.8	16.4	5.4	100
1969–70 to 1973–74	A	33.9	40.5	12.9	12.7	100
Fifth Plan	E	52.8	28.6	15.1	3.5	100
1974–75 to 1979–80	A	36.7	41.4	7.7	14.4	100
Sixth Plan	E	46.4	37.3	11.2	5.1	100
1980–81 to 1984–85	A	36.7	41.4	7.7	14.2	100
Seventh Plan	E	41.6	40.6	10.0	7.8	100
1985–86 to 1989–90	A	31.2	44.6	8.4	15.8	100

Sources: For the First to the Firth Plans, ESCAP (1983). *Integration of Tax Planning into Development Planning in the ESCAP Region* (section on India by A. Bagchi); for subsequent plans, L.K. Jha Memorial Lecture of 1988 by Shri R.N. Malhotra, Governor, Reserve Bank of India, December 1988.

while items (*iv*), (*v*) and (*vi*) are shown together as domestic capital. The Table clearly shows that own-resources of the government which should have contributed an increasingly higher share in the successive plans have come to play a much smaller role at the end of the four decades of planning. The share of own-resources in the total public sector plan outlay declined from 38.4 per cent during the First Plan to 31.3 per cent during the Seventh Plan. It may be mentioned that although it fluctuated widely during the intervening plan periods, the government's own-resources as a percentage of the total public sector plan outlay never reached the level attained during the First Plan in any subsequent period.

The Table also brings out the fact that the source which has assumed increasing importance in financing public sector plan outlay is domestic capital receipts, whose share in financing plans shot up from 35 per cent of public sector plan outlay during the First Plan period to 44.6 per cent during the Seventh Plan (although it was lower during the Second and the Third Plans than during the First Plan).

The Table further shows that the net inflow from abroad continued to play a minor role in financing Indian plans, at less than 10 per cent, except for the Second and the Third Plan periods, during which its role was quite significant. It may be added that its contribution was a little higher (12.9 per cent) than 10 per cent even during the Fourth Plan.

It can also be observed that deficit financing was resorted to in financing a significant portion of public sector plan outlay during the entire period. It did play a higher role during the First and Second Plans but declined to a lower level during the Third Plan and, since then, has tended to increase almost continuously. Deficit financing came to account for 15.8 per cent of the Seventh Plan outlay, which was the highest in the preceding five plans.

Having observed the declining importance of the government's own-resources in financing a plan, it will be useful to examine this source in greater detail.

As noted earlier, BCR is a component under the government's own-resources. The significance of BCR in financing a plan can be realised from the fact that non-plan expenditure is expected to be met out of the revenue from tax and non-tax sources with the base and the rate structure obtained in the base year of a plan, and the surplus (BCR), if any, is to be deployed for financing the subsequent plan. In other words, the built-in flexibility of the existing taxes was expected to more than meet non-plan expenditure, which also grows on account of the following factors: (i) normal increase in recurring expenditure for providing pure public goods such as maintenance of law and order, defence and administration of justice; (ii) maintenance and committed expenditure resulting from the completed projects during the preceding plan periods; (iii) interest charges due to market loans floated for financing the plans; and (iv) certain expenditure programmes which do not find a place under a plan but are considered important for one reason or another. It is apparent that maintenance and committed expenditure grows with every completed plan depending on the size of the previous plans and the composition of the projects implemented thereunder. On the other hand, interest charges increase depending on the quantum of market loans floated for financing a plan and the rate of interest stipulated on such loans. Thus, the growth of non-plan expenditure is linked to the size of plans and the composition of plan projects with a lag and the method of financing plans. But since the economy is expected to grow as a result of higher investment, a tax structure responsive to income changes should be able to meet not only growing non-plan expenditure, but also to release a part for financing public sector plan outlay in the subsequent period.

In reality, this has not happened. Beginning from 1979–80, the revenue account of the Government of India has consistently shown a negative balance. The deficit on the revenue account stood at as much as 2.8 per cent of the GDP of the country in 1987–88. This means that even expenditure of a housekeeping nature has now to be met by borrowed funds or by money creation.

DEFICITS DESPITE INCOME GROWTH

What is important to note is that this type of situation emerged during the Sixth and the Seventh Plan periods when growth targets set by the respective plans were achieved. What is more, the growth rate recorded during the 1980s was much higher (4.79 per cent per annum during 1980–81 to 1987–88 at 1980–81 prices) than that in the preceding three decades. Even so, the tax revenue of the union government grew at the rate of 16.59 per cent per annum while its revenue expenditure rose at the rate of 19.14 per cent per annum in the 1980s. The result has been growing revenue deficit, even in an environment of impressive growth of the national economy.

As regards additional resource mobilisation, which is another component of the government's own-resources, it can be stated that the actual ARM has been exceeding at varying degrees the targets set in all the seven plans. Nevertheless, the government continued to rely heavily on indirect taxes. It could not even attain targets of direct and indirect taxes set for the Seventh Plan in the long-term fiscal policy (LTFP), as can be seen from Table 2.

The importance of indirect taxes in the country's fiscal structure

Table 2: *Actuals and Targets of Direct and Indirect Taxes in LTFP*
(As per cent of GDP)

	1985–86		1986–87		1987–88		1988–89		1989–90	
	A/c	LTFP	A/c	LTFP	A/c	LTFP	RE	LTFP	BE	LTFP
Tax Revenue (net of state share)	8.7	7.8	8.9	8.2	9.1	8.7	9.0	9.2	9.6	9.4
(i) Direct taxes	1.5	1.5	1.5	1.7	1.3	1.8	1.5	2.0	1.5	2.1
(ii) Indirect taxes	7.1	6.3	7.4	6.5	7.7	6.9	7.5	7.2	8.1	7.3

Source: Government of India. *Economic Survey 1989–90*, p. 82.
Notes: RE: Revised Estimate.
BE: Budget Estimate.
A/c: Actuals.

is also noticeable in their growth performance. For example, while direct taxes like personal income tax and corporation tax recorded a growth at the rate of 9.1 and 12.9 per cent per annum, respectively, during 1980–81 through 1989–90 (BE), indirect taxes like union excise duties and customs grew at the rate of 14.1 and 21.0 per cent per annum, respectively, during the same period.

Similarly, the other component of own-resources, i.e., contributions of public undertakings (internal and extra-budgetary resources) significantly fell short of projections given in the LTFP document in every year of the Seventh Plan period, except 1985–86.

On the other hand, both market borrowings and budgetary deficit far exceeded the targets projected in the LTFP as can be seen in Table 3.

It may be pointed out that market borrowings as a source of financing a plan have two important consequences. First, market borrowings, when used in large measure to finance public sector outlay, may crowd out private sector investment thus affecting overall growth. Second, market borrowings is a more expensive instrument of financing a plan. It also affects income distribution adversely, particularly when interest payment is to be made with revenue collected through indirect taxes.

Deficit financing, which has been used liberally to finance public

Table 3: *Actual Market Borrowings and Budgetary Deficits vis-à-vis their Projection in the LFTP*

(As per cent of GDP)

	1985–86		1986–87		1987–88		1988–89		1989–90	
	A/c	LTFP	A/c	LTFP	A/c	LTFP	RE	LTFP	BE	LTFP
Marketing borrowing	2.0	2.1	2.0	1.6	1.9	1.5	2.0	1.5	1.8	1.5
Budgetary deficit	2.0	1.3	3.0	1.2	1.9	1.1	2.2	1.0	1.8	0.9

Source: Government of India. *Economic Survey 1989–90*, p. 82.

sector outlay throughout the planning era, has obvious price implications. In the ultimate analysis, it makes income distribution adverse and hurts the poor more through its price effects.

The above discussion drives home the point that with every successive plan, the country experienced a greater resource crunch in that the government's own-resources came to play a diminishing role. Faced with a situation like this, the country started relying more heavily on sources like market borrowings which further erodes BCR through interest liabilities, in addition to its adverse impact on income distribution and deficit financing with its obvious consequences on general prices and income distribution.

THE POLITICAL PROCESS BEHIND THE RESOURCE CRUNCH

Having shown the extent of the resource crunch the economy has faced while financing public sector plan outlay even in the period of higher growth, this section attempts to understand the process leading to such a situation, as also the forces underlying such a process.

We start with the proposition that the state represents various interest groups, and that it is the attempt at reconciliation of their conflicting interests which eventually leads to the allocation of public sector outlay, the appropriation of economic surplus for state purpose as well as to other economic interventions. We attempt to explain, illustratively, the problem of the resource crunch in the economy following this proposition.

Public sector plan outlay directed to agriculture and related activities, including irrigation and flood control, in the past three decades is shown in Table 4. It shows that the share of agriculture and related activities in the total public sector outlay ranged from 15.2 per cent (Seventh Plan) to 27.0 per cent (Annual Plan). Agriculture production also more than doubled during this period.

Table 4: *Plan Outlay on Agriculture and Related Activities (1961–90)* *(in per cent)*

	Agriculture and Allied Sectors*	Irrigation and Flood Control	Total
Third Plan 1961–66	12.7	7.8	20.5
Annual Plans 1966–69	16.7	7.1	23.8
Fourth Plan 1969–74	14.7	8.6	23.3
Fifth Plan 1974–79	12.3	9.8	22.1
Annual Plan 1979–80	16.4	10.6	27.0
Sixth Plan 1980–85	5.8	12.5	18.3
Seventh Plan 1985–90	5.8	9.4	15.2

Source: Government of India, *Economic Survey 1989–90*, pp. 41–45.
Note: * Excluding Rural Development and Special Areas Programme.

It can be observed that although the allocation of plan outlay for agricultural development was far less than the sector's contribution to national income, the farming community benefited from plan investment and other policy initiatives. It may be further stated that the direct benefits from such plan investment accrued particularly to the landed peasantry rather than to landless labour. They also benefited from various input subsidies such as water, power, fertilisers and concessional credits. Further, they succeeded in making land reform legislations infructuous. But the incremental income that resulted from productivity and price rises remained outside the tax net.

It can be argued that the large landowning peasantry which is increasingly being organised, particularly in the more developed regions of the country, shares decison-making powers directly or indirectly. The interest of industrialists in having access to cheap labour which is possible only with increasing supply of wage goods might have made it less difficult for policy slants to favour the landed peasantry.

Another sector which has not yielded the expected rate of returns on public sector investment is public enterprises. In its strategy to ensure commanding height, the public sector established and invested in a large number of public undertakings producing and selling goods as also rendering services. The total capital employed on 222 non-departmental public enterprises of the union government alone stood at Rs. 67,535 crores as on 31 March 1989. But the net profit (after tax) to the capital employed rose from $(-)1.1$ per cent in 1980–81 to a mere 4.4 per cent in 1988–89.

It was reasonable to expect that the public enterprises on which such a large investment was made over the years, apart from servicing several goals, would contribute to the public exchequer, which, in turn, would facilitate carrying ahead larger and larger public sector plan investment for economic development.

There are many reasons why public enterprises have been ailing. Two important amongst them are:

1. Public enterprises which require flexibility and continual innovations for their efficiency and performance are being managed as extended arms of the government bureaucracy which is generally deficient in professional and managerial acumen and training. Government bureaucracy being deeply entrenched in administrative and decision-making machinery could see to it that the public enterprises remained as havens for their occasional retreats particularly as escapes from their low-key placements.

2. Big industries and some other interest groups in collusion with government bureaucracy usually succeeded in gearing production, investment and pricing decisions of public enterprises to better subserve *their* interests. The result is there for all to see: public enterprises as a whole, instead of contributing to the country's resources to facilitate increasingly larger plan investment, are a dead-weight to the public exchequer.

In the past four decades the structure of the GDP has changed substantially. The decline in the share of the primary sector was accompanied by an increase in both the secondary and tertiary sectors, but by 1988–89 the tertiary sector came to claim a share (38.3 per cent) much larger than that of the secondary sector (26.9 per cent) and even of the primary sector (34.8 per cent). The tertiary sector undoubtedly expanded in response to the need to provide important services such as transport, communication, banking and insurance to both the primary and secondary sectors. It also expanded considerably as a result of the expansion of public administration and defence and other services that go for final consumption.

In addition, the tertiary sector must have been associated with a large income in white or black shades from speculative activities arising out of shortage situations in some sectors and many government interventions in the form of physical control such as rationing of goods in short supply and issuance of permits and licences. The generation of incomes of this nature must have found an outlet in speculative real estate deals. It is plausible that such incomes have assumed a large magnitude in the Indian economy. What is important to note is that all such incomes are possibly outside the tax net. Again, a part of the income originating in the supply of services for final consumption could not have been subjected to income tax.

The point is that when a large chunk of income generation takes place in a parallel economy and tax is evaded thereon, income tax cannot but be income inelastic. In fact, despite the reasonably high growth of the economy in the 1980s, the buoyancy of personal income tax was very low. One per cent increase in the GDP resulted in only 0.49 per cent increase in revenue from personal income tax. Large-scale tax evasion in the largest sector of the economy may be because of poor implementation of tax laws which, by itself, may be the result of collusion of tax gatherers with tax evaders, and because of loopholes in tax laws by design or by accident.

Coming to the secondary sector, a distinction between large, small and tiny or informal sector industries may be useful. Large-scale industries profited in many different ways. They operated in a seller's market for a long time because of protection. Many of them pre-empted possible competition by cornering licences. They obtained import permits, gained access to credit from public sector financial institutions, as also to public sector intermediate goods. They also maintained their relative strength in the domestic market by collaborating with multinational corporations.

Despite all this, the large-scale sector cannot be said to be buoyant. The registered sector which also includes small-scale industries accounted for only 13.2 per cent of the GDP in 1986–87. What is more, corporation tax did not show any buoyancy, probably because it provided for a large number of exemptions. In the 1980s, 1 per cent increase in the GDP led to a rise of only 0.99 per cent in revenue from corporation tax. It may also be mentioned that the present practice of treating net profit as a tax base is not particularly conducive to improving operational efficiency. In sum, it may be observed that large-scale industries with their clout in the decision-making process succeed in extracting many concessions and policy initiatives favouring them.

Historically, the small-scale sector was assigned a specific role in the economic development of the country on account of some of its important advantages like low capital intensity and high employment potential. In the Second Five-Year Plan it was clearly recognised that the small-scale sector would be engaged in producing wage goods that would be required in the economy. Accordingly, many policy instruments were adopted to develop this sector. But broadly speaking, small-scale industries that were linked with large houses in terms of ownership or in terms of production/distribution linkages were found to perform better than those not so linked. To that extent, concessions meant for the small-scale sectors benefited large industrialists eventually, and thus revenue sacrificed by the government provided an outlet for unintended quarters.

The tiny or informal sector which chronically suffers from market and technological constraints is probably not associated with the problem of tax evasion.

Coming back to the larger industrial sector, it can be observed that it is not only direct taxes on income which is not income responsive, but even the indirect taxes like union excise duty on commodities of this sector are not income elastic. In the 1980s, an increase of 1 per cent increase in the GDP led to a rise of only 0.98 per cent in the revenue from union excise duties. Such poor income responsiveness of union excise duties can be explained as follows: Because of the prevalence of differential tax rates across a large number of commodity groups combined with tax exemptions for certain similar commodity groups produced in the small-scale sector, there is wide scope for tax evasion. Poor implementation and loopholes in tax laws could be other reasons. In addition, a limited market for many industrial goods resulting from highly skewed distribution of purchasing power might have affected tax potentials.

In the light of the above discussion, it can be argued that the resource crunch as has been experienced in the Indian economy has been the product of a complex resolution of conflicting interests of various interest groups. In the process, large incomes accruing to the landed peasantry on account of productivity and price rises are not subject to income tax. Further, a large amount of subsidies benefit them. Even if the rate of return on capital employed in the public sector enterprises is dismally low, no serious attempt is made to free them from bureaucratic clutches. Rent-seeking activities arising from physical controls and shortage situations and speculative investment on real estate feed on each other. Large incomes arising out of them escape taxes and thus swell black money. Middle and high income groups have succeeded in raising the exemption limit of income tax, extracted a large number of tax-saving incentives and retained the benefit of tax assessment on an individual basis rather than on the basis of combined incomes of couples. Similarly, taxation on company and corporation incomes with net income as the base and a number of concessions and exemptions leave scope for tax avoidance and evasion. All this has rendered both personal and corporation taxes income inelastic. Thus, direct taxes have failed to syphon-off a part of incremental income into the public exchequer.

Although indirect taxes play a far more significant role in resource mobilisation, multiplicity of tax rates, differentiated tax rates by scale of production, concessions and exemptions and, of course, poor tax administration and loopholes in tax laws provide wide scope for tax evasion. Thus, even with the overwhelming importance of indirect taxes, they (at least union excise duties) are not income elastic.

What follows is that the tax structure requires a total overhauling so as to syphon-off a part of the incremental income for public sector investment. This would require hard decisions as regards widening the tax base, simplication and rationalisation of tax laws, eliminating or at least minimising various concessions and exemptions, streamlining tax administration, etc. Similarly, public sector undertakings have to be reorganised to instil innovations, flexibility and accountibility. But the question remains: Given the configuration of various interest groups, are such drastic tax reforms feasible?

15

The Capital Market in India

R.H. PATIL

The capital market plays a crucial role in all modern economies by enabling major borrowing entities, viz., the government and the corporate sector, to raise funds through securities and provide facilities for trading in such securities. The capital market is, therefore, an integral part of any sophisticated financial system. Prima facie, the role that the capital market is expected to play in a planned economy should be limited. However, this is not particularly true in the context of Indian planning as it does not formulate a strait-jacket investment plan for the private corporate sector. Although the licensing system, to some extent, influences the direction and volume of investment flow in different sectors/industries, the actual fructification of investments in the private sector depends primarily on market demand conditions and the framework of incentives as governed by cost–price relationships. Since the early 1980s the Indian economy has been increasingly liberalised. The rigour of the licensing system has been reduced and the government has minimised the extent of physical and discretionary controls. The capital market is also being assigned an increasingly greater role. The government policy framework is being modified to provide incentives aimed at rapid development of the capital market. The financial institutions are also encouraging the growth of the capital market as they are facing resource constraints and are, therefore, not in a position to meet the resource needs of all the borrowers. The institutions are keen that borrowers with better credit rating increasingly tap the capital market for the bulk of their resource requirements. It is in this context that the growth of the capital market is crucial to the growth of the corporate sector in our country.

Until recently, government securities dominated the capital market of our country. Since the early 1980s, the securities floated by the corporate sector have gained in importance in relation to government securities. The market value of central and state government securities listed on the stock exchanges amounted to Rs. 65,691 crores as against Rs. 70,521 crores of the corporate sector at the end of March 1990. Government securities are absorbed primarily by institutional investors like commercial banks, provident funds, trusts and insurance companies, as they are expected to invest a part of their aggregate resources in such securities for statutory reasons. Yet, however large and growing the market for government securities might be, it is not of much interest to study as its growth in India would continue to depend on statutory provisions. As far as common investors are concerned, investment and trading in the capital market are of prime importance only with regard to the corporate securities. Therefore, in what follows, the discussion is restricted to the functioning of the capital insofar as it is related to corporate securities.

The Companies Act of 1850 introduced the concept of limited liability company and the era of joint stock companies was ushered into the country. India has had a long history of stock exchanges, with the first stock exchange in the country starting its operations in Bombay in 1875. However, it is only since the beginning of the present decade that stock exchanges have begun to emerge as major mobilisers of funds by way of equity and debentures. This process of capital market transformation had, however, begun after the mid-1970s when a spate of issues by multinational corporations (MNCs) operating in India was made, providing a major impetus to the equity market. These issues offered an opportunity for instant price appreciation (as they were issued much below their market prices), attractive returns on investment, and created a new awareness among the small investors for industrial securities. The strengthening of the growth process in the economy since the beginning of 1980s and the major policy liberalisations introduced by the government have sustained the dynamism of the capital market and led to its widening and deepening.

GROWTH OF THE PRIMARY MARKET

For the sake of convenience, the capital market can be divided into two major components. The first is the primary market which enables the corporate sector to raise funds directly from the investors in exchange for its securities. The second component is the secondary market which lends liquidity to corporate securities by providing facilities for trading in corporate securities. There is, interestingly, a reverse umbilical linkage between the two segments of the capital market as it is the secondary market which influences the level of activity in the primary market. When the already issued securities are traded and appreciate in price, demand for new securities becomes buoyant, thereby stimulating activity on the primary market. Capital raised through the primary market is one of the important indicators of the growth of the capital market. Between 1985–86 and 1989–90, the total capital mobilised through new issues (i.e., excluding bonus shares) registered more than a four-fold increase from about Rs. 2,096 crores to Rs. 10,211 crores. This includes bonds raised by public sector undertakings. There has, however, been a sharp decline in 1990–91, as can be seen from the provisional figures given in Table 1. The total amount raised from the capital market declined sharply from Rs. 5,717 crores during 1989–90 to Rs. 2,267 crores during 1990–91. Equity capital accounted for Rs. 622 cores, convertible debentures for Rs. 1,490 crores, and non-convertible debentures for Rs. 154 crores. Various uncertainties in the policy areas and the industrial environment may have contributed to this decline. The Gulf and balance of payments crises appear to have caused a postponement in the plans entering the market, resulting in a decline in capital raised. Further, a large portion of the capital raised during 1989–90 was through mega issues while in 1990–91, there were hardly any mega issues. This could be another reason for the decline in capital raised, especially through debentures.

GROWTH OF DEBENTURES AND BONDS

Prior to 1980, the annual level of debenture issues was small, in the range of Rs. 10 crores to Rs. 40 crores. Over the period 1981–82 to 1983–84, funds mobilised through debentures grew sharply from Rs. 290 crores to Rs. 450 crores. There was an accelerated growth in the debenture market during the subsequent years. Composition of new issues reflected a distinct investor preference in favour of debentures. Funds raised by way of debentures amounted to

Table 1: Resources Raised Through the Capital Market
(Rs. crores)

	5th Plan 1974-75 to 1978-79	6th Plan 1980-81 to 1984-85	Seventh Plan						
			1985-86	1986-87	1987-88	1988-89	1989-90*	Total*	1990-91*
Equity preference	441 23	2570 20	898 1	1008 1	1103 7	1016 4	1052 8	5077 21	622 1
Convertible debentures	87	2100	85	1069	527	1743	4249	7673	1490
Non-Convertible debentures	–	–	758	487	137	390	408	2180	154
Total	**551**	**4690**	**1742**	**2565**	**1774**	**3153**	**5717**	**14951**	**2267**
PSU bonds	–	–	354	1791	2739	2498	4494†	11876	4933†
Grand Total	551	4690	2096	4356	4513	5651	10211	26827	7199

* Provisional   † Budget Estimates.

Rs. 4,656 cores in 1989–90 (Table 1). The tilt in favour of the debentures was undoubtedly the result of capital market responses to policy changes with regard to the terms and conditions of non-convertible debenture (NCD) issues. In the light of the recommendations of the Reserve Bank of India (RBI) Committee on Secondary Markets for Debentures (Pai Committee), return on NCDs was stepped up to 15 per cent. The three all-India investment institutions, viz., Unit Trust of India (UTI), GIC and Life Insurance Corporation (LIC) offer buy-back facilities as per the recommendations of the Pai Committee.

An interesting development in the debenture market in 1985–86 was the entry of the public sector companies into the bond market. These bonds carried income and wealth tax concessions. A beginning was when these enterprises raised a small amount of Rs. 354 crores in 1985–86. Thereafter, the public sector enterprises were permitted to raise a substantial amount of resources through the capital market. Funds raised through these bonds aggregated Rs. 4,933 crores in 1990–91. It may be noted that even when funds raised by the private corporate sector tended to decline, as in 1987–88 and 1990–91, PSU bonds continued to increase.

The public sector bonds are offering relatively higher returns than returns on similar types of instruments issued by private corporate entities. Attractive returns, coupled with the status enjoyed by public sector companies in the minds of average investors, put the public sector bonds in an advantageous position. Public sector banks are also giving preferential treatment to such public sector bonds. In several cases, the public sector banks absorbed the bulk of or the entire issues of some of the public sector bonds to eventually sell them to investors. The State Bank of India (SBI) regularly quotes bid and offer prices for some of the public sector bonds, and facilities for buy/sell transactions are available at a number of SBI branches.

SECONDARY MARKET

At present there are nineteen stock exchanges in the country. The Bombay Stock Exchange (BSE), the largest in terms of market capitalisation, was established in 1875. The stock exchanges are fairly well dispersed geographically in different parts of the country. In comparison with the markets of the US and Japan, the Indian capital market is relatively small. The USA with 6,727 listings had market capitalisation of US $3,506 billion as on 31 December 1989, while Japan with 2,019 listings had market capitalisation of US $4,393 billion. Among the emerging markets, South Korea with a market capitalisation of US $141 billion and Taiwan of US $237 billion were bigger than that of India, which has a market capitalisation of only US $27 billion (Table 2).

Table 2: *Selected Securities Markets (As on 31 December 1989)*

	Mature Markets				Emerging Markets			
	USA	UK	Japan	Canada	India	Brazil	South Korea	Taiwan
1. No. of stock exchanges	12	6	7	5	18	9	1	NA
2. OTC* markets	Yes	Yes	Yes	Yes	No	Yes	–	–
3. No. of listings	6727	2015	2019	1146	6000	592	626	181
4. Market capitalisation (US$ billion)	3506	827	4393	291	27†	44	141	237

Source: *The Wardley Guide to the World Securities Markets* (Euro Money Publication), and Quarterly Reports, International Finance Corporation, Washington.
* OTC = Over-the-Counter
† BSE only

Among the stock exchanges in the country, the BSE accounts for almost 70 per cent of the average daily trading turnover. In terms of market capitalisation, it accounts for about 89 per cent of the Indian market capitalisation. There are around 2,787 registered brokers on the stock exchanges, of which around 1,882 are reported to be active. Commensurate with its trading activity, the BSE has the largest number of active brokers.

GROWTH PATTERN OF LISTED SECURITIES

About one-third of the total number of public limited companies in the country are listed on the stock exchanges. The number of listed companies increased from 1,125 in 1946 to 1,203 in 1961 and further to 5,968 in 1990. The number of share and debenture issues of the listed companies increased from 1,506 in 1946 to 2,111 in 1961 and further to 8,289 in 1990. The paid-up capital of the listed companies increased from Rs. 270 crores in 1946 to Rs. 753 crores in 1961 and further to Rs. 2,614 crores in 1975. By 1990, this had risen to Rs. 27,750 crores. In 1988, the paid-up equity capital of listed companies constituted around 90 per cent of the paid-up equity capital of about 14,000 non-government public limited companies.

As shown in Table 3, market capitalisation of listed companies also rose from Rs. 970 crores in 1946 to Rs. 1,292 crores in 1961 and further to Rs. 70,521 crores in 1990. Comparing the growth rates of the number of listed companies and the paid-up capital with that of market capitalisation, it is reasonable to conclude that the capital appreciation was higher in the 1980s than in the preceding years. In relation to a country's national income, the market capitalisation continues to remain small as compared to the similar

Table 3: *Growth Pattern of Listed Stock*

As at December End	1946	1961	1975	1988	1990
1. No. of listed cos.	1,125	1,203	1,852	5,841	5,968
2. No. of issues of listed cos.	1,506	2,111	3,230	7,694	8,289
3. Paid-up capital of listed cos. (Rs crores)	270	753	2,614	21,465	27,750
4. Market value of paid-up capital of listed cos. (Rs crores)	970	1,292	3,273	51,379	70,521
5. Paid-up capital per listed co. (Rs lakhs)	24	63	141	367	465
6. Market value of paid-up capital per listed co. (Rs lakhs)	86	107	177	880	1,182

Source: Official Directory of the Bombay Stock Exchange.

ratios noted in the case of the mature markets and some of the emerging markets such as Malaysia, Hong Kong and Singapore.

The structure and market-wise pattern of listed stocks shows that the aggregate capital of listed companies was Rs. 27,750 crores, of which equity was Rs. 12,691 crores and preference capital Rs. 173 crores. The debenture capital outstanding was Rs. 14,886 crores, which is larger than equity capital. In terms of the total listed capital, the relative proportion of equity, preference and debenture capital was 45.7 per cent, 0.7 per cent and 53.6 per cent, respectively. The total listed capital of Rs. 27,750 crores of 8,289 listed companies was accounted for by 6,360 equity, 685 preference and 1,244 debenture issues.

The market-wise distribution pattern of listed companies as on 31 December 1986 is shown in Table 4. Out of 4,774 listed companies as on December 1986, 2,729 were listed on only one exchange, 1,305 on two, 465 on three, and 149 on four stock exchanges. Only four companies were listed on ten or more stock exchanges.

Table 4: *Number of Listings*

Listed On	No. of Cos. Listed	
	Dec. 1985—Dec. 1986	
1. Exchange	2,892	2,729
2. Exchanges	909	1,305
3. Exchanges	307	465
4. Exchanges	94	149
5. Exchanges	27	54
6. Exchanges	–	26
7. Exchanges	4	7
8. Exchanges	2	5
9. Exchanges	2	–
10. Exchanges	2	3
11. Exchanges	1	1
	4,240	4,744

COMPOSITION OF SECURITIES

As already noted, the Bombay Stock Exchange is the largest in the country and can be reasonably taken as a barometer indicating the direction and level of activity in the capital market. The security-wise composition of listed stocks of joint stock companies on the BSE is provided in Table 5. The proportion of equity and preference capital to total listed capital was around 92 per cent in 1961; it declined to 87 per cent in 1970, 77 per cent in 1980, 57 per cent in 1985 and further to 43 per cent in 1990. The continuous decline in the proportion of equity capital is indicative of the growth of the debenture issues and the increasing number of jumbo debenture issues on the market during the 1980s.

Table 5: *BSE: Paid-up Value of Securities*
(Rs crores)

At at 31 December	Equity	Preference	Debenture	Total
1961	295	56	31	381
	(77)	(15)	(8)	(100)
1970	852	123	141	1116
	(76)	(11)	(13)	(100)
1980	2114	145	671	2930
	(72)	(5)	(23)	(100)
1985	3764	108	3008	6880
	(55)	(2)	(44)	(100)
1988	8077	88	9740	17905
	(45)	(0.5)	(54.4)	(100)
1990	10426	89	13723	24238
	(43)	(0.4)	(56.6)	(100)

Note: Figures in brackets are percentage totals.

MARKET TURNOVER

The trading volume of securities on the secondary market is a useful indicator of the level of activity on the stock market. The annual turnover figures for the BSE are given in Table 6.

The first ten companies on the BSE which recorded the highest market turnover during 1988 are listed in Table 7. These ten companies alone accounted for over half of the turnover on the BSE. This is indicative of the high concentration of trading activity in a limited number of companies.

To develop a broad-based and active capital market it is necessary to create markets in other listed shares. This could be achieved

Table 6: *Growth in Volume of Trade on BSE*
(Rs crores)

1984–85	1985–86	1986–87	1987–88	1988–89	1989–90
4604	6952	13692	7912	20562	29385

Table 7: *Trade Volume of Ten Market Leaders (April 1989–March 1990)*

Name of the Company	Amount (in Rs crores)
1. Tata Iron & Steel Co. Ltd.	4051
2. Associated Cement Companies Ltd.	2808
3. Tata Engineering & Locomotive Co. Ltd.	2045
4. Reliance Industries Ltd.	2006
5. Bombay Dyeing & Manufacturing Co. Ltd.	1100
6. Hindustan Aluminium Corporation Ltd.	895
7. Bajaj Auto Ltd.	804
8. Tata Tea Ltd.	788
9. Grasim Industries Ltd.	672
10. Century Enka Ltd.	640

through appropriate investor education with the help of investment analysts and advisers as in other countries. A number of journals and newspapers are attempting to guide investors through their analysis on profitability prospects of different industries and companies. However, much needs to be done to encourage the emergence of qualified investment advisers, both by the stock exchange authorities and the Securities and Exchange Board of India (SEBI), by starting a system of granting recognition to qualified individuals and firms keen to be enrolled as investment advisers.

GEOGRAPHICAL SPREAD OF INVESTORS

Some of the studies on the spatial distribution of investors have pointed out that the major population of investors is concentrated in cities, particularly in a few metropolitan centres. Thus, over 50 per cent of the shareholdings are concentrated in three major metropolitan centres: Bombay (35 per cent), Delhi (9 per cent) and Calcutta (10 per cent) (Gupta 1987: 19–22).[1] Even if we take into account a few more urban centres like Ahmedabad and Madras, nearly two-thirds of the investor population is located in large cities. It is only during the last few years that an attempt has been made to tap savings from prosperous rural centres. An occupation-wise analysis of shareholdings indicates that major investors are professionals, salary earners and the self-employed. The spread of securities among other sections of investors such as rich farmers is extremely limited.

Thus, the culture of industrial securities has not spread geographically to all sections of society which have large saving potential. Efforts are, therefore, necessary to widen and deepen the market for industrial securities by covering semi-urban and prosperous rural centres and such major savers as rich farmers, doctors, lawyers and other self-employed people. Therefore, it is necessary to spread retail investment banking outlets through which potential investors can purchase industrial securities.

In countries like the USA, UK and Japan, there has been tremendous growth in financial services and investment banking, both with regard to the variety and quality of services and geographical spread. Stock broking companies and investment banking institutions like Meryll Lynch have spread their network to all places where large clusters of investors are located. These organisations offer broking services to institutions as well as individual investors and sell securities to clients over the counter. These investment bankers also manage security issues and are able to successfully sell them because of their wide branch network. These organisations are backed by investment research in the performance of corporate entities and mutual funds, and are manned by professionals in different areas of investment banking as also retail banking. They offer counselling services to clients and also provide portfolio management services.

As a first step in the direction of developing markets for industrial securities, it is desirable that banks and their investment subsidiaries encourage the growth of the bond market in the country by quoting bid/offer prices regularly in all major centres of the country. Investors located in the rural and semi-urban areas need to be initiated, in the beginning, into safe investments that fetch a regular and attractive rate of return. From this point of view, debentures/

[1] See L.C. Gupta (1987). *Shareholders' Survey: Geographic Distribution.* Manas: Delhi.

bonds of public and private sector companies would be the most suitable mode of investment for investors in semi-urban and prosperous rural areas.

To facilitate sale/purchase transactions, it is necessary to simplify the existing transfer arrangements and the physical movement of the transfer documents and debenture certificates to and from the investors to the company. To ensure quick, safe and less cumbersome systems of transfer of ownership of securities, a book entry system could be introduced. As a first step, perhaps, all the bonds being transacted by the bank may be held in its custody and the concerned bank should give the investors appropriate receipts stating that the bank is holding, on behalf of the investors, a specified number of bonds in custody. Only the investors who are keen to hold physical custody of the bonds may be given actual delivery of the bonds. Through effective counselling, investors may be persuaded not to insist on physical delivery of bonds as it involves undue expense and time delays in completing the process of transfer. It should not be difficult to develop confidence among the investors in this new system as they already have faith in the integrity and security of the public sector banks.

OVER-THE-COUNTER MARKET

Of the nineteen stock exchanges in the country, only five exchanges are active with the BSE now accounting for around two-thirds of the aggregate transactions on all stock exchanges. The trading on the BSE sets the tone for all the other stock exchanges. The dominance of the BSE is evident from the fact that prices of equities of companies listed even on other major stock exchanges are influenced by the BSE and any gap in the supply of and the demand for securities in any market is resolved with the help of dealers operating on the BSE. For instance, the price of the equity of a company located near Madras should normally be influenced mainly by trading on the Madras Stock Exchange (MSE). In practice, however, the BSE not only influences the prices of the MSE but the problem of a gap in demand or supply on the MSE is also often resolved through arbitrage transactions vis-à-vis the BSE. Such a situation is not peculiar to India alone. Even in the

US, the New York Stock Exchange (NYSE) dominates trading on other exchanges and accounts for the bulk of aggregate security trading in the US.

The Patel Committee, and prior to that the Pai Committee, recommended the opening of stock exchanges in a phased manner in all centres with a population of half a million or more. Prima facie, this appears to be an attractive proposal. But there are forty-four cities with a population of half a million or more in the country as per the 1991 Census. Opening stock exchanges in all such centres would be an expensive proposition. A stock exchange at a new place involves substantial fixed and variable costs in setting up and maintaining the facilities (including salaries of the minimum staff required). Given the small investor population at such centres, the volume of business that would be generated after the establishment of a stock exchange might not yield adequate revenue in the form of brokerage income, listing fees, etc. Such new stock exchanges are not likely to become financially viable for several years.

In this context it should be noted that stock exchanges are essentially auction markets and the level of their efficiency is determined by the number of buyers and sellers that could be brought together in the trading hall and the volume of business they would transact. Thinly traded markets are rarely efficient auction markets. Continuity in price formation and the narrowness of the spread between bid and offer prices cannot be ensured in thinly traded markets. It is for this very reason that a sizeable part of the business on other stock exchanges converges on the BSE on account of the large profits in arbitrage business.

A more economic way of taking the markets closer to the investors would be by linking such cities through dedicated tele-communication lines with major stock exchanges and arranging for a continuous display of prices as they form on the major stock exchanges. The dealers may be granted one or more teleprinter lines through which they could execute buy/sell orders with the help of their associate brokers on major stock exchanges. Although some elements of the transaction costs would be higher due to such an arrangement, the prices could still be fair to the investors. If it is possible to match buy/sell orders locally, the transactions can be completed at a price fair to both parties without involving a major stock exchange. The markets can be spread geographically in all major urban centres at less cost than by setting up new stock exchanges. With the help of modern technology and computer linkages, markets can be formed and made more efficient even without bringing buyers and sellers into physical proximity or contact.

A better geographical spread of markets can be brought about by developing an over-the-counter (OTC) markets in India. The OTC market of National Security Dealers Association in the USA would serve as good model for the purpose. The OTC market in the USA has made it possible to link all the security dealers and form a national market through National Security Dealers Automated Quotations (NASDAQ) arrangements. A number of market-makers continually quote their bid/offer prices to which all dealers have access. The best prices are formed as a result of continuous interaction among several market-makers' quotations. Since the OTC market is more flexible than the NYSE in its rules of listing and trading, several issues first get listed on the OTC market before they graduate to the NYSE. Several prominent securities are listed both on the OTC market and the NYSE, and many dealers operate on both markets. As a result, prices on the OTC market are quite competitive and the spreads are also narrow.

Instead of opening too many stock exchanges in India, an OTC market should be developed on a priority basis. The SEBI may formulate suitable regulations to govern trade on the OTC market to ensure that this market functions in an orderly fashion and the investors' interests are fully protected. As in the US, several small or unproven issues may be first listed on the OTC market on the condition that a designated dealer makes a market in it. At early stages such market-makers may be allowed flexibility through slightly higher spreads between bid and offer prices. The establishment of an OTC market would also help the stock exchanges to become more efficient markets. As in the US, an umbilical linkage may be established between the two markets so that good securities also become available to the investors operating through the OTC market. Recently, the financial institutions, in particular the Industrial Credit and Investment Corporation of India and Unit Trust of India, have promoted an OTC exchange which will initially focus on small greenfield companies. The operational modalities and policies governing their operations are being worked out. Once the OTC exchange commences its operations it holds out considerable promise for spreading the equity cult across the nation.

16

India in the World Economy: Challenges and Prospects in the Nineties

SUMITRA CHISHTI

INDIA'S PERFORMANCE IN THE WORLD CONTEXT

The purpose of this paper is to view India in the world economy and the issues that it would have to tackle in the context of developments in the world economy in the coming years.

With its large population and size, India has periodically attracted the attention of the world. In fact, its experiments with democracy with universal adult franchise, planned economic development and a non-aligned foreign policy have been a subject of both appreciation and criticism internationally.

In the field of economic achievement, India has not been a favoured country among the commentators. It is widely reported that the Indian economic planning strategy has not been effective in raising growth rates and in its poverty alleviation programmes. As a perceptive student of the Indian economy put it, 'India has regressed nearly in every major indicator in the world economy as a whole and particularly among the Third World countries' (Patel 1985). In this context, it is of significance to examine the performance of India in the 1980s. Is it still sliding down in the context of the world economy or has it shown some possibilities of growing faster and making it in the coming decade? What type of international economic environment is India going to confront in achieving this?

Table 1 gives a comparative picture of India's performance in selected areas with those of selected developing countries. It does not in any way change the picture that has been painted of India's performance over the last three decades. There are, however, a few aspects which deserve special attention.

Table 1: *Comparative Picture of India and Selected Developing Countries 1980–87*

		India	China	Brazil	South Korea
1. GNP per capita (1987, US.$)		300	290	2020	2690
2. Average annual growth rates (%) of					
a. GDP	1965–80	3.7	6.4	9.0	9.5
	1980–87	4.6	10.4	3.3	8.6
b. Per capita GNP	1965–87	1.8	5.2	4.1	6.4
c. Inflation	1965–80	7.6	0.0	31.3	18.8
	1980–87	7.7	4.2	166.3	5.0
d. Industrial production	1965–80	4.3	9.5	9.8	16.5
	1980–87	8.3	12.6	2.4	10.8
e. Exports	1965–80	3.7	5.5	9.3	27.2
	1980–87	3.6	11.7	5.6	14.3
3. International debt (billion $)		57.5	23.0	114.5	45.0
		(1989)	(1986)	(1987)	(1986)
4. Life expectancy (yrs.)		58	69	65	69

Source: World Bank (1989). *World Development Report and World Debt Tables.*

During the 1980s, India made serious attempts to change the economic strategy which had dominated its growth over the past three decades. The policy changes have been to provide increased competition to Indian industry, liberalisation of industrial and import policies, and increased reliance on market forces to direct economic development.

No doubt India faced a major drought in the year 1987–88; yet, the Indian economy performed well because of a good monsoon in the following year. It is estimated that India achieved a 5 per cent growth target during the Seventh Five-Year Plan period (World Bank 1989a). India's industrial growth picked up and was fairly comparable with other countries selected for the study.

INCREASED ECONOMIC VULNERABILITY

In the 1980s when the debt problem of developing countries surfaced, India was praised for its prudent borrowing. After 1980, however, the comfortable position that India enjoyed in debt repayment was lost and by 1989 India was faced with a serious debt problem. Though the *Economic Survey: 1988–89* disclosed that India had a debt of Rs. 55,000 crores, all other evidence pointed to a larger debt.[1] The next Finance Minister put the figure at Rs. 100,000 crores in his first interview to the press.[2] A recent publication of the World Bank revealed that India had a debt of US $57 billion. The debt to GNP ratio is 22.32 per cent, debt to export ratio 263 per cent, debt service to export ratio 29.23, the ratio of scheduled interest payments to exports 14 per cent (World Bank 1989b). These ratios prove that India is at the threshold of a debt trap. In fact, it was estimated by international financial institutions that India would have a debt of US $73.6 billion by March 1991,[3] which would make India's economic vulnerability more serious than it has been in the previous decades. This does not include defence loans estimated to the order of Rs. 15,000 crores (Dutt 1989). India has a failry low rate of inflation. Even in the 1980s, the rate of inflation as compared to previous decades was not alarming. Nevertheless, the years 1988 and 1989 witnessed a growth of inflation which, perhaps, has reached its tolerance limit in India.

Hence, in the 1980s India's dependence on the world economy grew. It now has to resolve a large number of issues arising out of this increased dependence. In searching for solutions, one must take into consideration the developments in the world economy which would determine India's course of action.

It has often been argued that India being a continental country with a small role for foreign trade need not worry about the international trading and economic environment. Table 2 gives the share of India's exports and imports in its national income and its share in world exports.

Further, India is a marginal exporter in a large number of products. This is another reason why it is generally expected that

[1] There has been tremendous controversy in India and abroad regarding the actual size of India's external debt. For more on the debate see Verghese (1988); Government of India, *Economic Survey, 1988–89*, p. 12; and 'India's External Debt Figures Controversy Centres on Scope and Definition', *The Economic Times*, 1 June 1989, p. 1.

[2] He said, 'More disturbing was the foreign debt burden of the government which, after including the NRI deposits, will carry Rs. 100,000 crores by the end of 1989–90'. Prof. Madhu Dandavate, Minister of Finance, Government of India, *Economic Times*, 14 December 1989, p. 1.

[3] Quoted in *Economic Times*, 1 June 1989.

Table 2: *India's Exports/Imports*

	1980–85 Average	1985–90 Average	1989–90	1990–91 Quick Estimate
Exports as % of GDP	5.0	5.1	6.3	6.3
Imports as % of GDP	8.4	8.2	9.0	9.1
Trade Balance as % of GDP	−3.4	−3.2	−2.8	−2.9
India's share in world exports (%)	0.4 (1980)	0.5 (1985)	0.5 (1988)	NA

Source: Government of India (1992). *Economic Survey 1991–92*, pp. 60 and S–90–91, New Delhi.
NA: Not Available.

the international economic environment will not affect India's export performance. However, this approach is particularly invalid in the circumstances in which India is placed today.

First, India needs to expand exports substantially not only to pay for its needed imports but also for its debt servicing. Second, however marginal the foreign trade sector may appear quantitatively, it has a critical importance for the Indian economy and its growth. Third, a large number of developments in the international economy are relevant to the strategies and policy framework, not only foreign trade policy, but the domestic economy policy of India as well, as will be seen subsequently.

The international trading environment is beset with certain long-term problems. These problems appear to persist despite increased world trade and income growth in the 1980s. International trade in the year 1988 was very high: the value of world exports grew by 9 per cent, the highest since 1984, and the growth of international trade has been higher than that of world production. Yet, neo-protectionism seems to persist. Nearly 50 per cent of world trade is covered by various regulatory measures such as voluntary export restrictions, the Multi-Fibre Agreement and quotas. Further, protection to domestic industry in advanced market economies has been granted through what is known as 'process protection' by initiating actions on imports from developing countries under countervailing and anti-dumping duties. The decade of the 1980s witnessed a spectacular growth in these actions. It is estimated by UNCTAD that nearly 578 measures have been initiated in the last eight years which affect the export of manufactures from developing countries (Chishti 1989). The question is: Can India, a marginal exporter, hope to remain unaffected? The answer to this question is a categorical 'no'.

First, India has already been affected by a large number of protectionist measures, especially in textiles, leather products and some agricultural products such as sugar. Second, India is facing a serious threat of unilateral action in the context of market access. The threat was prevalent in the 1970s and in the early 1980s, but as we entered the 1990s, this threat was concretised in the policy measures of the leading trading partner—the USA. The US has put India under what is popularly called the 'hit list' under clauses Super 301 and Special 301 of the United States Omnibus Trade and Competitive Act of 1988. The significance of including a marginal trader along with the leading trading partner, Japan, for retaliatory action if India does not change its trade, foreign direct investment and technology policies consistent with the US requirements is quite ominous. Thus, India is in the vortex of international trading being threatened substantially with regard to access to markets for its meagre exports in the context of world exports. Thus, in the 1990s India will face the challenge of an uncertain international trading environment which is not only restrictive but also has the serious potential of being highly discriminatory.

CHALLENGES

India is primarily an exporter of semi-processed and manufactured products. But it is also an important exporter of a number of primary products. The world trading environment for the export of primary products of interest to India is not very congenial. The steady decline in prices of primary products, particularly of those which it exported over the past six years, leaves hardly any basis to look for an expanding market in the 1990s.

While traditional sectors of export such as manufactures and primary products will face an uphill task in accelerating exports in the 1990s, the service sector—the new entrant in world trade—will face an uncertain future. India had been seeking non-inclusion of services in the Uruguay Round of Multilateral Trade Negotiations.

Despite India's efforts, liberalisation of international trade in services was brought under negotiation in the Uruguay Round. There are four important aspects of these negotiations which have a bearing not only on India's international trade in services and domestic policy pertaining to these services, but also to issues related to the role of international organisations that affects its merchandise trade.

First, it was decided at the Uruguay Round that discussion on services would be done sector-wise. Therefore, India would have to identify the sectors in which it would seek liberalisation and those in which it would offer liberalisation and adherence to certain requirements as demanded by the trading partners. India may, in its investment regulations, have to provide legal regimes for technology transfer, as also in regulations for the import of merchandise. India is moving towards a grand trade-off scheme with a large number of developed countries where it will be compelled to pursue trade, investment and technology policies which might not be consistent with its national interest. *Second,* in the event of its reluctance to go all the way in altering its national approach, there is every likelihood of India being excluded from the various trade liberalising measures. In fact, it has been anticipated that there could be a 'mini GATT Arrangement' with like-minded countries, thus overriding any of the obstacles posed by the decision-making process of the GATT. Thus, in the absence of an appropriate and cautious policy response, India may be left out of the liberalisation process. *Third,* the selection of sectors which will be treated for liberalisation is a vital aspect for India. While it may provide freer access to certain services like foreign direct investment, it is likely that the export of services in which it has a comparative advantage, such as skilled and unskilled labour, may not get adequate support. In fact, India has to strive to secure liberalised entry for our skilled and unskilled labour force in various countries. *Fourth,* there is also a threat to multilateralism. In the 1980s one witnessed the steady ascendancy of discriminatory bilateralism and the erosion of multilateralism. The 1990s may witness, especially in international trade in services, the growth of bilateralism. India, while keeping up its pressure to resurrect a truly non-discriminatory multilateral trading regime, might have to counter the ever-growing pressure of discriminatory bilateralism.

IMPLICATIONS OF CHANGES IN THE SOVIET UNION AND EASTERN EUROPE[4]

The 1980s experienced a major development in the world economy which is of great significance to India. The centrally planned economies of Eastern Europe and the Soviet Union had launched a major reform programme under Perestroika and the New Thinking of the Soviet Union. Under these, a large number of measures which had been shunned during the past seventy years were accepted. The Soviet Union with whom India has close political, defence and economic relations, has permitted increased marketisation of the economy, acceptance of integration of the Soviet Union in the world economy through expanded trade and participation in international economic institutions. It will now rely on the price mechanism to effect resource allocation. In this it is expected that the world price and convertibility of the rouble will play a significant role.

In this context, it is of great importance to examine how India's trade and economic relations with the Soviet Union will be shaped in the coming decade. There are three major components of the impact of these reforms in the Soviet Union on India's trade and economic relations with the former. *First,* India has not thus far been adversely affected by the introduction of these reforms. In fact, India's exports to the Soviet Union have actually gone up. It is expected that in the short-term, given payments arrangements, India will be able to expand its exports. *Second,* in the medium-term, there may arise the necessity to phase out payments arrangements when the Soviet Union moves to convertible currency trade. The impact on India's exports is uncertain. Whenever the Soviet Union has taken recourse to trade in convertible currency, it has enjoyed a trade surplus. There is no reason to believe that India will be an exception. India has to be prepared to face more competition in the market of the Soviet Union. *Third,* the Soviet Union gave India substantial aid during the period 1985 to 1988. There is every expectation that the Soviet Union may

---

[4] This paper was written before the recent break-up of the Soviet Union when it was still in existence. However, as will be evident to the readers, the discussion and remarks retain their relevance.—Editors.

continue to offer aid to India not only as a donor but to increase its exports of manufactures to India, especially machinery and equipment.

Besides these effects on bilateral relations, the Soviet Union's participation in GATT, IMF and the World Bank in the coming decade has important significance for both India and the Soviet Union. It is, however, difficult to exactly predict the course of this development. Only one substantial observation can be made at this point: that the Soviet Union in pursuit of its national interest in gaining economic advantages may encourage the forces of the market determining the role of aid, trade and technology transfer. It is believed in some quarters that the centrally planned economies of Eastern Europe and the Soviet Union be treated as developing countries and must be made eligible for the benefits that accrue to such countries. Hence, it has been suggested that they may emerge as competitors to developing countries. In the light of these developments, the 1990s may witness a dramatic change in the role of a major world power, thus raising questions about the traditionally accepted propositions about the response of this system to the needs of the developing countries. Hence, India must also make necessary adjustments in its traditional expectations from these countries.

ENVIRONMENT FOR CAPITAL FLOW

The environment for increased capital inflow is not going to be as congenial as India wintessed during the post-Independence period. It has already been seen that India has entered the 1990s with a huge external debt. Given this background, what would be its options to meet its foreign capital requirements? There are a few new issues that India has to tackle in the context of aid flow. Traditionally, India has borrowed both from governments as well as from multilateral lending institutions. The developed countries had reached a point of aid fatigue in the 1970s. Private lending by the international banks did not permit the impact of this to be felt by a number of developing countries. But the 1980s witnessed a virtual decline in private lending while official lending was not stepped up. It still stays at 0.38 per cent of the GDP, far below the expected rate of

0.75 per cent. Hence, India, in this environment, cannot expect any dramatic increase in the flow of resources through this channel.

There are new claimants to the funds, especially concessional funds, that are available from the donor governments and multinational financial institutions. The least developed countries had already come to the forefront in this regard. Now the East European countries and the Republics which constituted the former Soviet Union may crowd India out as a large beneficiary of such aid flows.

The international debt problem has directed the attention of donor countries and international financial institutions towards solving the problem of indebtedness which affects the lenders also. The borrowers, such as India, may not be on their priority list, a situation which has already been experienced by India.

While the lenders will also face problems, there are two problems whose creation can be traced to India. The lenders are getting considerably anxious about India's inability to utilise the aid. One of the major criticisms against India is that its utilisation rate declined substantially in the 1980s. It is estimated that India has Rs. 30,000 crores[5] in unutilised aid. Hence, the lenders rightly raise questions regarding the advisability of new commitments.

Further, India's balance of payments situation has recently deteriorated rapidly, with foreign exchange reserves which, at the time of writing, could meet only six weeks' import bill. This has been accompanied by a serious deterioration in government finance with accumulation of a huge internal debt and large budget deficits. In this context, the lending international financial institutions obviously wish to bring India under the discipline of conditionalities of structural adjustment programmes as and when it seeks assistance from them. India will thus be in a dilemma regarding seeking assistance from international financial institutions. The IMF and World Bank report that even IDA assistance is being brought under conditionality which will affect India considerably.

India did not borrow from commercial banks abroad till 1980. However, the 1980s saw the growth of a substantial debt owing to international commercial banks. Nearly 30.8 per cent of India's total debt can be accounted for by borrowings from commercial

[5] Mr. S.B. Chavan, the then Finance Minister of India, in an interview to the *Economic Times*, 30 September 1989.

banks. The figure stood at US $19,147 crores in 1989.[6] The servicing of this debt would cost the government an equivalent of Rs. 5,000 crores annually. Just to service this debt the government has to borrow Rs. 5,000 crores annually from the commercial banks. The government is also borrowing short-term credit at a very high rate of interest of 13 per cent.[7]

There are two important questions that India has to answer. Will India now borrow from the commercial banks to avoid loans from the international financial institutions which are loaded with conditionalities? Second, will the international commercial banks still consider India a creditworthy country to which to lend substantial sums? There is little choice between the two sources. The latter option will only postpone India's coming under conditionality, perhaps with more rigorous conditionality.

Under these circumstances, it has been suggested that India take recourse increasingly to foreign direct investment, an alternative source of external finance which in the context of India has been very limited. In fact, in the past three decades, the total foreign direct investment has been around Rs. 3,000 crores. The role of foreign direct investment as an alternative source of external capital has been important only in the case of a few developing countries such as Thailand, Malaysia and China in the 1980s. But the bulk of foreign direct investment has gone to developed countries either as direct investment or trade-related investment. Further, the major investors, especially transnational corporations, have preferred not to risk investing too much in the developing countries while taking recourse to new forms of international investment (Oman 1984). In India, despite selective foreign direct investment policies, most of the major foreign companies are controlling the Indian market through new forms of direct investment by taking resource to Indian capital. Thus, there will be little incentive in the coming decade for the foreign investor to invest large sums of capital in India. The investor has thus far enjoyed all the advantages with little risk capital and he will enjoy the same in the coming years as well.

It is important in this context to look into a number of problems that India will have to contend with while pursuing an independent foreign direct investment policy. National policies towards foreign

---

[6] *Economic Times*, 9 November 1989.

[7] 'No more a distant threat', *Economic and Political Weekly*, 25 November 1989, p. 2575.

direct investment are no longer free of international interference. The US has been trying to bring trade-related investment measures under the GATT. If the US position is totally accepted by the GATT, then there will be an 'investment framework' imposed by the GATT to meet the requirements of developed countries. India will be adversely affected by this development.[8] While India has taken a reasonable stand on retaining independence of national policies, it is difficult to expect that it will not be under severe pressure to modify its domestic policy if it wants access to markets for the export of its merchandise and services. This is an important issue that needs to be tackled within the next year or two.

TECHNOLOGY TRANSFER

Another area of great concern to India in the 1990s is the vastly changed international environment for technology transfer. The 1960s and 1970s witnessed the interest of developing countries in technology transfer. Hence, endeavours were made at the national and international levels to promote technology transfer to developing countries on less onerous terms to enable them to pursue self-reliant technology development. They were encouraged to have legal regimes affecting technology transfer consistent with their national needs. All this has changed in the 1980s. There has been an onslaught from the developed countries coercing the developing countries to adopt legal regimes for technology transfer to meet the needs of the sellers. This coercion is evident at both the national and international fora. The proposal to bring Trade-Related Intellectual Property Rights in GATT for discussion and policy programmes is one such attempt at an international forum. The Super 301 and Special 301 clauses of the US Trade Act (1988) are examples at the national level. Under this the developing countries have been asked to create a legal regime consisting of more stringent patent rights to sellers, and limited protection to the buyers, compelling developing countries to pursue these measures in order to get market access in the USA. India has adhered to many international norms. Only in the case of patent

---

[8] For details, see 'India's stand on Trade Related Investment Measures' (Document), *Mainstream*, 2 December 1989.

protection does India have a divergent view from the developed countries, i.e., it does not provide product patent protection. India has reiterated the necessity of observing the national interest with regard to coverage and duration of patent rights and the need for compulsory licensing.[9] India will have to resolve this crisis in the 1990s.

CONCLUSION

The 1980s witnessed a major erosion in the solidarity of developing countries in seeking collective solutions to their international economic problems. Due to various problems such as heavy debt, decline in prices of primary products, breakdown of the OPEC, and radical shifts in the attitude of developed countries, the solidarity of developing countries has been undermined. Now these countries are seeking national solutions. The 1990s with the existing international trading and economic environment, may witness further erosion.

It must be the task of India to revitalise the sagging morale of the developing countries by fostering the solidarity required while carefully pursuing an international economic policy consistent with its national interest in the fast-changing international economic environment.

REFERENCES

Chishti, Sumitra (1989). 'State of the Health of the World Economy in the 1990s: Perspective of the Developing Countries', *International Studies*, vol. 26, no. 3: 233–45. July–September.

Dutt, Ruddar (1989). 'Debt Trap and India's External Debt', *Mainstream*, vol. 27, no. 46: 7–10, 12 August.

Oman, Charles (1984). *New Forms of International Investment in the Developing Countries*, OECD: Paris.

Petel, S.J. (1985). 'India's Regression in the World Economy', *Economic and Political Weekly*, 28 September.

Verghese, S.K. (1988). 'India's Mounting External Debt and Servicing Burden', *Economic and Political Weekly*, 26 November.

World Bank. (1989a). *India Consortium*, 15 June.

—— (1989b). *Debt Tables*.

[9] See 'India's stand on Intellectual Property Rights Controversy' (Documents), *Mainstream*, 5 August 1989.

and appropriate to take up planning exercises in full measure. At the higher level, rightly or wrongly, the planning approach is guided by macro estimates. How far these approaches are relevant in the development of local areas is not clear. Yet, the task of balancing local and overall priorities at different levels is very delicate. Various issues which are either assumed or do not attract attention in macro planning, acquire greater relevance at the level of grass-roots planning. While these issues cannot be bypassed in the preparation of local plans, serious information gaps regarding these local matters have rendered local planning less fruitful.

Efforts to realise district planning in the past have not yielded adequate results. This is because instead of doing the groundwork to build up local institutions, the Planning Commission concentrated more on details of local planning, resources to be provided, etc. The earlier National Service Scheme (NSS), National Extension Service (NES) as well as the Community Development Programme which were originally conceived to realise popular participation have virtually become bureaucratic programmes. A knowledge of plan programmes was not within the reach of even enlightened people. Even today this condition has not altered much and information regarding planning at the grass-roots level is particularly lacking. As a result, the figures which appear on the numerous forms (and which are transmitted upwards to provide planning information to the higher administrative levels) are frequently the product of invention. There were no proper institutional arrangements for popular participation. *Gram panchayats* or *taluk* development boards had to depend on the bureaucracy to evolve plan proposals. It was the bureaucracy at the state level which used to sanction the schemes, provide funds and implement the programmes through local machinery.

The basic reason for the weakness of decentralised planning lies in the planning process in India. Planning in India has been centralised and vertical rather than decentralised and horizontal. The centralised plan begins with certain predetermined objectives with regard to the rate of growth, poverty alleviation, etc. The growth rate is further related to sectoral growth rates. To bring about a predetermined growth rate a certain size of plan investment is planned on the basis of data available on the capital–output ratio. Thereafter, the total investment is divided into the central and state plans. The detailed plans for the states are then prepared by various departments which, in turn, propose the break-up for the districts. Planning at the district level therefore amounts to nothing more than the allocation of sectoral and departmental investments.

Thus, district-level planning did not work as expected due to lack of precise information, expertise, institutional arrangements, heavy dependence of local institutions on the bureaucracy and almost total dependence on the state government for resources. The approach to planning was basically sectoral which is largely managed by the departments. The following factors should receive attention while evolving a framework to start decentralised development:

1. Decentralised planning should consist of both planning and implementation at the grass-roots level;
2. Planning and implementation responsibilities should rest with the representatives of the local people. The local bureaucracy should help the representative bodies responsible to the local people;
3. This involves division of functions, responsibilities, powers and resources between the state/union governments and local governments;
4. There is also a need to have effective coordination among plans involved at different levels;
5. The matter of accountability of the local government to the state government should be seriously taken note of.

Regarding the pattern of decentralised planning that should emerge, Dr. D.M. Nanjundappa observes: Every one of the institutions (i.e., village panchayat samitis and zilla parishads) is intended to serve a three-fold purpose. First, each of them, being mainly an elected body, has to be self-governing and autonomous to some extent. A certain degree of autonomy is essential for the developmental function. Second, they have to play an effective part in the preparation and implementation of programmes needed for the area under their jurisdiction. Their voice should be heard in determining the local plans. Third, while implementing the programmes, they should have sufficient scope for initiative and readjustment in accordance with the people's desires and [the] locality's changing needs while conforming to the accepted national pattern (Nanjundappa 1976: 143).

KARNATAKA'S EXPERIMENT—1978 TO 1987

It is not that states including Karnataka have not made any effort
to build up state plans on the basis of district and local plans. The
question of building the development process from the local level
had assumed new vigour in the 1970s. In Karnataka, villages,
blocks (*taluks*) and districts were considered the natural choice of
units of area planning, as some administrative infrastructure was
already available. Village *panchayats, Taluk* Development Boards
and District Development Councils were the popular organisations
already created and supported by Block Development Officers at
the block level and the Deputy Commissioners at the district level.
At the same time, efforts were also made to deploy experts from
universities and research institutions to prepare district and block
plans.

In 1978–79, Karnataka initiated district planning with this basic
infrastructure already in existence. The plan programmes were
classified as district sector and state sector schemes. A lump sum
provision was made on objective criteria for each district every
year for the formulation of the district sector plan. The district
planning committee distributed the lump sum provision among
various development sectors and the concerned heads of departments at the district level formulated programmes. The proposals
emanating from the districts were scrutinised by the heads of
departments at the state level. After their approval, the finalised
plans were communicated to the districts. This process continued
for a considerable time with some modification. However, there
was some arrangement to consult the local authorities, both officials
and non-officials. The only change that took place was that the
origin of the proposals was the districts. At the same time, it
should be noted that the state's annual plan was formulated independent of district plans. Due to large-scale changes in district
priorities brought about at the state level, the priorities which
ultimately emerged in the district plans were totally different from
those accorded by the District Development Council. Even the
proposals for locations underwent changes. Due to inadequate
arrangements for closer interaction between the state- and district-
level authorities and inadequate institutional arrangements for
people's participation, popular participation in the planning and

implementation of district development programmes was at a very low ebb, despite tall claims of taking planning to the grass-roots.

Subsequently, an effort was made to curtail the freedom given under lump sum allocations in order to overcome difficulties arising out of differences in local and state priorities. Inter-sectoral allocations for each district were made at the state level with some provision to choose schemes for the district within the sectoral outlays determined at the state level. This freedom was also further curtailed when, during 1983–84, the state government took up on its own the allocation of outlays even on minor categories of development schemes.

These developments had their own adverse implications on resource utilisation in the district. The district authorities were no more than glorified spending agencies along the pattern provided by the government. In many sectors, the utilisation of plan funds was very poor, largely on account of procedural delays and incorrect application of priorities. Ultimately, in 1984–85, the Deputy Commissioners were given the power of allocating outlays to the departments as per the budget provisions and of reappropriating from one scheme to another within a particular sector to the extent of 10 per cent of the budgeted outlay. This has to some extent eased the rigidity in implementation which came about as a result of detailed schematic distribution of outlays made at the state headquarters.

It did not take much time for the district authorities to realise that the liberty available to give effect to their priorities and to take up new programmes was limited due to a large share of the outlay being committed to on-going programmes. This problem was repeatedly voiced. Hence, through the Annual Plans in 1983–84, the District Development Councils were provided with a discretionary outlay to take up small works/schemes at the choice of the District Development Councils in each district. This continued till 1988–89, when full-fledged decentralised district planning was introduced in Karnataka by the promulgation of an Act.

Thus, district planning in Karnataka, for about a decade since 1978–79, was in a period of experimenting, but it was still the state headquarters that provided directions, resources and implementing machinery. More than this, popular participation in districts was not effective to the extent desired. In short, this was a period of transition from a system of state planning for the districts to district authorities planning for the districts. The sequence of events ultimately led to the birth of democratic decentralised planning in the middle of the 1980s.

ZILLA PARISHADS AND MANDAL PANCHAYATS

The basic question prior to the commencement of full-fledged decentralised planning in Karnataka in 1987 was to strike a balance between decentralisation and a reasonable degree of discipline, accountability and coordinated action. A series of decisions were to be taken regarding jurisdiction for various levels of planning and administration, mix of bureaucracy and popular participation, bifurcation of functions, resources and powers, distribution of development administration machinery between state and local authorities, and coordination between these developmental activities at different levels. Decentralisation is thus a complex political and administrative problem and a considerable amount of pragmatism has to be brought into its solution. A satisfactory answer cannot be found within the confines of mere ideological considerations and one may have to accept an amalgam of centralisation and decentralisation to ensure the success of decentralised planning in its functioning.

DECENTRALISED STRUCTURE

The Karnataka *Zilla Parishad, Taluk Panchayat Samiti, Mandal Panchayat* and *Nyaya Panchayat* Act, 1983, is one of the bold steps taken to evolve a structure and modalities to realise democratic decentralisation in the state. The institutional structure is basically two-tiered, consisting of *mandal panchayats* and *zilla parishads*. The size of these units is essentially reflected in two fundamental factors: area and population. While the size of the *zilla parishads* is almost historically determined, the *mandal panchayats* were to be made viable by defining the area and population which come within the *mandal*. The *taluk panchayat samitis* only play the role of an advisory body. This is a significant departure from the previous set-up. From the point of view of planning, while districts are considered as an ideal size in terms of area and population, there can hardly be any comprehensive plan for *mandal panchayats*. At best, only certain works and schemes that benefit local people can be proposed at this level under the present set-up. The details of these institutions are given in Table 1.

Table 1: *Zilla Parishads and Mandal Panchayats in Karnataka*

	Zilla Parishads	Mandal Panchayats
Number of Organisations	19	2536
Number of Members (Elected)	887	55188

The *mandal panchayats* and *zilla parishads* have been made democratic local governments with popular representation. A member of the *zilla parishad* is elected from among 28,000 people and a *mandal panchayat* member from among 400 people in all districts except Kodagu, where a smaller number of people are represented due to a sparse population. Weaker sections of society are assured reasonable representation in these institutions by providing reservation for women (25 per cent) and Scheduled Castes and Tribes to an extent of their proportion in the population. Members of the Legislative Assembly (MLAs) and Members of Parliament (MPs) are the ex-officio members of the *zilla parishads*. The President of the *zilla parishad* is given the status of a Minister of State.

RESPONSIBILITY AND POWER

The powers to the *zilla parishads* and *mandal panchayats* are devolved by (*i*) dividing subjects between the state government and the *zilla parishads* and *mandal panchayats* for planning and implementation; (*ii*) devolving block assistance and per capita grants for their plans; and (*iii*) delegating powers to district authorities to take decisions regarding various programmes. According to the Act, *zilla parishads* are given thirteen important subjects which could be operated at the district level. The *mandal panchayats* have been allocated five subjects of local relevance. The *zilla parishads* and *mandal panchayats* also implement centrally sponsored and central sector schemes as per guidelines. In order to facilitate the formulation of plans, district planning units were strengthened in every district. *Mandal panchayats* have taxation powers whereas *zilla parishads* do not. Resources for non-plan expenditure are devolved on the basis obtained just prior to the constitution of the *zilla parishads*. The block assistance for plans to each district is worked out on the basis of objective criteria, and is arrived at on the basis of population (50 per cent weightage) and backwardness as reflected in different indicators (50 per cent weightage). Apart from block assistance, *mandal panchayats* and *zilla parishads* are provided per capita grants of Rs. 2.5 and Rs. 7.5 crores, respectively. The *zilla parishads* are to devolve a part of the block assistance for plans to the *mandal panchayats* on the basis of objective criteria. The present modality is a stop-gap arrangement. Ultimately, it is the Finance Commission which guides the devolution of funds. The Finance Commission, already constituted, has submitted its award.

The *zilla parishads* and *mandal panchayats* are given full powers of sanctioning and reappropriation along with financial powers. Prior to the establishment of these institutions, no district head of department with the exception of Public Works Department (PWD) officers had the power of according technical sanction to any scheme. Under the scheme of *zilla parishads*, these officers are given the power of according technical sanction to any scheme/project involving an outlay up to Rs. 2 lakhs. The *zilla parishads* are given the power of according administrative sanctions for all the on-going schemes and new schemes with an outlay up to Rs. 10 lakhs in each case. If the *zilla parishads* and *mandal panchayats* wish to modify rules governing any on-going scheme or to introduce a new scheme, such a modification will be mutually agreed upon by the state government and the *zilla parishad/mandal panchayat* before the *zilla parishad's* plans are finalised. *Mandal panchayats* are also given the power of reappropriation up to 10 per cent of their approved budget.

Thus, the *zilla parishads* and *mandal panchayats* have extensive developmental functions and adequate powers. Regulatory functions have been retained by the state administration. However, the development functions of the *zilla parishads* are further supported by providing non-plan grants to maintain the administrative machinery, assets, etc.

PLANNING PROCESS

For the first time in 1988–89, the state's annual plan was formulated on the basis of plans prepared at the level of the *mandal panchayats* and *zilla parishads*. In order to start the work of plan formulation from this level, the government adopted a calendar for planning which starts from the middle of July every year. A tentative size for the *zilla parishad* and *mandal panchayat* sector was adopted by the state government and the size of the plan of each district is determined on the basis of objective criteria. The *zilla parishads* are required to formulate their plan involving the *mandal panchayats*, within the size indicated, in the middle of July. The government also holds discussions during the first half of October with the *zilla parishads* on their draft plans. To facilitate discussion, a small committee has been constituted with the Planning Commissioner as Chairperson, the Finance Commissioner, Secretaries or Heads of Departments and Joint Secretary, Planning, as members, and the Director, District and Regional Planning, as Member Secretary. The principal objectives of this meeting with the authorities of the *zilla parishad* are to ensure adequate outlay for the Minimum Needs Programme (MNP), Special Component Plan (SCP) and Tribal Sub-Plan (TSP), as also the commitment of the staff in the district sector plan. At this meeting, the state government is able to understand the reasons for the changes in priorities and facilitate heads of departments to offer their advice. Thus, the *zilla parishad* plans are firmed-up and the finalised plans are integrated with the state sector plans in each sector by November. Following this, the state's annual plan emerges with the combined priorities. Thereafter, the state annual plan is discussed at the Planning Commission level and if there is any modification in the outlay, suitable adjustments are made first in the state sector and, if necessary, in the district sector.

WORKING OF THE SYSTEM

The district sector outlay forms around 25 per cent of the state plan outlay and 67 per cent of the outlay for the central sector and centrally sponsored schemes, as seen in Table 2. Thus, the districts

Table 2: *Proportion of District Sector Outlay to State Central Plan*
Outlay 1987–88 to 1989–90
(last three years of Seventh Plan)

Year		Total State Plan Outlay (Rs crores)	District Sector Outlay	Proportion of District Sector Outlay to Total State Outlay (per cent)
1987–88	State	917.00	220.69	24.1
	Centre	215.47	144.16	66.9
	Total	1132.47	364.85	32.2
1988–89	State	900.00	239.78	26.6
	Centre	252.00	153.13	60.6
	Total	1152.00	392.91	34.0
1989–90	State	1040.00	265.07	25.5
	Centre	266.41	179.75	67.5
	Total	1306.41	444.82	34.0

have been investing about one-third of the total combined plan investment of the state sector and centrally sponsored programmes.

As shown in Table 3, the *zilla parishads* have given priority to programmes of economic and social infrastructural development. These include health, education, roads and veterinary services. But production-oriented activities like agriculture, horticulture, fisheries and minor irrigation, soil and water conservation have been dropped by all *zilla parishads* uniformly. Nominal or token provision for these works is almost absent in their proposals. On the other hand, the requirements of each sector are fully assessed and outlays provided. Allocations for primary and secondary education, rural health and sericulture are cases in point. Sectors like Indian systems of medicine, animal husbandry and youth services, which received lower allocations in the past, have now got a better deal. Above all, with the establishment of these institutions, the spread of information about plan programmes has percolated down to *mandal panchayat* level. All the members of the *mandal panchayats* and *zilla parishads* (about 55,000) have now become aware of the different plan programmes implemented in the state and are actively involved in plan formulation and

Table 3: *Sector-wise State Plan Outlay for Zilla Parishads*
(Rs. in lakhs)

Sector	1987–88	1988–89
1. Primary and secondary education	860.90	1546.00
2. Adult education	132.60	187.26
3. Indian systems of medicine	12.98	33.00
4. Rural health	1140.00	1276.12
5. Family welfare	96.00	102.50
6. Rural water supply	1819.00	1825.74
7. Housing	1233.75	1322.92
8. Welfare of SCs/STs	288.47	351.00
9. Welfare of BCM	246.29	307.55
10. Tribal sub-plan	313.00	373.35
11. Special component plan	1538.70	2040.99
12. Stipendary employment scheme	450.00	506.00
13. District planning units	30.00	33.35
14. Women and children welfare	108.50	160.92
15. Nutrition		
a) SNP	699.50	501.34
b) Mid-day meals	79.40	19.77
c) Foodgrains for poor	286.97	335.50
16. Agriculture	571.16	532.93
17. Horticulture	126.40	110.32
18. Soil and water conservation	628.51	630.61
19. Animal husbandry	122.59	252.20
20. Fisheries	108.54	169.00
21. Forest	949.45	852.00
22. Cooperation	469.42	475.25
23. Rural development programme	6769.53	6638.33
24. Minor irrigation	730.00	792.54
25. Sericulture	487.75	647.86
26. Village and small-scale industries	261.50	279.82
27. Roads and bridges	1463.52	1629.24
28. Youth services	6.85	18.00
29. Ground-water development	27.69	26.01
Total	22058.97	23977.42

implementation. This is the single most important gain achieved through the decentralised planning process.

District sector programmes are composed of *zilla parishad* programmes, *mandal panchayat* (1) programmes (*mandal panchayats* are responsible for planning and implementation with the approval of the *zilla parishads*), and *mandal panchayats* (2) programmes

(wherein *mandals* are responsible for planning, including identification of location and selection of beneficiaries, but the implementation rests with the *zilla parishads*). Out of the total state plan
outlay of Rs. 1,145 crores for 1990–91 the district sector outlay for
different programmes is shown in Table 4.

Table 4: *Investment Pattern of Distrct Plan Outlay (1990–91)*

Programme		Rs crores	% to District Sector Total	No. of Schemes Implemented
Zilla parishad Programme	Planned and implemented by zilla parishads	125.88	43	264
Mandal panchayat (1) Programme	Planned and imple- mented by *mandal panchayats* with zilla parishad approval	38.60	13	22
Mandal panchayat (2) Programme	Planned by *mandal panchayats* and implemented by zilla parishads	128.65	44	68

An Evaluation Committee appointed to assess the working of
the *zilla parishads* and *mandal panchayats* observed that the performance of the former was good with respect to a large number of
programmes including schools, health facilities, and other economic
activities. They were capable of mobilising resources; but women
and other weaker sections were hesitant in their participation in
decision-making; *gram sabhas*, from where works and programmes
originate, did not meet regularly. The Committee suggested that
more schemes should be transferred from the *zilla parishads* to the
mandal panchayats.

Soon after the constitution of the *zilla parishads* and *mandal
panchayats* the government appointed a Finance Commission to
look into the various issues connected with *zilla parishad* finances,
as also to make suitable recommendations. The Commission
favoured an assured share of state resources to the *zilla parishads*
by way of sharing certain taxes. The Commission was not in favour
of providing any taxation powers to the *zilla parishads*, largely on

account of its fear that the *zilla parishads* might be diverted from development efforts to tax administration.

MAJOR ISSUES

The issues are two-fold: First, there are a few general issues which impede functioning within the present set-up. They largely cover the issues related to lack of liberty in bringing about changes in local priorities. For instance, out of an outlay of Rs. 240 crores for the district sector in the 1988–89 Plan, only Rs. 34 crores or 14 per cent was available for new schemes. The *zilla parishads* also face the problem of exercising power to modify the norms and the structure of a large number of programmes handed over to them for implementation. The question is to what extent can the *zilla parishads* modify the norms either individually or collectively? Apart from all this, there was dissatisfaction with regard to the set-up, functioning and the powers given to the *zilla parishads* and *mandal panchayats*.

The district planning process now followed is not very different from the previous procedure. The block assistance for different districts is decided at the state level; the district planning units prepare annual and five-year plans and send these to the state government after the formal approval of the *zilla parishads*. In the discussions regarding the district plan at the state level only officers participate; they do not take place at the level of the *zilla parishad* President or the level of the state Planning Minister. After the Planning Commission's approval, the district plan proposals are modified at the state headquarters and are put to vote in the state legislature. Added to this, outlays for a number of sectors are earmarked for the district sector programmes at the state level. Programme implementation is strictly according to the guidelines issued by the state and central governments. In the light of this, even though greater liberty and power are conceived for the *zilla parishads* and *mandal panchayats*, it remains on paper alone.

In the preparation of district plans/programmes, greater technical inputs appear to be necessary. In fact, the development of the district could be realised by integrating various investment activities—both public and private—the district, state and centre, and also the investment flowing in through banking and other national financing institutions. The present set-up could result in different organisations falling into the trap of planning for the subject and the areas which come under *their* jurisdiction alone, without establishing linkages with the different kinds of investments and activities. Therefore, it is necessary to build within the system a process of realising inter se links among the development activities.

There are no clear-cut guidelines to determine the magnitude of the funds which should go to the *zilla parishads* and *mandal panchayats* annually. In Karnataka, as said earlier, the resources flowing down to the district sector are of the order of about 25 to 28 per cent of the state plan outlay. There are those of the view that the share of the district sector should be at least one-third of the state plan outlay. If uncertainties continue regarding their share, planning from below would undoubtedly encounter serious problems of ad hocism. Similarly, the share of funds flowing to the *mandal panchayats* in the total assistance provided to the districts is also not stabilised. While there are criteria to make inter-*mandal panchayat* allocations, the total quantum will have to be settled on the basis of a certain rationale in order to avoid uncertainties or apprehension of discrimination.

There is growing opinion that the *mandals* are far too small in size and far too many in number for their development activities to be overseen at the district level. As said earlier, *mandals* are less than viable units both in terms of area and population for any full-fledged planning exercise to be undertaken. Nor are they small enough to make them homogeneous and apprehend their problems at the household level. Therefore, it is felt that the *taluk* can continue as a unit of planning below the district level.

The allocation of schemes and programmes for the *zilla parishads* and *mandal panchayats* requires a fresh look. Most of the programmes have both district sector and state sector components. Some of the schemes on which neither the *zilla parishads* nor the *mandal panchayats* have been able to take any decisions nor implement them have gone to the district sector under the present dispensation. A number of instances can be quoted in this regard. Therefore, the allocation of development programmes will have to be reviewed and the *zilla parishads* should be provided with programmes which are truly of local importance, benefiting a larger section of people, and which should be handled by the machinery available to them. *Zilla parishads* do not at present have the resource-raising power to supplement the block assistance provided to them. The need to provide them with this also has to be examined.

Minimum expertise in planning at various levels is the basic requirement for the successful working of the system. While collective participation of the local people would, to some extent, help in identifying the felt needs of the people, it is equally essential to involve the local intelligentsia in the planning process so that a proper perspective can be evolved for the district economy.

Of late, there has been growing dissatisfaction regarding the style of functioning of the *zilla parishads* and *mandal panchayats*. This time, it is the turn of the state legislators to express their discontent. It should be noted that under the present circumstances, the *zilla parishads* and *mandals* are very much a part of the state body of governance. Their budgets are voted in the state legislature and are therefore accountable to it at least indirectly through the concerned Minister. With respect to the technical aspects of plan expenditure and its effectiveness, they are accountable to various planning authorities at the higher levels. The *zilla parishads* and *mandal panchayats* cannot go on with their programmes unmindful of national and state priorities. In short, they are not independent of the state government; instead, they, and the state government should complement each other and endeavour towards achieving the stated objectives. In the course of their functioning, a number of issues are likely to come up which should be settled through an exchange of views on such forums as the State Development Council.

REFERENCES

Nanjundappa, D.M. (1976). *Development with Social Justice*. Oxford and IBH: New Delhi.

18

Economic and Planning Council: An Insider's Evaluation[1]

G. THIMMAIAH

BACKGROUND

The introduction of government-sponsored economic planning necessitated the creation of the Planning Commission at the national level to formulate public sector plans for the country and to monitor their implementation, which was expected to take place primarily at the state level. The Planning Commission was conceived as an independent organisation but with an ideal mix of top political leaders and experts. The Prime Minister was made the Chairperson and some Union Cabinet Ministers also came to be nominated as members. The presence of these high-level political leaders conferred on the Commission the required power and influence. But the technical work expected from the Commission required expertise in economics/statistics, physical science, technology and administration. Accordingly, such subject experts were also nominated as members. This organisation has been kept outside the union government but has been made to interact very closely with the union and state governments.

However, at the state level no such organisation was created to undertake the task of formulating and monitoring the implementation of state plans. No doubt, the Chief Ministers of the states were made ex-officio members of the National Development Council, which too was created at the national level, to approve

---

[1] The responsibility for the views expressed here lies with author alone.

the plans formulated by the Planning Commission and to review the progress of their implementation at the state level. At the state level only Planning Departments were created to keep official records of plan programmes, schemes and projects allotted to the state governments for implementation. In the initial period these state Planning Departments remained rudimentary without qualified personnel to interact with the Planning Commission. They were not in a position to suggest any modifications in the programmes and schemes formulated by the Planning Commission, let alone any *new* programmes and projects. Most of the state Planning Departments came to be manned by the officers of the Indian Administrative Service (IAS), supported only by office clerks. It was only during the Fourth Plan period that the Planning Commission realised the importance of having state-level Planning Departments manned by experts in charge of formulating state-level plans and monitoring the progress of their implementation. Accordingly, the Planning Commission decided to provide financial assistance to the state governments to strengthen the then existing Planning Departments. Most of the state governments strengthened the state Planning Departments by inducting experts who were locally available. Besides, the state Planning Boards were also constituted with the Chief Minister as the Chairperson, the Planning Minister as the Vice-Chairperson, and the Secretary, Planning Department, as the ex-officio Member Secretary. A few experts were drawn from local universities and research institutions to serve as part-time members of the state Planning Boards. Subsequently, one state, (Tamil Nadu), created a full-fledged state Planning Commission with full-time experts as members. Despite this, the state Planning Boards rarely functioned. Perhaps the bureaucrats in the state Planning Departments did not want a parallel organisation consisting of outside experts to function alongside Planning Departments as advisory bodies. Consequently, this bureaucratic dislike reduced the state Planning Boards to mere ornamental bodies and they remained on paper alone. Such non-functioning state Planning Boards continued only to satisfy the Planning Commission. There was some sort of concealed resistance in the state bureaucracy to allow the state-level planning organisation to function effectively and assist the state governments in the formulation of plans, take decisions regarding the priorities of state plans and review the progress in implementation. The state bureaucracy has not encouraged the entry of subject experts with high-ranking positions into the policy-making bodies like the state Planning Departments. This situation prevailed even in Karnataka.

COMPOSITION AND ROLE

It was against this background that Mr. Ramakrishna Hegde, Chief Minister of Karnataka in 1983, decided to constitute the Economic and Planning Council (EPC) in place of the state Planning Board. The EPC came to be known as the Think Tank of Karnataka. This organisation was broad-based, high-powered expert body which was created by a resolution of the state Cabinet to advise the state government on all policy matters including planning. The EPC also became an expert body for monitoring the progress of the implementation of the Seventh Five-Year Plan.

This organisation was headed by the Chief Minister and the Vice-Chairperson was a distinguished administrator who had served as a member of the Planning Commission. There were full-time as well as part-time members; the latter included economists, a political scientist, an architect, a Gandhian activist and administrators. Full-time members were mostly senior officers of the state government, i.e., the Chief Secretary, Development Commissioner, Finance Commissioner and Planning Commissioner, all of whom were appointed as ex-officio members. The Planning Commissioner was made the Member Secretary. The Cabinet Ministers and other departmental secretaries were invited to participate in the deliberations of the EPC whenever the subjects relating to their portfolios came up for discussion.

In the beginning, the EPC appeared to have too many IAS officers, as a consequence of which it was feared to have become a Stink Tank! Subsequently, however, after the induction of some distinguished economists like I.G. Patel and Raj Krishna, this lacuna was rectified. The Secretariat of the EPC was located in the Planning Department. An additional post of Under Secretary with a few supporting staff members was created to provide administrative support to the EPC. This was only obvious as the Planning Commissioner was the ex-officio Member Secretary of the EPC.

The meetings of the EPC were held according to the convenience of the Chief Minister and according to the need to discuss policy matters. In the beginning, the Planning Department was asked to prepare status papers on specific issues like urbanisation, energy policy and the approach to the Seventh Plan for deliberations by the EPC. Initially the Planning Department prepared these documents enthusiastically, but this enthusiasm gradually waned. The ideas and policy issues presented in the status papers prepared by the Planning Department were not shared by the secretaries/heads of the conventional departments of the state government, which offended the Planning Department. At one of the meetings of the EPC, a status paper on energy prepared by the Joint Secretary of the Planning Department was severely criticised. From that time it was decided that the EPC should ask the concerned departments of the state governments to prepare the status papers whenever the EPC wanted these papers on different policy issues. Accordingly, the agriculture department was asked to prepare a status paper on the strategy for agricultural development. Similarly, the industry department was asked to prepare a status paper on industrial development policy. But the quality of these departmentally-prepared status papers was not uniform and some of them were no more than departmental notes with statistical tables appended to a few pages of descriptive presentation. Therefore, the EPC began to commission the services of outside experts to prepare research papers. Even that effort proved fruitless as some of them did not produce new and workable ideas or analyses. Probably irked by some disappointments with less than serious research documents, the EPC later appointed an Experts' Group to prepare a Perspective Plan for the state.

The EPC's contribution to the formulation of the policy of political decentralisation was noteworthy. The issue was debated in the EPC at length and those discussions immensely helped the state government in preparing the Karnataka *Zilla Parishads*, *Taluk Panchayat Samitis, Mandal Panchayats* and *Nyaya Panchayats* Act, 1983. The next policy thrust recommended by the EPC and accepted by the state government was to accord greater priority to the Minimum Needs Programme rather than to sink huge funds into money-guzzling major irrigation and power projects. This shift in development priority was no doubt resented by some powerful ministers and bureaucrats, but the EPC carried the day.

The EPC also started reviewing the progress of the implementation of projects and programmes in the state. This task scared the government officers as they were subjected to searching questions and embarrassing comments by outside experts. It appeared as though Mr. Hegde used the EPC to curb the monopoly of IAS officers in development administration. Their policy advice was not automatically accepted by the Chief Minister or the Cabinet Ministers. Hegde's popularity in the state was so high that he was prepared to take the risk of antagonising the IAS lobby. Not surprisingly, there were also time-servers in the state administration, some of whom even competed to please the EPC and Hegde. Most of the policies, whether suggested by the department or conceived by the state Cabinet, were always discussed in the EPC before according the state government's approval. This process created a countervailing administrative process within the administration. To that extent, the EPC brought about an alertness among the top officers heading the developmental departments. Another by-product of the EPC was that a lot of information, data and discriptive material relating to various aspects of the economy of Karnataka came to be presented before the EPC and, subsequently, it was decided to publish all the status papers and other documents in the form of EPC Proceedings. (They are published in three volumes but do not include the documents which were discussed after 1986.) These documents became easily available to scholars for understanding the economy of Karnataka—both its strengths and weaknesses.

Towards the end of 1986, the EPC started deliberating on the Eighth Plan of Karnataka. For that purpose, the EPC appointed an Experts' Group to prepare a Perspective Plan for the development of Karnataka. This Group submitted its report after a prolonged period of two years, and that too in a hurry, by which time Mr. Hegde was no longer Chief Minister. Although the Perspective Plan contained a number of well-conceived ideas, it was not a coherent document. Decentralised democracy was overemphasised and the perspectives of development presented in the document were not properly integrated into the decentralised development strategy. However, the background papers which were prepared for the benefit of this Experts' Group were also published along with this document. They contained a lot of information and indicated specific perspectives for Karnataka's development.

DRAWBACKS

Several criticisms were levelled against the EPC from the time of its inception. One long-standing criticism was that it consisted of experts drawn mostly from Delhi, thus ignoring local experts. This criticism was found to be valid to the end. Mr. Hegde wanted national level experts to serve on the EPC to give it a high status comparable to that of the Planning Commission. While his intentions were laudable, the experts whom he appointed from Delhi had hardly any time to devote to the work of the EPC. Some members of the EPC from Delhi were in that position mainly because of their political proximity to Hegde. Some of them used to offer him political advice. In fact, when Hegde resigned in 1986 because of the Supreme Court's observations on an excise case, some of his followers in Bangalore held Hegde's political advisers from Delhi responsible for advising him to resign. The other experts hardly found time to attend all the meetings. For the convenience of these Delhi-based experts, one or two meetings of the EPC used to be held in New Delhi, disregarding the immense cost incurred by the state government. Despite this, some of them did not take the EPC seriously after 1986. It should be mentioned in this context that Mr. Hegde responded positively to the criticism, as a result of which the composition of the EPC kept changing, making it a really dynamic expert body. Because of this continuous change in its composition, the Think Thank did not become a Stink Tank as was earlier feared.

Whenver he attended the meetings, Mr. Hegde made it a point to listen to all the discussions and debates which took place through-out the day. He came to be known as a great listener. It was also true that like Nehru, he liked the company of intellectuals. The discussions and debates at the EPC were also useful and beneficial to the officers. Quite a number of these deliberations were highly educative for even senior officers. Perhaps they were equally educative for Hegde and, in retrospect, we could say that his experience with the EPC subsequently made him a better-informed Deputy Chairperson of the Planning Commission. It is true that some members did not bother to read the documents even when they were circulated in advance. Thus, the EPC wasted a lot of time in explaining the contents of these papers. In spite of all these minor deficiencies, the EPC was a well-conceived idea and a well-implemented scheme of creating a broad-based intellectual forum to deliberate on the policies and programmes of development in Karnataka.

ACHIEVEMENTS

The relevance, usefulness and impact of the EPC should be judged against the background of the absence of any independent policy-advising body within the state government before the establishment of the EPC. The Planning Department then in existence no doubt included some expertise but was hardly adequate in assisting policy formulation and, more importantly, in wielding influence on the state government to consider its recommendations on various policy issues. The state Planning Board was either not reconstituted or hardly met even for the limited purpose of deliberating on the issues relating to planning. Under these circumstances, the only policy advice that was available to the state government, particularly to various development departments, was that tendered by the departmental secretaries who happened to be from the IAS. It is a well-known fact that the IAS is not adequately equipped to give policy advice. It is only meant to implement the policy decisions taken by the government. But over the years, the IAS has come to dominate policy-making to such an extent that it has almost usurped the role of policy adviser which, in other countries, is reserved for specialists. Such usurpation has also been encouraged by the government because of the absence of any substantial change in the development policies of the country. Since the IAS erected a strong fortress around itself in the government, and since the political leaders became so preoccupied with their own power and influence, there was hardly any scope for specialised experts to offer advice on various policy matters to the state governments.

The situation no doubt has been slightly better at the national level. Since the IAS could not give advice on science and technology, it had to tolerate the entry of distinguished scientists into the central government, particularly in the area of telecommunications, energy, defence and space research. But with regard to the policies relating to economic planning and development, the IAS put on the garb of an all-knowing expert body. This is evident from the dominant posts of IAS officers as advisers in the Planning Commission. This prevented the second line of advice, particularly to the political leaders at the state level, from making any impact. It is in this context that the creation of the EPC in Karnataka by Mr. Hegde, though not well-received in the beginning, came to be regarded as a welcome step in the right direction in order to improve the quality of advice offered to the state government.

The very fact that the EPC was mainly responsible for advising the state government on the nature and content of the PRI Act, as also for initiating a debate on long-term development perspectives for Karnataka, proves its valuable contribution. This well-conceived effort of Mr. Hegde to constitute the EPC deserves praise and emulation. It was the best forum for offering better quality advice on policy issues to the state government. It is true that this forum was mostly confined to state-level policies. However, the Experts Groups' Perspective Plan has very clearly recommended the creation of such Think Tanks at the district level to give the expertise at that level an opportunity to participate in the thinking process regarding the development of the districts. Over the years, such district-level Think Tanks are expected to develop into well-equipped organisations to think and deliberate on the policies which are appropriate for the development of the districts.

As soon as President's Rule was imposed in 1989, policy-making power passed into the hands of the bureaucracy. They saw to it that the EPC was not revived. Subsequently, the Congress (I) government which was elected to power decided to abolish the EPC altogether. Thus, a novel and fruitful experiment ended in 1990.

WHAT NEXT?

There is today no state Planning Board to advise the state government on the formulation of the plan, prioritisation of its programmes, and ways and means of mobilising resources. The EPC discussed the Perspective Plan prepared by the Experts' Group. It was not properly structured and the discussion was pale. The approach to the Eighth Five-Year Plan was prepared at the time

Writings of Professor D.M. Nanjundappa

BOOKS

Community Development and Employment (1963). Karnatak University: Dharwad.

Local Taxation in Urban Areas, jointly with M.V. Nadkarni (1967). Karnatak University: Dharwad.

Surplus Rural Manpower and Economic Development in Mysore, Foreword by V.K.R.V. Rao (1971). Government of Mysore: Bangalore.

Resale Price Maintenance in a Developing Economy (1971). Karnatak University: Dharwad.

Road User Taxation and Road Finance in Indian Economy, Foreword by Lady Ursula K. Hicks (1973). Nehru Memorial Institute of Development Studies: Bombay, and Popular Prakashan: Bombay.

Transport Planning and Finance, ed. (1973). Karnatak University: Dharwad.

Some Aspects of Karnatak's Economy (1973). Bharat Prakashan: Dharwad.

Inter-Governmental Financial Relations in India (1974). Sterling Publishers: New Delhi.

Budgeting of Road Expenditures (1974). Mysore University: Mysore.

Studies in Public Finance (1976). Asia publishing House: Calcutta.

Rural Development in Karnataka: Antyodaya Model (1975). Kaujalgi Hanumantha Rao Memorial Trust: Bangalore.

Development with Social Justice, Foreword by S. Chakravarty (1976). Oxford and IBH Publishing Company: New Delhi.

Abhivruddhiya Bugge (Kannada) (1976). India Book House: Bangalore.

Working of University Finances, Foreword by Malcolm S. Adiseshiah (1976). Sterling Publishers: New Delhi.

Planning and Panchayatraj Finances (1977). Submitted to University Grants Commission: New Delhi (mimeographed).

Area Planning and Rural Development (1981). Associated Publishing House: New Delhi.

Draft Guidelines for Local Level Planning, UN: ESCAP project (1980). Submitted to ESCAP: Bangkok (mimeographed).

Indian Economic Development and Policy, ed. with P.R. Brahmananda and B.K. Narayan (1979). Vikas Publishing House: New Delhi.

Planning and Management of Higher Education (1983). Karnatak University: Dharwad.

Backward Area Development—Problems and Prospects, ed. with R.K. Sinha (1982). Sterling Publishers: New Delhi.

Gramina Abhivrudhige Samsthika Choukattu (Kannada) (1986). Sahyadri Prakashana: Mysore.

Irrigation Investment and Income Distribution (1987). Bangalore University: Bangalore.

Essays in Indian Economic Problems (in press).

BOOKLETS

Leadership for Rural Development (1987). Mangalore University: Mangalore.

University Finances—Search for New Perspectives (1990). Bangalore University: Bangalore.

BOOKS IN PROGRESS

Plan Finance: Theory and Control
Management of Universities
Decentralised Planning—A Manual

PAPERS

(This is not an exhaustive list and includes only salient papers. Reports prepared by him as a government economist are excluded here.)

Abbreviations: *IEJ—Indian Economic Journal; JKU—The Journal of Karnatak University; SE—Southern Economist; ET—Economic Times; DH—Deccan Herald.*

'Financing of Small Enterprises', *Journal of Small Scale Industries*, 1958.

'Debt Management as an Instrument of Employment Policy', *IEJ*, vol. 6, no. 8, January 1959.

'Company Taxation and Economic Growth', *JKU*—Humanities, vol. VI, 1962.

'Rural Economy of Mysore State', *Khadi Gramodyog*, vol. 9, no. 3, December 1962.

'Towards a More Realistic Wage Policy', *JKU*—Humanities, vol. VII, 1963.

'Educational Expenditures in Mysore', *Mysore Economic Review*, 1963.

'Engineering Industry in a Developing City', jointly with M.V. Nadkarni, *JKU*—Humanities, vol. VIII, 1964.

'Expenditure on Education', *JKU*—Social Sciences, vol. I, 1965.

'An Appraisal of the Criteria for Investment in Education', *IEJ*, 48th Annual Conference Number, December 1965.

'Restrictive Trade Practices and Public Policy', *IEJ*, 49th Annual Conference Number, December 1966.

'Capital Gains Tax and Development Finance', *JKU*—Social Sciences, vol. II, 1966.

'Resource Transfer from the Union to the States—Case for Lesser Centralisation and More Flexible Scheme of Devolution', *IEJ*, vol. 14, no. 3, October–December 1966.

'Fiscal Policy and Planning', in G.S. Halappa (ed), *Freedom for Progress*. Dharwad, 1966.

'Survey as a Decision Tool for Entrepreneurs', *Commerce*, 18 March 1967.

'Untapped Resources of Karnataka', *Industrial Mysore, DH*, Special Number 1967.

'Incidence of Site-Value Rating in a Developing Country', *IEJ*, 50th Annual Conference Number, December 1967.

'Incidence of Taxation', Rapporteur's Report, *IEJ*, 50th Annual Conference Number, December 1967.

'Tax Incentives for Entrepreneurs', *Industrial Mysore, DH*, Special Number, 1967.

'Expenditure Patterns in Developing Regions', with M. Basavana Goud, *JKU*—Social Sciences, vol. IV, 1968.

'A note on Rural Economy of Raichur District: A Scheme for Agricultural Estates', with M. Basavana Goud, *Journal of the Institute of Economic Research*, vol. III, no. 2, July 1968.

'Some Aspects of Town and Country Planning', *DH*, 16 June 1968.

'Changing Structure of Industrial Finance in India' (Review Article), *Manchester School Journal*, 1969.

'Rural Manpower Programme in the Fourth Plan', *Yojana*, 1969.

'Budgetary Classification—A Reform', with A.D. Shilledar, *SE*, vol. 8, no. 22, 15 March 1970.

'How Recent is Resale Price Maintenance in Indian Industries?', *The Indian Journal of Economics*, 1971.

'Employment Objectives in Economic Policy', *JKU*—Social Sciences, vol. VII, 1971.

'Development of North Karnatak After Integration', *Industrial Mysore, DH*, Special Number, 1971.

'Towards a Dynamic Employment Policy', *The Hindu*, 18 October 1971.

'Balanced Growth of Mysore's Economy', *ET*, 1971.

'Impact of Roads on Development in India', in Ashok V. Bhuleshkar (ed.), *Towards Socialist Transformation of Indian Economy*. Popular Prakashan: Bombay, 1972.

'An Instrument of War-cum-Development Finance: National Reserve Fund', *Young Indian*, 1972.

'Economic Progress and Social Justice in India', Multicultural Understanding Programme, USEFI and Karnatak University, Dharwad, June 1972 (mimeographed).

'Co-operative Banks and Rural Finance', *Yojana*, 1972.

'Pricing of Road Services', *Southern Economic Review*, vol. 1, no. 4, June 1972.

'Economics of Dry Farming', *Industrial Mysore, DH*, Special Number, 1972.

'Toll Finance', *The Indian Roads Transport Development Association Journal*, vol. XLI, no. 16, August 1972.

'Panchayat Raj and Development Finance', *IEJ*, vol. 20, no. 2, October–December 1972.

'Tax Effort and Resource Transfer Under Fiscal Federalism in India', *JKU*—Social Sciences, vol. VIII, 1972.

'Basis of Resource Transfer from Centre to States', with G.V.K. Rao, *Economic and Political Weekly*, vol. VIII, no. 37, 15 September 1973.

'Rural Income Distribution', paper presented at an international seminar at the Institute of Development Studies, Sussex, UK, 1973.

'A Note on Ceiling on Land Holdings with Reference to Dry Farming and Private Source of Irrigation', with Y.L. Inamdar, in *Seminar on Land Reforms*, published by Administrative Training Institute: Mysore, December 1973.

'Land Reforms: Need for a New Perspective', with Y.L. Inamdar, in *Seminar on Land Reforms*, published by Administrative Training Institute: Mysore, December 1973.

'A New Pattern of Finance for Development', with G.V.K. Rao, *ET*, 13 August 1974.

'Karnataka's Economy: Growth and Potential', *Southern Economic Review*, vol. 4, no. 2, October 1974.

'Need for Financing Higher Education', *ET*, 24 June 1975.

'An Alternative System of Financing Higher Education', *ET*, 25 June 1975.

'Urbanisation: Tunnel Vision Policy', *Seminar*, July 1975.

'Innovation in Institutional Credit', *SE*, November 1975.

'Note on Working of Karnatak University Finances', *Journal of Higher Education*, UGC Journal, vol. II, no. 2, Autumn 1975.

'Export Potential of Karnataka', *Commerce*, November 1975.

'Planning for Farmers' Service Societies', paper presented at the Workshop on Decentralised Planning, organised by the Government of Karnataka at Bangalore, 28–29 January 1976 (mimeographed).

'Commercial Banks and Co-operative Finance', *Journal of the Land Development Bank*, December 1976.

'Karnataka—Perspectives for the 80s', *SE*, 1 November 1977.

'Planning Priorities in Karnataka 1978–83', *Yojana*, 26 January 1978.

'Some Policy Options in an Agricultural Economy', *SE*, January 1978.

'Sixth Plan of Karnataka', with R. Anandakrishna, *SE*, 15 January 1979.

'Savings Behaviour in Karnataka', *IEJ*, 62nd Annual Conference Number, December 1979.

'Taxation of Urban Land', in P.R. Brahmananda et al. (eds.), *Indian Economic Development and Policy*. Vikas Publishing House: New Delhi, 1979.

'Centralisation, Decentralisation and Administrative Systems', *DH*, 10 January 1980.

'National Farm Price Policy and Land Reforms', *DH*, 11 January 1980.

'Low Wage Price Syndrome in Agriculture and Class Conflicts', paper presented at an international seminar at Sussex University, UK, January–February 1980.

'Business Managers and Social Obligations', *DH*, 8 August 1980.

'Development of Infrastructure in Karnataka', *Commerce*, December 1980.

'Linkages between Education, Employment and Development', paper prepared for the Planning Commission's Working Group on the subject, *DH*, 7 and 9 February 1981.

'Karnataka Job Scheme', *ET*, 15–16 April 1981.

'Educational Outlays—Cost Effectiveness and Policy', *DH*, 28 April 1981.

'Utilisation of Local Resources and Regional Balance', *Financial Express*, 13–14 May 1981.

'Indo-Soviet Economic Co-operation and Its Influence on the Economic Development of India', paper presented as a member of the Indian delegation to the USSR to celebrate the 10th Anniversary of the Indo-Soviet Peace Treaty at Moscow, sponsored by Indo-Soviet Cultural Society, August 1981 (mimeographed).

'Administrative Systems for Rural Development', *DH*, 19 and 20 October 1981.

'Karnataka Block Planning: Methodology and Project Criteria', *ET*, 2 January 1982.

'Rural-Urban Conundrum in Indian Planning', Presidential Address to the All-India Economic Association, *IEJ*, April–June 1982.

'Some Critical Issues in Planning and Management of Higher Education', paper presented at the international seminar at Berlin, GDR, *University News*, India, 15 June 1983.

'Costs-Fee of Medical Education', paper submitted to the Committee on the Abolition of Capitation Fees in Private Medical Colleges, Government of Karnataka, 1983.

'Revision of Gadgil Formula for Central Assistance for State Plans', paper presented at the National Seminar on Centre-State Relations, organised by the Economic and Planning Council, Government of Karnataka, at the Institute for Social and Economic Change, Bangalore, 5–7 August 1983.

'Employment and Unemployment in Karnataka', jointly with M.A. Srinivas, in Austin Robinson, et al. (eds.), *Employment Policy in a Developing Country*, vol. 2, Macmillan Press: London, 1983 (for the International Economic Association).

'Decentralised Planning: Problems of Administration and Co-ordination', *Indian Economic Almanac*, April–June 1985, and *ET*, 23–24 April 1985.

'Pricing of Roads', in S. Chandrasekhar (ed.), *Readings in Public Economics and Planning*, Chugh Publications, 1985.

'Incidence of Urban Site Value Rating in a Developing Economy', in S. Chandrasekhar (ed.), *Readings in Public Economics and Planning*, Chugh Publications, 1985.

'Karnataka's Growth: Perspectives and Problems', *ET*, 1 October 1985.

'Link Education with Development', *Yojana*, 26 January 1986.

'Rural–Urban Dichotomy in Indian Planning', in N.K. Thingalaya (ed.), *Rural India—Real India*, Himalaya Publishing House, 1986.

'Monitoring and Information Systems for Planning', keynote paper at the Workshop on Monitoring, organised by the Government of Assam at Gauhati, 30–31 October 1986 (mimeographed).

'Irrigation Investment', *ET*, 2–4 December 1986.

'Regional Rural Banks: Problems and Prospects', 10th Bank Economists' Meet, Papers and Proceedings, published by Vijaya Bank, Bangalore, 1987.

'Rural Bias for Development', in P.R. Brahmananda et al. (eds.), *Dimensions of Rural Development in India*, Himalaya Publishing House: Bombay, 1987.

'Financing On-Farm Development—Command Area Development Approach' in Ashok A. Bhuleshkar (ed.), *Indian Economy in the World Setting*, Jawaharlal Nehru Memorial, Volume V. Himalaya Publishing House: Bombay, 1988.

'Issues in University Financial Administration', keynote paper at the Workshop on Financial Administration in Universities, organised by the Association of Indian Universities, Pune, 6 June 1988 (mimeographed).

'Growth and Income Distribution', in V.S. Mahajan (ed.), *Studies in Indian Planning*. Deep and Deep Publications: New Delhi, 1988.

'Radical Change in Planning Process Necessary', *ET*, 1 October 1988.

'Panchayat Raj and Decentralised Planning—An Attempt to give People their own Socialism', paper presented at the 71st Annual Conference of the Indian Economic Association, Jadhavpur University, Calcutta, 29–31 December 1988.

'Planning from Below', *Yojana*, vol. 33, nos. 1 and 2, 26 January 1989.

'Geosynthetics in the Development of Irrigation', valedictory address at the International Conference of Geotextices, Bangalore, 29 November 1989 (mimeographed).

'Priorities in Eighth Plan Approach: Education', *DH*, 2–3 August 1990.

'Trading Partnership: India and Pacific Basin Countries', paper presented at the US Fulbright Association 13th Annual Meeting and National Conference on 'Pacific Focus 1990: Change and Challenge', held at the University of Hawaii—East West Centre, Honolulu, Hawaii, USA, 5–7 October 1990.

'When Degrees Get Out of Synch with Jobs', *ET* and *The Times of India*, 10 October 1990.

'Trade Policy' (three parts), *The Times of India*, 23, 24 and 25 November 1990.

'Decentralised Planning' (two parts), *ET*, 10 and 11 December 1990.

'Employee Ownership for a Stable Industrial Base', presidential address to the 32nd Annual Conference of the Indian Society of Labour Economics, held at Utkal University, Bhubaneswar, Orissa, 23–25 December 1990, published in the *Indian Journal of Labour Economics*, January–March 1991.

'Devolution and its Redistributive Role', in M.V. Nadkarni, A.S. Seetharamu and Abdul Aziz (eds.), *India: The Emerging Challenges—Essays in Honour of Prof. V.K.R.V. Rao*. Sage Publications India: New Delhi, 1991.

About the Contributors

Malcolm S. Adiseshiah is Chairperson, Madras Institute of Development Studies, Madras.

Abdul Aziz is Professor and Head of the Economics Unit, Institute for Social and Economic Change, Bangalore.

K.K. Balachandran is Technical Coordinator at the Department of Economics, University of Bombay, Bombay.

R. Bharadwaj is Director, Department of Economics, and Professor of Econometrics, University of Bombay, Bombay.

S. Bisaliah is Professor and Head, Department of Economics, University of Agricultural Sciences, Bangalore.

S.G. Bhat is Director, Planning Department, Government of Karnataka, Bangalore.

Sumitra Chishti is Chairperson of the Centre for International Politics, Organisation and Disarmament, School of International Studies, Jawaharlal Nehru University, New Delhi.

T.R. Satish Chandran is Director of the Institute for Social and Economic Change, Bangalore.

Ramesh Kanbargi is at the Institute for Social and Economic Change, Bangalore.

Shanta Kanbargi is at the Institute for Social and Economic Change, Bangalore.

M.V. Nadkarni is Professor and Head of the Ecology Economics Unit, Institute for Social and Economic Change, Bangalore.

G. Nagaraju is at the Institute for Social and Economic Change, Bangalore.

R.H. Patil is Economic Adviser and Executive Director, Industrial Development Bank of India, Bombay.

R. Radhakrishna is Director of the Centre for Economic and Social Studies, Hyderabad.

V.K.R.V. Rao is Founder-Director and ex-Chairperson of the Institute for Social and Economic Change, Bangalore; Institute for Economic Growth, Delhi; and Delhi School of Economics. He was Cabinet Minister, Government of India (1967–71) and Member, Planning Commission (1963–66). Prof. Rao was awarded the Padma Vibhushan in 1974.

V.M. Rao is Member, Agricultural Costs and Prices Commission. He was formerly Professor and Head of the Rural Economics Unit, Institute for Social and Economic Change, Bangalore.

C. Ravi is at the Centre for Economic and Social Studies, Hyderabad.

P. Hanumantha Rayappa is Professor and Head of the Population Research Centre, Institute for Social and Economic Change, Bangalore.

Atul Sarma is Professor of Economics, Indian Statistical Institute, New Delhi.

G. Thimmaiah is Economic Adviser to the Government of Karnataka, Bangalore.

Index